Interpersonal Skills and Project Managers

Interpersonal Skills for Portfolio, Program, and Project Managers

Ginger Levin, DPA, PMP, PgMP

MANAGEMENTCONCEPTS

MANAGEMENTCONCEPTS

8230 Leesburg Pike, Suite 800
Vienna, VA 22182
(703) 790-9595
Fax: (703) 790-1371
www.managementconcepts.com

PMI, PMP, Program Management Professional (PgMP), CAPM, *OPM3*, *OPM3* ProductSuite, PMI Certified *OPM3* Assessor, PMI Certified *OPM3* Consultant, PMI global standards, and PMI-ISSIG are registered marks of the Project Management Institute, Inc.

Portions of this book are excerpted or adapted from *People Skills for Project Managers* (2001) and *Essential People Skills for Project Managers* (2005), by Steven W. Flannes and Ginger Levin. © Management Concepts, Inc. All rights reserved.

Printed in the United States of America

Library of Congress Cataloging-in-Publication Data

Levin, Ginger.
    Interpersonal skills for portfolio, program, and project managers / Ginger Levin.
       p. cm.
    ISBN 978-1-56726-288-9
1. Project management. 2. Personnel management. 3. Interpersonal relations. 4. Interpersonal communication. I. Title.
HD69.P75L4834 2010
658.4'094–dc22

                                                              2010019620

10   9   8   7   6   5   4   3   2   1

About the Author

Dr. Ginger Levin is a senior consultant and educator in project management. Her specialty areas include portfolio management, program management, the project management office, metrics, and maturity assessments. She is certified as a PMP, PgMP, and *OPM3* consultant and assessor. She was the second person in the world to receive the PgMP designation.

In addition, Dr. Levin is an adjunct professor for the University of Wisconsin–Platteville, where she teaches in the master's in project management program, and for SKEMA (formerly Esc Lille) University, France, in the project management program at the master's and doctoral levels. She is also a visiting professor for RMIT in Melbourne, Australia, at the doctoral level.

In consulting, Dr. Levin has served as project manager in numerous efforts for Fortune 500 and public-sector clients, including BAE Systems, UPS, Citibank, the Food and Drug Administration, General Electric, SAP, EADS, John Deere, Schreiber Foods, TRW, New York City Transit Authority, the U.S. Joint Forces Command, and the U.S. Department of Agriculture. Prior to her work in consulting, she held positions of increasing responsibility with the U.S. government, including the Federal Aviation Administration, Office of Personnel Management, and General Accounting Office.

She is the coauthor of *Implementing Program Management: Forms and Templates Aligned with the Standard for Program Management,* second edition; *Project Portfolio Management; Metrics for Project Management; Achieving Project Management Success with Virtual Teams; Advanced Project Management Office: A Comprehensive Look at Function and Implementation; People Skills for Project Managers; Essential People Skills for Project Managers; The Business Development Capability Maturity Model;* and the *PMP Challenge! PMP Study Guide* and *PgMP Study Guide.*

Dr. Levin received her doctorate in information systems technology and public administration from The George Washington University, receiving the *Outstanding Dissertation Award* for her research on large organizations.

To my husband, Morris, for his continuing encouragement, support, and love.

Contents

Preface

Interpersonal issues tend to be the most frustrating aspect of the work portfolio managers, program managers, and project managers do. For the project manager, interpersonal issues can hinder project success, especially in terms of meeting the project's schedule and budget. They can also jeopardize achieving customer satisfaction with the project's scope and quality requirements. In program management, interpersonal issues can get in the way of the delivery of benefits not only from the individual projects that constitute the program but also more importantly, from the program as a whole. They can also interfere with governance approval and the ability to meet and manage stakeholder expectations. The overall value of the program's deliverables can diminish. In portfolio management, interpersonal issues can impede the development of a portfolio management process that is followed consistently throughout the organization and can delay and even prevent communication about the programs and projects and their priorities to others in the organization.

This book is dedicated to giving you, the project professional—whether at the portfolio, program, or individual project level—professional, tangible, and tested interpersonal skills that will help you address the many people issues you encounter in your work and with your team, while also helping you manage your own career direction. The differences in working with people at the various levels—portfolio, program, and project—are stressed, as are the differences (and similarities) in working on virtual and co-located teams. This book presents a set of specific, practical skills that you can use to resolve the difficult people issues managers so often encounter and to turn them from challenges and problems into opportunities.

The interpersonal skills addressed in the chapters of this book include:

- The ability to provide strong leadership and to comfortably implement four key leadership roles critical to success

- Different strategies for building effective and high-performing teams, whether the teams are virtual or co-located

- Proven methods for motivating your team as well as understanding your own motivation style

- Best practices for communicating, with an emphasis on developing concrete communications skills and recognizing what not to do

- Approaches for building and maintaining relationships with stakeholders at all levels, both internal and external

- Decision-making approaches and managing relationships with people who have dominant sources of power

- Proven methods for handling stress and responding to unexpected critical incidents

- Best practices for resolving conflict in the most productive and effective manner, along with ways to manage agreement to avoid groupthink

- Specific career management skills and approaches to follow in light of the complexities inherent in our working environment.

Why are interpersonal skills so critical? We are under extreme pressure to complete programs and projects faster than ever before and to achieve ever higher levels of customer satisfaction. We also are under pressure to select programs and projects that truly will make a difference to our organization in an environment of limited resources and necessary capacity planning. Our work is increasingly complex, often relying on new and unproven technologies and requiring greater interaction with an increasingly large number of stakeholders, many of whom may not be identified until the later stages of our work. In addition, we often perform our work in a global environment, with some of our teams never meeting face-to-face during the course of their work. It is also rare for most people to work on only a single program or project, so effective time management is essential.

Interpersonal Skills for Portfolio, Program, and Project Managers is based on two earlier books, *Essential People Skills for Project Managers* (2005) and *People Skills for Project Managers* (2001), both coauthored with Steven Flannes, Ph.D., and published by Management Concepts. This book incorporates some of the key ideas presented in the two earlier books, broadening the focus to include portfolio and program managers and to discuss work with virtual teams. Additionally, this book includes some new techniques developed to meet challenges that were not common in 2005. Like the two earlier books, this book recognizes that portfolio, program, and project managers need information they can grasp quickly and apply immediately to their work. The discussion questions at the end of the first nine chapters can be used in universities or in organizational seminars addressing interpersonal skills.

Parts of this book, plus those of the other two books, have been presented at conferences in the United States, Canada, Europe, South Africa, New Zealand, and Australia at Project Management Institute (PMI) chapters, during workshops for various organizations, and at PMI Congresses and International Project Management Association (IPMA) conferences. In these and similar settings, project professionals note how much more attention is being paid throughout the world to the interpersonal aspects of portfolio, program, and project work; this emphasis is also evident in the 2008 PMI standards in these three areas.

* * *

I would like to express sincere thanks to the staff at Management Concepts for working with me for over a decade and especially to Myra Strauss, Mary Cowell, and Courtney Chiaparas for their tremendous assistance to me in publishing this book.

Ginger Levin
September 2010

Introduction

Interpersonal issues in projects and programs as well as in portfolio management can be messy and uncomfortable. Most significantly for the project manager, people issues can hinder project success; in particular, they can make it difficult to meet the project's schedule and budget and can jeopardize customer satisfaction with the project's scope and quality requirements. In program management, people issues can get in the way of the delivery of benefits, not only from the individual projects that compose the program but, more importantly, from the program as a whole. They also can interfere with governance approval and the ability to meet and manage stakeholder expectations. The overall value of the program's deliverables may decrease. In portfolio management, people issues can impede the development of a portfolio management process that people in the organization consistently follow and can delay and even prevent the plan from being communicated to the members of the organization.

As a project, program, or portfolio manager, you can, however, develop and refine skills that will enable you to address people issues successfully when they surface within a team setting. Equipped with these skills, you will not only bring added value to your organization but also find more personal enjoyment and fulfillment in your work as you proactively manage your career.

Projects: Technical Problems with Human Dimensions

Projects are technical problems with significant human dimensions. Cleland and Ireland (2007) note that most problems in organizations can be traced to people. They point to the importance of communication skills and note that there are many personal barriers to good communication that people must overcome. Management consultant Peters (2004) writes, "These days, it's the people skills that matter and will increasingly determine an organization's success." He also notes that "only putting people first wins in the long haul, good times and especially tough times" (2008).

Unfortunately, many project professionals have not had training in the people skills required for success and career advancement; instead, they must develop these skills informally as they proceed through their careers.

The Importance of People Skills

There are a number of key reasons why people skills are so important:

- We are under pressure to complete projects and programs faster than before; in today's competitive world, cycle times must be reduced in order to ensure customers' satisfaction exceeds their expectations.

- We are working in a global environment. It is rare to work with a team of people who are co-located. Even if we do have the luxury of working with a co-located team, our stakeholders and customers may not be in the same location as we are. We may never see some of our team members, stakeholders, and customers face-to-face.

- Projects and programs are more complex, often using unproven technology, and we may not recognize the complex elements of our projects and programs early in the life cycle.

- The number of stakeholders we must interact with seems to increase as more and more interest is involved in each project and program. In other words, projects and programs have to reflect the interests of more stakeholders now than in the past.

- While more and more organizations are operating in a matrix environment, this kind of environment still presents challenges, not only for the project and program managers but also for the team members and functional managers.

- Offshoring and outsourcing are frequently used to decrease costs, and they increase the time required to complete projects.

- It is rare to work on only a single project, which means we must interact with more people than ever before.

- Many organizations have not completely defined the roles and responsibilities of program and project managers, and there may not be a portfolio management focus in the organization.

The Program and Project Life Cycles

Both projects and programs have life cycles, regardless of their size or complexity and regardless of whether they are performed by virtual or co-located teams. These life cycles are sequential and show the major phases that need to be performed. Typically, the specific life cycle is part of the overall program and project management methodologies used in the organization. Groups of individuals become a team as they progress through these life cycles. Each phase requires that project or program managers, and their respective team members, have finely honed people skills to succeed at the highest level.

Table I-1 shows how the five stages of the Tuckman team development model correspond to the Project Management Institute's (PMI) five life cycle stages for projects and programs and PMI's portfolio sub-processes.

We will look at these stages from the vantage point of how people working on projects, programs, and portfolios become effective teams. This discussion introduces specific people skills that will be covered in subsequent chapters. Over the course of any project or program, and in various phases of portfolio management, all of the people skills discussed in this book are employed simultaneously, though some skills are more heavily relied on in one stage than in another, and some are more essential in co-located or in virtual environments.

Forming Stage

A team begins as a collection of individuals with different motivations and expectations. Unless the team has worked together successfully in the past, there is limited trust among team members. Some members may not even want to be part of the team. They may have competing priorities because of

Table I-1 The Tuckman Team Development Model and Project, Program, and Portfolio Management

Tuckman Model (1965, 1977)	Project Management (PMI 2008a)	Program Management (PMI 2008c)	Portfolio Management (PMI 2008b)
Forming	Initiating	Pre-Program Preparations	Identify Components
			Categorize Components
			Classify Components
			Identify Portfolio Risks
Storming	Planning	Program Initiation Program Setup	Evaluate Components
			Select Components
			Analyze Portfolio Risks
Norming	Executing	Delivery of Program Benefits	Prioritize Components
			Authorize Components
			Develop Portfolio Risk Responses
			Review and Report Portfolio Performance
			Monitor Business Strategy Changes
Performing	Monitoring and Controlling	Delivery of Program Benefits	Balance Portfolio
			Communicate Portfolio Adjustments
			Monitor and Control Portfolio Risks
Adjourning	Closing	Program Closure	

their work on other programs or projects or in ongoing operations. Each team member brings his or her own ideas and perspectives about the purpose of the project and his or her specific roles and responsibilities. The team does not yet have specific processes for effective operation.

In this stage, people are gathering information about their fellow team members. Some may hold opinions of their teammates that are based on stereotypes, which may pertain to cultural differences or may be long-held assumptions based on job function (e.g., generalizations about "the auditors," "the engineers," or "the IT staff").

Additional people-related challenges affect programs. Team members may not be sure why their project is part of the program in the first place and why it is being managed in a program structure. They may not recognize the benefits that can be derived from a program management approach and may not know how their project relates to other projects in the program. They may wonder whether they will interact with the program manager and, if so, how often this interaction will occur. However, because it is early in the process, conflicts are not usually a major issue.

Portfolio management is an ongoing process, as new programs and projects are selected for inclusion in the portfolio, and other programs and projects are terminated or successfully come to completion. Identifying the specific components (programs, projects, and other work) that will compose the portfolio and determining how best to categorize them are, nevertheless, concerns in the forming stage. Members of a portfolio review board or similar organization may resist the inclusion of certain components in the portfolio, or they may believe that certain categories in the portfolio are no longer relevant given changing business conditions and need revision. They may be concerned that the portfolio management process is not being followed throughout the organization. (If it is not, they may wonder why they are serving as board members, and they will try to figure out how to make the process more effective.) New board members may be uncertain about the board's operating procedures, its specific roles and responsibilities, and the organization's portfolio management process.

Leaders in project, program, and portfolio management during the forming stage must resist the tendency to make any assumptions about the personalities, values, sources of motivation, interests, and agendas of each of the team members. The ability to perceive and appreciate individual differences is an essential people skill that is discussed more fully in Chapter 4. The forming stage is a time for leaders to really get to know their team members.

Working with their teams, leaders must articulate the vision or end state for each program or project such that each team member can personally identify with it and support it. The vision explains why the program or project adds value to the organization, the desired end state of the program or project, and why it is part of the organization's portfolio. Focusing on the vision, rather than emphasizing specific deliverables, technical specifications, and the details of the work to be done, shows how the program or project contributes to the overall goals and objectives of the organization.

The people skills managers must have for crafting and communicating the vision include:

- The ability to comfortably inhabit four distinct leadership roles: leading, managing, facilitating, and mentoring. The manager acts as a leader to communicate the vision (see Chapter 1).

- Effective communication skills (such as listening actively and asking open-ended questions (see Chapter 4).

- Effective political skills, which enable the manager to work with a diverse group of stakeholders to clarify the vision and ensure commitment to it (presented in Chapter 5).

Storming Stage

The second stage, as described by Tuckman (1965) and Tuckman and Jensen (1977), is the storming stage. This stage is marked by conflict and disagreement among team members and the program and project manager. Some people may not like the roles and responsibilities they are assigned to perform and may prefer those assigned to other team members. They may challenge their peers for specific niches and identities in the project. Many may be anxious about the new project or program. The assignment represents change, which may surface self-doubt or old grievances. Team members so affected may try to resist the changes.

Conflict may be even more common in virtual teams because some people, based on their style of motivation, may be uncomfortable with their specific assignments. Some minor confrontations may occur. For example, a person who is motivated more by close connections and associations may resist his or her assignment to a virtual team because it does not offer the day-to-day interpersonal contact with team members. Or a person who is motivated more by a need for power may also resist his or her assignment to a virtual team because it is less conducive to involvement in multiple project activities and awareness of the specific assignments of others.

The project manager may be able to handle some of these confrontations, but some may have to be escalated to the project sponsor. At the program level, project managers may raise issues to the program manager for resolution, and often, he or she may need to involve the program's governance board or steering committee for assistance.

At the portfolio level, disagreements are especially likely if portfolio management is being introduced to the organization. Board members may question the methods used to identify portfolio components, and the selection process often is marked by extensive discussion and controversy, especially if a key member of the portfolio review board supports a project that is not selected for inclusion in the portfolio. Company employees may not know about the plan to introduce portfolio management, and if they are aware of it, they may feel threatened by its formal approach.

Project, program, and portfolio managers with an assertive and facilitative style can help the team create not just solutions to individual conflicts but also processes the team can use to resolve them directly.

Five distinct people skills are required to resolve conflicts and to model positive conflict-resolution behaviors:

- The ability to identify the motivational styles of team members (addressed in Chapter 3)
- The ability to use the most appropriate communications skills (addressed in Chapter 4)
- The ability to apply six distinct conflict resolution strategies and to know when to apply each of them (addressed in Chapter 8)
- The ability to guide the team as it forms and to employ various team-building approaches (addressed in Chapter 2)
- The ability to take on the manager role, one of the four basic leadership competencies, to help the team prepare a team charter that will define the methods it will use to resolve conflict (discussed in Chapters 2 and 3).

A team charter can help managers and team members determine how to address crisis situations—for example, if a critical incident, such as a serious illness, death, or a natural disaster, strikes a team member. At the portfolio level, major business changes, such as mergers and acquisitions, using offshoring for the first time, or a need to downsize staffing, can constitute critical incidents.

To effectively respond to a critical incident, portfolio, program, or project managers should be able to:

- Assess whether a critical incident debriefing—a facilitated team meeting that is intended to allow team members to talk through the crisis—is warranted, given the nature of the critical incident. Debriefings can be held in either a co-located or virtual environment.

- Be empathetic to the team members' personal reactions to the event while still keeping a business-oriented, task-completion focus.

- Determine when a project or program recovery plan is needed and identify the qualities of the ideal recovery manager. At the portfolio level, a manager should be able to decide whether an outside person should be brought in as a recovery manager for the organization.

A potential downside of creating group standards and norms through a team charter or a set of operating procedures is that the team may display conformity, obedience, or groupthink in decision-making. Groupthink, as defined by Harvey (1974), also called management by agreement, is a major source of portfolio, project, or program dysfunction. In teams under the influence of groupthink, people take action based on what they believe the team desires, but in reality no one supports the decision that was made. Groupthink happens because many people do not express their true feelings about situations. When it becomes evident that the group's decision was ineffective or wrong, team members then blame others, a typical reaction during the storming stage. Obviously, such a situation damages team cohesiveness.

To mitigate the risk of groupthink or management by agreement, the project, program, or portfolio manager needs to achieve a balance of cohesion and dissent. The people skills required for managing agreement involve the five conflict resolution skills and the influencing skills discussed in Chapter 8.

Norming Stage

By the time a team reaches the norming stage, the work of the program or project is underway and people are accustomed to their roles and responsibilities. Team members have a greater sense of trust in each other, and they work to resolve conflicts. However, challenges remain. The program or project manager must ensure that team members do not lose sight of the overall vision or end state and that they maintain momentum to complete the required activities. At the portfolio level, it is incumbent to ensure that only those projects and programs that continue to support the organization's strategic goals and objectives are pursued, and pet projects or ones that do not meet the criteria in the portfolio system are not considered or continued.

It is easy at this stage for the team members to revert back to the storming stage, so the manager must foster an environment conducive to success and harmony for the team and continually engage stakeholders in a proactive fashion. The team must not be resource constrained and must remain motivated.

The people skills a manager must have during the norming stage include:

- The ability to operate as a facilitator, one of the four roles of a leader (discussed in Chapter 1), which involves pursuing needed resources and negotiating for these resources (discussed in Chapter 5)

- The ability to use a variety of motivational approaches, based on team members' styles and the unique characteristics of the project or program (discussed in Chapter 3)

- Determining how best to involve each stakeholder on the project and how best to manage each stakeholder's expectations (discussed in Chapter 5).

Performing Stage

While many groups do not reach this stage because of team turnover or because of the short duration of many projects, those that do still need the project or program manager's active involvement. This stage is extremely important at the portfolio level because the portfolio management process is ongoing throughout the life of the organization.

In the performing stage, the team's identity is established, and it is empowered. Team members trust one another, and work proceeds in a fashion. When conflicts occur, or when changes affect the project or program, they are handled through a defined process. The key people skill in this stage is decision-making, discussed in detail in Chapter 6.

If the team is not operating at the expected level of efficiency during this stage, people issues affecting the team may be to blame. At the portfolio level, for example, there may be a new person in a key role on the portfolio review board or, at the program level, on the governance board. Or the team may have lost a key technical resource, which is affecting its morale. A "people issues" audit may be appropriate. Such an audit also can be helpful even if the team is performing at its peak level to document best practices to follow and replicate on future teams.

Further, a people issues audit can help ensure that team members are working on activities that best support their own competencies, skills, and abilities. It can also be used to determine whether tasks are sequenced effectively, so that if a particular team member's skills are needed to support several of the projects within a program, this individual will not be overloaded and can perform at peak efficiency. Finally, it can be used to evaluate the team's work—whether it is contributing to the project or program and to the work of the performing organization, the customer, or both. The results of this audit, then, are used to promote overall team building, which is discussed in Chapter 2.

Adjourning Stage

In the adjourning or closing stage of a project or program, team members, especially if the project or program has been underway for some time, may not wish to leave their current assignment. They may enjoy the team's camaraderie. Some people may not have another assignment in the organization and may need to look elsewhere for work; others may wish to move on quickly to the next assignment. This stage affects people differently, and team members' reactions, positive or negative, may be directed toward the project or program manager.

During this stage, the project or program manager should remember that:

- Team members may display a variety of emotions, ranging from anger if they do not have another project or program to look forward to, to dismay if they believe they are missing out on an opportunity because they need to stay with the project or program to complete all of the closure tasks.

- Team members' feelings may not be logical and may have little to do with the work the team has done.

Project or program team members who have a positive attitude about the next opportunity may be candidates for a project management career path. These people might benefit from mentorship, in which the program or project manager, the team member, and his or her functional manager work together to determine the team member's next assignment and guide his or her advancement in the organization. (Mentoring is discussed in detail in Chapter 1.)

Given the importance of proactive stakeholder engagement, the project or program manager must ensure that stakeholders are satisfied with the end result. Whoever is assigned to work with each stakeholder should meet with him or her to determine whether he or she is satisfied with the project deliverable or result or the benefits of the program.

Project and program managers also must ensure that all of the closing activities are completed successfully. Someone who is skilled in and enjoys closing activities may stand in for the manager, though the manager should assist this person. He or she makes sure that the administrative and contract closure processes are followed. For a program, a process must be in place for benefit sustainment.

Therefore, to maximize performance during the adjourning/closing stage, the project or program manager must:

- Craft tailored motivational strategies that address the needs of each team member, stakeholders, and, in a program setting, those who will be responsible for benefit sustainment (discussed in Chapter 3)

- Offer suggestions as appropriate to help team members deal with stress to help keep team performance at an optimal level (discussed in Chapter 7).

The program or project manager must have various interpersonal skills to address the people issues that arise during each of the stages of a typical program or project. While the successful program or project manager uses almost all of these people skills during each stage, this book highlights the most important skills needed during each stage.

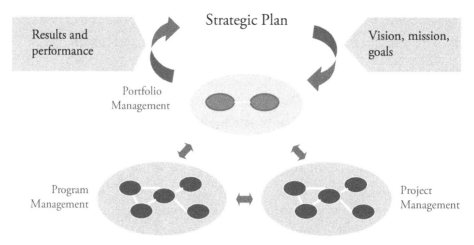

Figure I-1   The Project-Based Organization

The Project-Based Organization

In many organizations, programs and projects are now seen as organizational assets. In the public and private sectors, leading organizations recognize that programs and projects are critical to growth and organizational sustainment. In fact, without programs and projects, some private-sector companies could not continue to ensure their competitive position in the marketplace. (See Figure I-1.)

This movement toward the project-based organization means that:

- Communications can no longer be conducted in a hierarchical way, based on organizational silos. Instead, communications cross organizational lines.

- People are assigned to programs and projects based on what they can contribute rather than where they are located in the organization.

- Often, assignments are short-term. Team members must build trust as rapidly as possible; there is not enough time to develop the working relationships of the past.

- Motivation may be more team oriented than individual oriented.

In project-based organizations, there has been a definite shift in management style at all organizational levels. There is a growing emphasis on consensus and participation, calling for the project manager to serve not solely as a manager but also as a facilitator, team member, team player, and mentor. The manager's ability to demonstrate effective people skills in a variety of circumstances has become paramount.

This trend toward management-by-projects is further evidenced by the growing membership of the Project Management Institute. When Management Concepts *People Skills for Project Managers* book was published in 2001, PMI had approximately 77,000 members. At press time, PMI had more than 300,000 members in more than 275 countries. The number of certified Project Management Professionals (PMPs) has increased dramatically and a new credential the Program Management Professionals (PgMPs) is growing in the recognition of its importance by people in the profession. Such a trend is expected to continue, which is due in part to the completion of the International Organization for Standardization (ISO) initiative in project management, along with the cooperative agreement signed in 2008 between PMI and the International Project Management Association (IPMA). These developments show that project management is a recognized profession across the globe, as management-by-projects continues to increase worldwide, and that project management is recognized as a desired career path for many professionals.

The Importance of Project and Program Stakeholders

Programs and projects always have been customer-driven because they are performed for stakeholders—customers and end users, who may be internal or external to the organization. And, increasingly, customers are playing a far more active role in programs and projects. Their support cannot be taken for granted. Proactive stakeholder management is essential for overall program success in terms of deliverables and benefits. It is a continual process starting at project initiation (in the project management life cycle) or the pre-program preparations phase (in the program management life cycle).

Program and project managers must have strong people skills to understand customers' requirements, manage relationships with customers, and ensure customer retention. Often, they are measured by their success in these areas. But maintaining customer relationships can be challenging because managers often have to communicate with so many stakeholders. It is easy in such a fast-paced environment to become overloaded with nonessential information, miss critical metrics and indicators of program or project success, or overlook the requirements of critical stakeholders.

In its discussion of project manager-stakeholder relationships, the *PMBOK® Guide* (PMI 2008a) emphasizes the need to proactively manage stakeholder expectations by continually working with stakeholders and using effective communications skills and consistent messages to clarify and resolve issues of concern.

At the program level, the priority in stakeholder management is ensuring that stakeholders will actively support and accept program objectives and benefits as they accrue throughout the program's life cycle. Interpersonal skills facilitate the identification and recognition of stakeholders (PMI 2008c).

At the portfolio management level, portfolio managers must use interpersonal skills at a variety of levels, working with senior executives as well as other internal and external stakeholders to maximize the performance of programs, projects, and the overall portfolio (PMI 2008b). This requires the portfolio manager to interact effectively with an even greater number of internal and external stakeholders. Portfolio managers can prepare a communications management plan as part of their stakeholder management strategy to show the requirements of each stakeholder group and to rank the importance of each stakeholder group in gaining overall approval of the portfolio management process.

Program and Project Complexity

Interpersonal skills are even more important as programs and projects become increasingly complex. The norm today in program and project work is to work faster with fewer resources, turning out products, services, and results with multiple applications and uses. It has become harder and harder for project managers to produce the promised deliverables and for program managers to ensure program benefits are attained. From a people perspective, complexity often results in a loss of team morale, presenting motivational challenges for the program and project manager. At the portfolio level, there is more pressure to ensure the "right" programs and projects are pursued—ones that will best enable the organization to meet its strategic objectives.

This complexity also is evident in the continuous advancement of technology. Given the length of some projects, and especially at the program level, it is not uncommon for the technologies used on programs and projects to change during their life cycles. The program or project manager may be struggling to maintain an adequate understanding of the current technology while facing pressure to implement newer technology (and still responding to the human factors of the team) in an atmosphere of intense competition from other organizations.

Technology and the use of virtual teams on programs and projects have enabled global teams to employ a 24-hour workday. Constant communication between managers, team members, and stakeholders is expected, and programs and projects must be completed faster than in the past, which often leads to team burnout as well as increased stress for program and project managers.

Program and project managers must be comfortable with approaches such as fast tracking, concurrent engineering, and agile methods to enable a faster time to market while still emphasizing quality products, services, and results. Program managers must focus on the interdependencies between projects in the program and must be prepared to deploy staff from one project to another, when necessary. And portfolio managers must recognize the interdependences between all of the current programs and projects, especially from a resource-allocation perspective.

Continual Downsizing, Outsourcing, and Offshoring

Not long ago, downsizing, outsourcing, and offshoring were the exception rather than the norm and occurred only in times of economic slowdown. People joined an organization and expected to remain with it for their careers. It was rare to change jobs and even rarer to move outside one's initial selected field.

Downsizing, outsourcing, and offshoring now are a way of life. While competency in one's chosen field has always been important, it is necessary today for program and project professionals to continue to enhance their skills and competencies so that they remain essential to their current organization and are in demand by other organizations. Movement of people both within the organization and to other organizations is common and expected.

Outsourcing and offshoring are often necessary for companies to remain competitive. The work done by the performing organization itself should be the work it is most suited for, and suppliers and valued partners should do any work outside the organization's typical lines of business. Offshoring can enable the 24-hour day to become a reality, and it allows companies to take advantage of lower currency exchange rates to reduce overall program and project costs.

When companies outsource, program and project managers must be able to rapidly establish teams of people who may never meet face-to-face and who represent different cultures. They must be able to merge diverse perspectives to develop common solutions and make effective decisions when there is not enough time to gain consensus among all the parties involved. Program and project managers also face interpersonal issues such as:

- Finding ways to motivate the surviving employees, who may be wondering whether they will be part of the next wave of layoffs within the organization

- Motivating these employees, who feel overburdened and must "do more with less"

- Motivating outsourcing and offshoring partners to become part of the team and to work under the team's operating procedures and charters.

Leading in a Matrix Structure

Some form of matrix management is used in most organizations, ranging from the weak matrix to the strong matrix and various approaches in between. The matrix organization has emerged as *the* organizational structure for programs and projects. In a matrix organization, the project manager and the functional manager share responsibility for resource allocation and reporting, and project team members thus tend to have two bosses in most cases.

Although matrix management has become a given, the roles and responsibilities of functional managers, project managers, and team members are still uncertain. In fact, this uncertainty has increased, since each organization tends to use a variety of organizational structures based on the nature and complexity of its programs and projects.

The matrix structure often tends to discourage team members from committing to a program or project, especially if they are also doing ongoing work within their functional organization. Team members recognize that program and project work is temporary, while the ongoing work remains. They may never work again for the program or project manager or with their teammates as a collective unit on future programs or projects. Also, it is rare to work on only one program or project, so team members have several managers to whom they must report. This further diffuses their commitment to a single manager. The portfolio manager must recognize when allocating resources that some individuals may resist assignments to certain programs or projects if they prefer to remain within their functional units.

Kerzner (2009) highlights the motivational issues facing the project manager:

* Project managers have little real authority; functional managers have considerable authority.
* Project managers may not have input into team members' performance evaluations; functional managers are responsible for employee evaluations.

Milosevic, Martinelli, and Waddell (2007) note there are additional challenges at the program level because program managers often do not have resources reporting directly to them, which means program managers must use strong leadership skills that focus on building relationships to influence, focus, and motivate the team.

The portfolio manager may have a small staff who are direct reports but, as noted by PMI (PMI 2008b), portfolio managers must be adept in managing people and may need to use mentoring, coaching, motivating, and training skills to develop employees. They also must focus on recruitment and retention, goal setting, performance evaluation, reward and recognition, and succession planning.

Virtual Teams and a Distributed Workplace

The growing popularity of virtual organizations is a response to the unprecedented growth in program and project management, customer and other stakeholder expectations, global competition, complexity, rapid change, and time-to-market compression. At the same time, the growth of virtual teams has *led* to the increase in organizations practicing management-by-projects.

Customers, suppliers, and employees no longer need to reside in the same location or the same city and can be located anywhere in the world. While the virtual organization does present a number of challenges, the benefits far outweigh the disadvantages. Virtual work enables an organization to quickly deploy its resources to form teams capable of responding to emerging program or project work or to a change in the strategic direction of the organization's portfolio.

However, while there are commonalities between work in co-located environments and work in virtual environments, on virtual teams people-oriented issues take on greater importance and need faster resolution, which often is difficult given that people may be located all over the globe. The program and project manager must set the stage for success and facilitate effective communication, recognizing that most communication will be asynchronous and that communications must be especially succinct and explicit so they are not easily misconstrued.

As noted by Rad and Levin (2003), because the virtual team may span multiple cultural and language boundaries, team procedures must ensure that diversity among team members is an asset and not a liability by making sure team members are aware of each other's cultural backgrounds. Additionally, if programs and projects follow a 24-hour workday, managers must ensure that team members pay strict attention to documentation and configuration management as a matter of course. For example, if a team member located in Asia completes a portion of the deliverable and then passes it to someone in North America to continue working, the team member in Asia must refrain from further work on the deliverable until it again is his or her turn.

For overall success in virtual teams, and in a management-by-projects environment, there really is insufficient time to build trust in the normal way because team members must quickly form as a team and assume others have a comparable commitment to the project's vision, mission, and values. Also, on most virtual teams, the conditions required to develop trust simply do not exist; physical proximity, daily informal and unplanned interactions, and face-to-face meetings are lacking.

Program and project managers must ensure that virtual team members have the same level of commitment to the virtual program or project as they would if the team were co-located. This necessitates communicating effectively to motivate each team member to participate actively and not develop an "out of sight, out of mind" mentality, and it necessitates an issue resolution process because the manager obviously cannot use a "management-by-walking-around" approach.

The virtual program and project manager must:

- Lead by influence, rather than through control or supervision
- Encourage team members to collaborate on work
- Reduce the stress that often exists on a virtual team and help create an environment in which membership on a virtual team is as valued as membership on a co-located team by emphasizing the importance of the program or project to the organization's overall strategic goals and by emphasizing the program or project's vision or mission
- Help build trust and a team identity
- Ensure that team members feel free to discuss ideas.

Continual Organizational Change and People Skills

Because of global competition and technological obsolescence, as well as the natural tendency for stakeholders to change their ideas about priorities, leaders in organizations must continually make changes, and members of the organization must embrace change. Change is to be expected in today's environment; it will happen, though its timing is uncertain.

While incremental changes to a strategic plan in an organization may not require changes in the portfolio, significant changes certainly will have a definite impact. Portfolio, program, and project managers are expected to be change agents. Portfolio managers must rebalance the portfolio based on changes that are made, and at the program or project level, changes may lead to reallocation of resources, a change in priorities, and even, in some situations, to program and project termination.

Most people resist change. This resistance causes tension, lower morale, higher anxiety, more stress, and reduced productivity. Change, coupled with the temporary uncertainty of program and project work, may lead to employee dissatisfaction; in some cases, valued staff members may decide to leave the organization. They may feel that their own well-being is not being considered amid constant and continual organizational change.

Further, when an organizational culture is made more project-oriented—even if the change is limited to establishing a program or project management office (PMO) or a portfolio management system—even the most senior managers may resist. (Sometimes, even Chief Executive Officers (CEOs) who promote management by projects put up resistance to actually making the necessary changes.) Structural changes shape a new organizational environment, and senior leaders may view the program and project models as a threat to the power they have accumulated over the years within the functional organization.

Because the personal consequences of resisting change, such as stress and decreased motivation, are detrimental, portfolio, program, and project managers must work to develop motivational strategies to help team members and other stakeholders cope with change and the resulting stress in a positive manner. As change agents, managers must:

- Articulate the vision of the program or project to internal and external stakeholders at different levels

- Be assertive and persistent in pursuing the organizational transformation

- Develop and use good listening skills

- Mentor team members as the change is implemented.

People Skills and Risk Management

Portfolios, programs, and projects all encounter risks of some type. The sheer size of many programs and projects places increased emphasis on managing risks and also on thinking of risks not only as potential problems but also as possible opportunities for the organization to pursue. While risk management usually focuses on the deliverables of the project or the benefits of the program, it also must focus on the people component; after all, programs and projects are performed by people.

To be effective as a portfolio manager, one must understand "how to manage risks and opportunities" (PMI 2008b, p. 16). These include fiscal and budgetary constraints, resource constraints, stakeholder dynamics and risk tolerances, and constraints affecting programs, projects, and nonproject work. PMI (2008b) further explains that assessing risks and reporting the risk level of the portfolio is critical in making decisions about whether to include a program or project in a portfolio, keep it in the portfolio, and determine how a risk to one component will affect others in the portfolio or those planned for future inclusion. Portfolio risk monitoring and control is paramount to organizational success.

Risks are identified and quantified, responses are prepared, and then the risks are monitored and controlled primarily because of their impact on project deliverables or program benefits. These risks typically involve the technical aspects of the program or project. Risks that could affect the people who are working on projects are often overlooked, but they are also important. For example, a key subject matter expert may decide to leave the organization or may have an accident or serious illness. What would the team do if this person were unable to contribute as planned?

Frame (2002) suggests that if one compiled a list of risks for a project, the list of possible human risks would be the longest. He also believes it is difficult to determine appropriate risk management responses for these risks in advance, creating the need for spontaneous, people skills-based solutions, rather than implementing predefined contingency plans.

The effective program or project manager must have strong interpersonal skills to manage the people risks in the organization and, if possible, turn these risks into potential opportunities. Managers must have the skills to effectively handle:

- Grievances, harassment complaints, and Equal Employment Opportunity Commission complaints

- Politics within the organization

- Union activity

- Violence in the workplace

- Loss of key staff members and other retention issues

- Time lost to injuries.

People Skills and Business Development

Previously, most organizations relied solely upon their strategic planning, sales staff, and marketing staff to determine the programs and projects to pursue.

Program and project managers were not part of this process, and if they were included, it was an afterthought, or they were, for example, asked to craft a potential technical solution to a customer's request to help secure a business opportunity. Managers were rarely involved until after a program or project was initiated.

Now, most programs and projects have multiple customers to satisfy, and customers cannot be taken for granted. There is no guarantee that even long-term customer relationships will continue in the future. Competition may dictate that the customer, no matter how satisfied it is with the program or project team, look elsewhere.

This means that everyone involved must be committed to business development, supporting adaptability, innovation, and customer-oriented solutions as strategic values of the organization. Effective and proactive communication with customers is needed at all levels, and program and project managers must be involved in solution development to foster customer collaboration, ensure that solutions yield customer value, and maintain customer interaction as long as possible to make sure customers are deriving value from the deliverables. At all levels, best practices and plans should be developed collaboratively with customers for innovative solutions.

Competencies in business development must now be part of a program or project manager's skill set and career development plan. Program and project managers must:

- Conduct numerous targeted customer meetings to nurture customer relationships over the long term

- Instill confidence in customers about the organization

- Understand the customer's business plan in order to relate program benefits and project deliverables to the plan

- Regularly obtain customer feedback to adjust benefits and deliverables as needed

- Lead the implementation of customer-focused, collaborative approaches and strategies—before the customer asks other organizations to provide these solutions.

People Skills and Knowledge Management

Knowledge is a strategic asset for organizations. Knowledge management (KM), previously called *information resource management*, can enhance productivity and increase profitability if knowledge assets are used effectively. But while everyone possesses some key knowledge assets, people tend not to share their knowledge with others even though they realize that sharing could serve the organization and lead to exemplary performance. Too often, people hoard knowledge or think of it as a private power, rather than leveraging the power of knowledge as an integral part of portfolio, program, and project management. The problem, then, is that most knowledge assets are not articulated.

KM should be part of people's daily work, but this can happen only in an organizational culture in which knowledge assets are regularly shared. Information must be easy and quick to access, and people must be able to use it to improve program and project effectiveness and efficiency. In such a culture, people assess a knowledge asset and consider how it might benefit others in the organization. The emphasis is on sharing and connecting people to people and people to knowledge.

Portfolios, programs, and projects are an excellent source of vital historical data that can be used for future programs and projects, which often must be completed in as short a time as is feasible with limited budgets and resources. Also, KM can facilitate rich communication and collaboration in virtual teams, on which project team members may never meet face to face, or co-located teams, even if team members do not know each other well.

Reich (2007) says that on teams in which members have a variety of specialties, "the project manager's primary task is to manage the knowledge bases of the team members and stakeholders so that they combine in the best possible way to successfully accomplish their assignment" (p. 6). (Team members, for their part, must learn how to transfer knowledge to others.) The effective portfolio, program, and project manager must be able to facilitate knowledge sharing and management, not only for the individual program or project but throughout the organization. These include:

- Leading knowledge asset creation and sharing by example, so that it becomes a routine way of working throughout the program and project life cycles

- Fostering an environment that emphasizes knowledge sharing, not knowledge hoarding

- Recognizing not only team members who developed breakthrough innovations that contributed to program or project success, but also those who worked with the technical team member to document what was done in an easily accessible format for future reference

- Emphasizing the importance of sharing knowledge to career advancement; i.e., sharing knowledge so others can pursue interesting and innovative tasks.

Leadership

1

Success on any program or project requires strong leadership from the program or project manager. According to the Project Management Institute (PMI):

- A leader "guides, inspires, and motivates team members and other project stakeholders to manage and overcome issues to effectively achieve project objectives" (2007, p. 23). Leadership is a key personal competency for the project manager.

- Leadership is important throughout all phases of a project's life cycle, but it is especially essential for communicating the project's vision and then inspiring the team to achieve high performance (2008a, p. 240).

- Leadership "is the process that will facilitate project goal achievement" (1987, p. F-6).

- "Leadership skills are needed for managing multiple project teams throughout the program life cycle" (2008c, p.13). Program managers must establish the overall direction of the program through their leadership of the program management team.

In the third edition of the *PMBOK® Guide* (PMI 2004), John Kotter writes that both leadership and management are necessary in order to produce outstanding results, but management is more concerned with "consistently producing key results expected by stakeholders" (p. 24), while leadership involves establishing direction and aligning, motivating, and inspiring people. This edition of the *PMBOK® Guide* stresses the importance of project managers as leaders, especially on large projects, but it also emphasizes that any team member can demonstrate leadership at any time in a variety of ways.

Adams and Campbell (1982) write that the "most important function of a manager, but oftentimes the least mentioned, is the leadership function. This is also true for the manager of a project" (p. 3). They explain that leading a project team requires skills, knowledge, and the ability to communicate with a diverse group of people who represent different functions and backgrounds. They understand the challenges of leading in a matrix management environment but warn that project managers without leadership ability may never see their projects completed.

Project managers tend to gradually acquire leadership skills early in their project careers and then sharpen them as they work on more complex projects and with more seasoned project managers. Project managers must be not only leaders but also managers, facilitators, and mentors. This chapter describes these key roles.

The Importance of Leadership in Program and Project Management

In many ways, program and project managers face more leadership challenges than functional or operational managers. Programs and projects may have more stakeholders than functional or operational teams, and they may not all be easy to identify. Organizational structures are often less clear in a program or project environment.

The primary difference between relationships in a program and project management environment and those in a functional or operational management structure is that the latter are more stable. The relationship between the functional or operational manager and the employee is ongoing. This means they can work together to formulate a career path for the employee that enhances his or her skills and enables him or her to pursue roles with greater responsibility over time. The employee is not concerned about what his or her role will be in the organization once the program or project ends or when his or her specific tasks on the program and project are completed. He or she has security in the organization. Also, the mission the employee must fulfill is generally clear, and the employee can relate to the strategic goals of the organization and the vision or desired state from his or her position within the functional unit. Formal and informal operating methods tend to remain constant. Additionally, program and project work requires people to work with others whom they may not have worked with in the past, but within the functional unit, the employee can develop longer-lasting relationships with peers. These help build lasting trust and can make the work experience a more enjoyable one.

Identifying Stakeholders

The functional or operational manager tends to have fewer stakeholders than does a program or project manager. This means that it is not necessary for functional or operational managers to prepare a stakeholder management plan, and over time, people get to know the key stakeholders with whom they work on a daily basis. Because the reporting relationships are known, it is easier to manage upward.

Relationships are less clear cut in program or project situations. For each new program or project, the program and project managers must identify the key stakeholders that will be involved and must ensure that a key stakeholder is not overlooked.

A project manager working on a major project for a transit authority believed that she had successfully completed the project. The project was a challenging one. It had involved an organizational restructuring, which are usually met with significant resistance from the employees involved. The project manager had mitigated this situation by explaining the purpose of the restructuring to the people involved and continually communicating with everyone regarding the project's progress.

When the restructuring was complete, the point of contact at the transit authority was pleased with the team's work and invited the project manager and her team to present their results to the executive staff. When the meeting began, before the project manager even started to present, one individual said that it was not necessary to do the presentation because he was totally dissatisfied with the results. He stated that he had not been consulted about the project and was not interviewed to share his views, and he told the team that it could meet with him and redo the project so that it met his needs or terminate the contract.

This person—whom the project manager had never seen before—was the transit authority's executive vice president for finance. He was a stakeholder who was not included in the stakeholder inventory the team prepared, and he was not part of the stakeholder management plan and strategy. His involvement was critical to the project's success.

This project manager learned the hard way about the importance of thorough stakeholder identification and the need to work with each stakeholder throughout the project to ensure his or her requirements are met.

PMI (2008a) suggests several ways project managers can identify stakeholders and determine the influence and impact they may have on the project. These include using power/interest, power/influence, or influence/impact grids or a salience model. The power/interest approach evaluates the stakeholder's level of authority and his or her level of concern. The power/influence approach assesses the stakeholder's power on the project versus his or her active involvement. The influence/impact grid evaluates the stakeholder's active involvement and his or her ability to effect change on the project. The salience model evaluates the stakeholder's power—e.g., the ability to impose his or her will, his or her level of urgency, his or her legitimacy, or his or her level of involvement in the project.

Using Smith's (2000) approach, project managers identify each stakeholder's interests in the project and estimate each stakeholder's priority and the potential impact (high, medium, or low) he or she will have on the project. Smith then suggests that project managers prepare a stakeholder importance/ influence matrix and describe the extent of stakeholders' participation in the project in each phase (initiating, planning, executing, monitoring and controlling, and closing). The project manager can then use this information to determine how best to work with each stakeholder and to prepare a stakeholder register and a stakeholder management strategy, which are both outputs of the "identify stakeholders" process outlined in the *PMBOK® Guide* (PMI 2008a).

But it is not enough to identify the stakeholders and prepare a strategy. Project managers must actively engage stakeholders throughout the project as planned and manage communications with them to see if they are interested in other aspects of the project. This active management of stakeholder expectations, as noted in the *PMBOK® Guide* (PMI 2008a), can increase the likelihood of project success because the stakeholders will feel a sense of ownership in the project.

Cleland and Ireland (2007) also note the importance of active stakeholder involvement in their five-step model, in which the project manager defines the key issues, then determines the underlying factors surrounding these issues, identifies the key stakeholders, identifies the specific "stake" each one has in the project, and finally modifies the project's strategy in light of the stakeholder analysis and the stakeholders' commitment to the project.

Milosevic (2003) recommends that project managers prepare a stakeholder matrix, listing stakeholders and the factors that are keys to success for the project. Table 1-1 presents an example.

To prepare this matrix, the project manager can use tools such as brainstorming (all team members discuss ideas freely), the nominal group technique (all team members speak without interruption or criticism), and Delphi analysis (experts participate anonymously, assisted by a facilitator, to help the group reach consensus and to prevent one person from dominating the discussion). The project manager must then document the matrix and update it throughout the project's life cycle. Milosevic explains that such a matrix is particularly useful while planning a project, but it also helps foster overall project team development because it informs the team members of the stakeholders' key success factors, which will help the team develop a stakeholder management strategy.

Table 1-1 Example Stakeholder Matrix

Stakeholder	Key Success Factor
Sponsor	Meeting the business case goals for the project
Project Manager	Ensuring the project is on time, within budget, according to specifications
Portfolio Manager	Ensuring the project supports the organization's strategic goals and objectives
Team Members	Completing their assigned tasks
Functional Managers	Ensuring team members complete work quickly so they can return to the functional unit
Finance Managers	Ensuring the project achieves its desired return on investment
Marketing Managers	Ensuring the deliverable is the first to market
Customers	Ensuring the project meets their needs and expectations

At the program level, PMI (2008c) devotes a knowledge area to stakeholder management. This knowledge area focuses on identifying the program's stakeholders in terms of how each one affects or will affect the program—for example, a stakeholder's influence on the culture of the organization, as well as any major issues associated with a stakeholder—and then developing a strategy to promote active stakeholder engagement, which will ensure acceptance of the program's deliverables, objectives, and benefits. At the program level, the emphasis is broader; in most cases, programs, which have a larger scope and longer duration, involve far more stakeholders and interdependencies than projects. PMI also notes the importance of stakeholder management to successfully implementing changes in an organization.

Both program and project managers must recognize that stakeholder management is a key success factor. It cannot be addressed in a document prepared at the beginning of the life cycle. It is an iterative and ongoing process. New stakeholders will become interested in or gain influence over the program or project, while others may no longer have an interest in the program or project at certain points.

The key stakeholder management skills required of program and project managers include:

- The ability to quickly identify the needs and expectations of a stakeholder.

- A high level of personal confidence. Program and project managers must be able to effectively work with stakeholders who hold various positions in the organization, customers, and the public.

- An ability to adapt their style of communication when interacting with stakeholders, given their personalities and specific interests and influence on the program or project.

- A willingness to embrace change and diverse points of view, which will help the program or project manager develop mutually agreeable solutions to problems or issues that may arise.

Clarifying Organizational Structure

Another key challenge for program and project managers is the lack of clarity of the structure of the organization. Program and project teams, whether they work virtually or are co-located, come together for a certain period of time and then disband. Especially in a virtual environment, team members may be subject matter experts that only join the program or project team for certain specific tasks. Further, it is rare for people to work on only a single program or project, unless they are a member of its core team and assigned to it for much of its duration. The organizational structure of programs and projects is, therefore, nebulous.

Further, in matrix environments (discussed in more detail in the introduction), the program or project manager's authority can range from low to high. A weak matrix or project-coordinator–type structure in which the project manager does not have much authority is typical for smaller projects, while for larger programs and projects, working within a strong matrix, and, sometimes, using a projectized approach, is more common and gives program or project managers a higher degree of authority. The organizational structure may change during the life of the program or project, especially if the program's or project's priority in terms of the organization's portfolio changes. As noted by PMI (2008c), different types of organizational structures may be used for the project and nonproject work that composes a program. Still, the project or program manager's level of authority may not be equal to that of a functional or operational manager. Both the nebulous organizational structures and the different levels of authority mean program and project managers must have sophisticated people skills, including:

- A high tolerance for ambiguity
- Personal comfort in operating with a dual focus (such as applying technical skills while also operating as a generalist)
- The ability to change direction quickly if needed and to lead the change within the team
- Skill in creating group cohesion, without encouraging groupthink or "management by agreement" (see Chapter 8 for more on the risks of too much agreement)
- Personal confidence that enables the program or project manager to undertake a significant endeavor without knowing in advance all the issues, risks, and other problems that may arise

Program and project managers can develop skills such as tolerance for ambiguity, strong self-confidence, and comfort with relinquishing control by:

- Becoming involved in mentoring relationships

- Volunteering for assignments outside their usual work

- Seeking open and honest feedback from peers and others in the organization regarding the effectiveness of their work

- Taking classes and workshops in other fields to get exposure to new ideas and new ways of working.

Leveraging Resources

The functional manager also benefits more from greater consistency of resources than does the program or project manager. While this book's focus is on human resources, other resources also are required at certain phases in the life cycle of a program or project. Because the functional manager has a long-term working relationship with those in his or her department, he or she is aware of the technical and interpersonal strengths and weaknesses of each employee and may have worked with individuals on developing their prospective career paths. This relationship enables the functional or operational manager to:

- Apply the strengths of the people in the unit more effectively

- Avoid problems by assigning people to tasks they are likely to perform successfully.

Also, because the working relationship at the functional or operational level is ongoing, a manager can develop the human resources of the unit. He or she may:

- Create and monitor ongoing personal development plans for each employee to enhance his or her technical and interpersonal skills, thus improving the talent pool

- Be involved in hiring and promoting individuals in the unit

- Provide other rewards and recognition in addition to salary advances.

Program and project managers face different challenges. First, they must establish at the inception of the program or project the knowledge, skills, and competencies required to achieve the program's or project's goals and complete the deliverables. Then they must determine how they will acquire the needed resources, when the resources will be needed, for how long they will be needed, and how they will be released to their functional or operational unit at the program's or project's conclusion. This information constitutes the resource management plan.

Research in the information systems arena illustrates the importance of team members having both domain and technology knowledge. Cheney and Lyons (1980) and Byrd and Turner (2001) note that insufficient personnel resources are a primary reason so many information systems projects fail. They suggest that the quality of the people who work on a project is of far greater value in project success than are the tools and techniques that those people use. Bruce and Pederson's (1982) assertion that selecting an outstanding project team is one of the more critical factors for the overall success of projects underscores this conclusion.

Then the program or project manager must negotiate with functional and operational managers, as well as with the human resources department, to acquire the needed human resources and to ensure that they are available when they are needed. Outsourcing may be necessary, so make-or-buy decisions may have to be made for both human resources and other resources.

Once the resources have been acquired, there are other challenges. The program or project manager:

- Must quickly assess the strengths and weaknesses of each team member (usually, team members have not previously worked for the program or project manager).

- Has little control over the human resource component; often, the resources are preassigned to the team by someone else.

- Has little time or authority to prepare long-term professional development plans for a poorly performing team member—or any team member. Often, the program or project manager must work with whoever is assigned to a specific work package but may not be able to provide training to team members to improve their skills and competencies while program or project work is underway.

- Must determine through a resource assignment matrix the specific roles and responsibilities of the team members for the various tasks or activities to be performed on the program or project.

- Has limited control over recognition and rewards for outstanding work done by the team as a whole or by specific individuals on the team.

To be able to work effectively within these human resource constraints, the program or project manager must have:

- The ability to quickly and accurately assess the strengths, weaknesses, and personalities of people he or she may never even meet, especially if work is performed in a virtual environment
- The ability to focus more on the *strengths* of each team member.

It is difficult to develop these skills, but there are approaches that can help:

- Becoming familiar with a system that describes individual personality differences, such as the Myers-Briggs Type Indicator or McClelland's achievement motivation approach.
- Making a conscious effort to identify some positive aspects of all negative professional situations.

Leveraging Motivation

It is simpler for the functional or operational manager to motivate his or her employees than it is for the program or project manager. In a functional or operational unit, relationships are long-term. Employees realize that they need to meet the expectations of their manager: He or she has the power to give raises, promotions, and assignments, and he or she also has a significant impact on each employee's career direction. Employees' performance development plans or management by objectives plans usually support those of their departmental manager, and their contributions further the department's goals and objectives. They prepare these plans with assistance from their manager. As they work to execute these plans, they can seek managerial feedback on ways to improve and to meet their goals and objectives. Contrast this situation with that of the program or project manager, who often has no opportunity to contribute formal feedback on team members' performance to the functional or operational manager.

Program and project managers face a far more difficult task in motivating team members. In a matrix setting, whether it is strong or weak, the program or project manager has little control over team member assignments and availability and must lead the team through influence and motivation rather than through direction. These managers must truly be skilled in influencing behavior creatively, using "carrots" as often as possible. To motivate team members effectively through influence, program and project managers need two key people skills:

- The ability to motivate team members through knowledge of their personal styles and their career stage

- The ability to apply sophisticated interpersonal communications skills.

The Four Key Leadership Functions of Program and Project Managers

A project manager must be able to play four different leadership roles throughout the project or program life cycle to complete a project on time, within budget, according to specifications, and to the customer's satisfaction. The program manager must take on these roles to deliver the program's intended benefits along with its deliverables (Flannes and Levin 2001, 2005). The roles include:

- Leader

- Manager

- Facilitator

- Mentor.

These four key roles are summarized in Table 1-2.

It is important not to think of these four roles as occurring in isolation. Instead, the program or project manager must recognize he or she is fulfilling these roles each day under different circumstances. Even as a project manager, for example, is having a one-on-one conversation with a team member, he or she may need to seamlessly move from one role to another.

Generally, project or program managers are comfortable operating in one or two of the four roles. In one's own development, one should concentrate on improving competencies in all of the four roles, but especially in those one does not use on a regular basis. Developing improved competencies in these areas may be an element the program or project manager includes in his or her individual development plan.

Table 1-2   The Four Roles of a Leader

Role	Key Behaviors
Leader	• Conceptualize and articulate the program or project vision
	• Motivate team members throughout the program or project toward the vision
	• Represent the team to stakeholders and motivate stakeholders throughout the program and project to work toward the vision
	• Embrace and cope with change
Manager	• Create a program or project administrative structure to bring consistency to the program or project
	• Track compliance with program and project performance
	• Report progress to stakeholders in a timely way
Facilitator	• Communicate clearly, both verbally and in writing
	• Listen attentively to team members, sponsors, and other stakeholders
	• Model and create methods for conflict resolution
	• Proactively obtain needed human resources
Mentor	• Model appropriate team, professional, and organizational behaviors
	• Help team members identify possibilities for problem-solving and career path development
	• Display a genuine personal interest in team members' performance and development, as individuals and as team members

The Program or Project Manager as Leader

The leadership role is critical to program and project success. As noted by Shenhar, Levy, Dvir, and Maltz (2007), it is necessary to "turn project managers into leaders" and "make them responsible for business results" (p. 25). To do so, the authors suggest that project managers must create an "inspiring vision, and develop an appropriate project spirit" (p. 28).

For example, when a program begins, the vision or end state is articulated in a business case for the program. It is further developed in the program manager's charter. When the charter is approved and the program manager is appointed, he or she then expands this charter by developing the program management plan. Each component project in the program must also have its own business case, and the program manager must ensure that this business case supports the overall program's vision or desired end state. This vision is *why* the program or project is undertaken and shows the added value of the program or project not only to the organization but also to its customers and any valued partners. This vision further must support the organization's objectives as shown in its strategic plan and in its portfolio.

In working to describe the vision, the program or project manager (or the sponsor, if the program or project management plan is prepared before the program or project manager is assigned) must integrate the perspectives of numerous stakeholders, most importantly those of the customer, the organization's executives, the portfolio review board or similar group, and other key stakeholders. To determine the vision, the program or project manager must actively engage these individuals to ensure that the true purpose is captured and that it is one they will support throughout the life cycle. If the program or project manager does not develop a clear statement of the overall vision, this only will lead to problems, such as scope creep, lack of customer acceptance of the final products, extensive change requests, and poor team morale.

Then the program or project manager must describe the vision in explicit terms so that the team members understand it, are committed to it, and understand why the program or project is being undertaken. (Regarding a case study of a high-tech project, Shenhar et al. (2007) noted that because the project vision that was part of the proposal was not well articulated to the project teams, it was essentially "lost," and the program plan had to be redesigned twice.) The program or project manager must also note any implied goals that may not be obviously stated and the customer's definition of added value. If the program or project manager is confident that executive management and the customer support the vision, the program and project will begin with motivation and purpose.

The statement of work for a particular project indicated that the project's purpose was to improve the safety of milk in the U.S. However, the real purpose of the project was to develop a database containing test data used to detect animal drug residues in milk and to assess the effectiveness of the various testing methods. Obviously, such an initiative could help improve the safety of milk in the U.S. but the vision—improving the safety of the milk supply—was stated in a way that was too broad for this project.

During the kickoff meeting held with the team and customer representatives, the project manager asked everyone to state his or her vision for the project. Interestingly, everyone believed that the vision was to ensure the safety of the nation's milk supply. Through an active discussion, the team and customer representatives crafted a more specific vision that everyone could support: developing a database to assess the effectiveness of testing methods used to identify animal drug residues in milk.

Once the team agreed on the initial vision, it worked closely with the customer, then worked to develop the needed planning documents and successfully executed the project, which involved several hundred stakeholders.

At your program or project team's kickoff meeting, ensure that everyone is comfortable with the overall vision and has a common understanding of it. Discuss the vision with the team, then craft it into a statement that the team will support and will sign off on in the team's charter.

To make sure everyone involved understands and agrees to the program or project vision, the program or project manager should:

- Ask probing questions that demonstrate an interest in taking initial discussions beyond the general level.

- Notice what the customer is saying and not saying. If there are multiple customers, talk with each of them to define objectives and requirements.

- Clarify perceptions of the program or project's purpose, ensuring that the program or project manager, the customer, and other key stakeholders are all working toward the same goals and objectives.

While it is important to discuss the vision at the program's or project's kickoff meeting, this is not a one-time discussion. At each team meeting, the vision should be reviewed, especially if the program or project is long and complex. External or internal environmental changes may necessitate changing the vision in some way or altering the overall priority of the program or project in the organization's portfolio.

This discussion is not a one-way discussion in which the leader makes a formal briefing; instead, it is interactive. Each team member should be encouraged to participate and define the vision in his or her own words. This approach has more meaning for each team member and allows the team to be more engaged in the process.

The program or project manager also demonstrates his or her role as a leader in the early stage of the program or project as he or she establishes personal credibility with the team members. Establishing such credibility—or "walking the talk"—involves demonstrating actions and behaviors that are consistent with verbally espoused values or decision-making processes.

For project managers, leadership as a personal competency involves creating a team environment that fosters high performance, building and maintaining relationships, motivating and mentoring team members, taking accountability for the project, and using influencing skills as needed (PMI 2007).

Congruence between actions and spoken values, including maintaining commitments, demonstrating fair treatment, acting with integrity, and taking ownership for adverse project outcomes, is essential to creating a motivating climate. Leaders striving for congruence:

- Demonstrate their own values through their day-to-day work

- Refrain from making promises that may not be possible to keep because of organizational resource limitations, political constraints, or internal or external factors outside one's control. Instead, they explain why it is not possible to promise to do so.

- Seek feedback from a mentor, coach, or supportive peer regarding how congruent one's behavior is with one's stated values.

Leadership for both program and project managers also involves serving as the team's voice when communicating with external stakeholders, including the public. The leader should communicate actively and consistently with internal and external stakeholders by:

- Supporting and obtaining buy-in to program or project goals and benefits

- Providing updates and progress reports regularly and upon request

- Addressing conflict and resolving issues in a proactive, productive, and forthright manner.

In summary, the program or project manager's leader role involves answering the question "Why are we doing this program or project?" by describing the program's or project's vision and mission and the added value and benefits the completed program or project will bring.

The Program or Project Manager as Manager

One of the people-related challenges program and project managers face is creating an administrative system that has enough structure and discipline to complete the program or project but is not excessively bureaucratic. According to PMI, the manager's role is to "effectively administer . . . the project through the deployment and use of human, financial, material, intellectual, and intangible resources" (2007, p. 23). More specifically, PMI says that managing requires building and maintaining a team, planning and managing for project success in an organized way, and resolving conflicts involving the team or other stakeholders.

It is difficult to create an effective administrative system. The balance between structure and freedom for team members varies from project to project or program to program, depending on the mix of the individuals on the team, even if the organization already has an administrative system in place that is supported by its enterprise program management office (EPMO). Such structures often need tailoring to meet the specific needs of each program or project; some aspects of the system may be appropriate, while others may not be needed. The program or project manager must determine, in conjunction with the team, what should be retained and what is not needed, given the uniqueness of the program and project.

There are a number of indications that program or project managers are successfully executing the manager role:

- Team member roles and responsibilities provide a clear source of direction, while still giving each team member opportunities to define his or her own plan to complete them. This can be done by using a resource assignment matrix (or responsible, accountable, consult, inform [RACI] chart) tied to the work breakdown structure that shows specific responsibilities for each team member (e.g., approve, coordinate, review, perform, accountable, or consult) based on specific work packages that have been assigned.

- Processes and procedures state clear behavioral and performance expectations as guidelines rather than as strict rules that must be followed without exception. Managers should carefully consider which aspects of a methodology must be followed and which are optional based on the specific requirements of the program or project.

- Meetings are purposeful and focused, providing opportunities to balance the need to dissent and discuss decisions and seek closure. As appropriate, a meeting can even be held to review the structure and methodologies in place to see if improvements are needed.

The program or project manager who successfully functions as a manager explains to team members the rationale for what some may think is excessive structure. Managers should recognize that some team members have difficulty operating in a structured environment. In these discussions, managers can discuss making structures more flexible if possible (after consulting with the EPMO, if applicable), and they should make clear that they want to complete the program or project and transition it to the customer or an operational function with minimal bureaucracy.

Personal preferences and style will also affect the way the program or project manager executes the managerial role. Some people have a tendency to create excessive structure (in other words, become too controlling), while others may create too little structure, adopting a more laissez-faire approach to managing, even if this lack of structure diverges from the EPMO's or organization's requirements.

An overcontrolling manager has difficulty prioritizing how best to spend his or her time and often focuses on tasks that may better be handled by others. Although well-intentioned, such a program or project manager strives for excessive structure and order, perhaps reflecting his or her doubt that things will work out as planned. This type of leader often struggles with anxiety and personal stress and is frequently unaware of how his or her behavior affects the attitude and morale of program and project team members.

One manager who was working with a telecommunications company set up a methodology that team members considered to be overly controlling. For example, team members were required to complete detailed progress reports and email them to this manager every week. The program was large, so this manager received about 300 different reports via email each Wednesday. He was pleased to receive so many emails, and the team knew he reviewed each one. Also, while the project leads were empowered to conduct regular meetings with customers via teleconferences, this overcontrolling manager often listened in without the project lead's knowledge. Once people realized that the manager might listen in, communications with the customer became more formal, and the teleconferences lacked the dynamic they previously had when open communication was the norm.

Team members working for such a micromanager may:

- Feel frustrated and angry about being overstructured or overmanaged, especially if they have extensive experience in successful program or project management

- Lose motivation to complete assigned work packages and activities

- Believe that they are undervalued or unappreciated or that the manager does not trust them to do their assigned work.

If a program or project manager suspects that he or she is at risk of becoming a micromanager, he or she should seek regular feedback from the team. Ask direct questions, because team members tend not to volunteer their opinions of their managers, or send out an anonymous survey, perhaps from an independent source such as the EPMO, to gather honest opinions.

Conversely, the laissez-faire manager tends to create too little structure for the team, allowing many details or processes to drift. This person may place too much trust in the team members, especially if he or she has worked with the team members in the past and knows their strengths and weaknesses. This type of manager also may overlook matters such as compliance with the program or project management methodology required by EPMO (or a comparable group) and may not be concerned with timely completion of work packages and activities. Laissez-fare managers often enjoy creating the program or project vision but are less interested in implementing the vision on a tactical level.

If a manager errs on the side of creating too little structure, there are several risks:

- Deliverables, compliance, and monitoring may suffer.

- New team members may not know what is required of them; no one will show them the team's operating guidelines.

- Team members may be anxious and hesitant about how to proceed because they believe they do not have sufficiently specific guidance to be successful.

- Stakeholders may not receive the information they need, so they may not support the program or project in a positive way, becoming uninterested, uninvolved, or even outwardly negative.

Clearly, the "right" place to be on the continuum between overcontrol and undercontrol is in the middle. A manager who takes a moderate approach establishes a structure that team members follow, but he or she allows enough autonomy and flexibility to enable team members to be creative when completing their assigned work. It is difficult to define the ideal point on the continuum between overcontrol and undercontrol, but there are several indicators of an appropriate balance between extremes:

- Team members report that appropriate procedures are in place for the team to operate autonomously.

- These procedures are documented in a team charter, which all members sign to demonstrate their commitment to them.

- Key work can be tracked and monitored.

- Team members demonstrate positive attitudes, initiative, and creativity.

- The team prepares basic reports to stakeholders that are easy to read and understand, are not time consuming to prepare and read, and provide the stakeholders with the necessary information on progress and status.

The Program or Project Manager as Facilitator

Facilitation is one of the most subtle yet profound roles program and project managers can assume. As a program or project facilitator, the manager demonstrates behaviors and attitudes that can help others get their work done. The program or project manager does not do team members' work for them; instead, he or she sets the stage for success. PMI (2008c) recommends that the program manager prepare high-level plans to guide project and operational managers working on the program and specifically states that the role of the program manager is *not* to do the work of other managers working on the program.

Facilitation often is achieved through the art of influencing others. It entails communicating effectively, resolving conflicts, obtaining needed resources, and motivating people, both individually and as a team. A key role of the program manager is to resolve any conflicts a project manager feels he or she cannot resolve on his or her own, especially if these conflicts may affect another project or other work on the program. A program manager may also step in to help a project manager determine the most appropriate response to a risk, whether the risk is perceived as an opportunity or as a threat, particularly if the risk might affect another project in the program.

Facilitators make use of the following people skills:

- Using clear, explicit statements to get to the point

- Asking open-ended questions, such as "What else do you think our team should do to be successful on this project?" or "How can I best help you to resolve your conflict?"

- Being a good listener by trying to recognize the key points of the speaker's message

- Asking for clarification as needed by asking if their understanding is correct

- Demonstrating a willingness to behave assertively and to do whatever it takes, considering professional and social responsibility, to assist the project manager or the team member, even if this means not being liked by a key stakeholder.

Facilitation as a management skill can be compared with the task of planning and orchestrating the details for a dinner party. The host of the party does his or her best to consider the needs of the guests, to obtain the items needed for the event, and to create an atmosphere appropriate for the gathering. As the guests arrive, the host continues facilitating the event by offering choices to the guests and doing what he or she can to create a positive experience.

However, this is where "facilitation" ends. The host cannot make the people have a good time. Facilitation provides them with the resources they need, but the creation of fun is up to the guests themselves.

The goal of facilitation is to provide team members with choices, options, and a conductive setting and then trust that the team will create the sought-after outcomes and benefits. It is *not* the program or project manager's job to create the solution on his or her own—that is up to the team.

Further, as the program or project manager helps team members resolve conflicts, responds to potential risks, and acquires needed resources in a productive and effective manner, he or she demonstrates that he or she is an adept facilitator. If the program or project manager is able to respond to potential resource issues—e.g., the program or project requires a specialized technical expert—in advance and successfully attains the needed resources, the team will see that the program or project manager supports and is dedicated to them and their work.

Facilitation requires that the program or project manager not get too involved in the details or substance of the program or project. Such immersion in the details, while intellectually stimulating, can become a way to avoid some of the less pleasant aspects of being a facilitator, such as the need to be assertive to make things happen for the team and stakeholders. The assertiveness component of the facilitator role can be developed through training, feedback from sponsors or peers, reading books, mentoring and coaching, and in workshops on assertive behavior. In addition to assertiveness, PMI (2007) urges project managers to take the initiative when needed and assume calculated risks to expedite the completion of a project.

As facilitators, program, and project managers should prevent inconclusive discussions by recognizing that consensus, while desirable, often cannot be obtained, and appropriate actions and decisions must be taken, especially if the program or project is in a crisis situation. They also must make timely decisions, be persistent, and show consistency in their actions.

The Program or Project Manager as Mentor

Mentoring is the process by which one person (the mentor) assists another person (the mentee) either formally or informally in various tasks related to professional development and growth. The purpose of mentoring is to share the lessons the program or project manager has learned from experience to improve the capability of other individuals or the program or project team as a whole. Mentoring relationships can be informal or more formal, designed to emphasize improvements in knowledge, skills, and competencies.

Establishing mentoring relationships with team members is a PMI leadership performance criterion (2007). Mentoring is a valuable contribution to team member performance and development, but it is a service that needs to be offered with care. Some team members may not wish to be in a mentoring relationship, especially if it is with their program or project manager; they may prefer to work with someone who is not part of the program or project team, perhaps in their functional organization or even in another business unit or department. Nonetheless, the program or project manager can informally mentor a current team member by offering the mentoring input in a casual and indirect manner that aids the team member's growth and also addresses current work on the program or project. This kind of informal mentoring is especially useful when new people join the team so they can understand the purpose of the program or project, the methods the team is using to do its work, and the overall policies, procedures, and guidelines in place in the organization.

Mentoring may call upon the program or project manager to demonstrate the following people skills, depending on the needs of the individual and the current needs of the program or project.

- Serving as a role model: the program or project leader clearly demonstrates skills, behaviors, and attitudes whose adoption may benefit team members

- Demonstrating a genuine, personal interest in the welfare and professional growth of team members and, as appropriate, providing counseling or advice concerning team members' problems and one-on-one personal attention

- Offering suggestions, possibilities, resources, problem-solving approaches, and opportunities to discuss with team members how certain situations were handled, current and future issues regarding their assigned work, and improvements team members can make in the use of processes, tools, and techniques

- Providing feedback that is supportive yet frank and accurate, reinforcing successes while portraying failures as learning opportunities that can spur team members to improve their knowledge, skills, and competencies

- Motivating team members to set and achieve long-term professional goals and to overcome any barriers that may impact career growth, including identifying any needed changes in attitudes or interpersonal style.

During the more intense periods of a project, for example in a program during the delivery of program benefits phase, most interactions between the program or project manager and team members are focused on real-time issues and risks. Focusing on mentoring during these periods is not appropriate and should wait until work demands are lessened. During quieter times, the program or project manager, in the mentor's role, and the team member can debrief each other about recent work. The mentor can then offer formal or informal guidance about how the team member could approach particular situations in the future.

In program management, often the mentoring relationship is between the program manager and his or her project managers. Sometimes the projects are already underway before the program is officially approved. Then the mentor's role may be to help the project managers see how their projects fit into the program, to assist the project managers in their work with their teams, and to help the project managers understand the vision for the program and why the projects are now being managed as part of the program.

The program manager also can help the project manager develop various project management plans to ensure that the project plans support the benefits and goals of the program and to point out interdependencies with other projects in the program. Additionally, program managers can help project managers resolve issues, respond to risks, or resolve conflicts.

Sometimes a team member will request feedback from the program or project manager; other times, he or she will not ask for feedback but will be receptive if it is offered. Program and project managers should pay attention to the team members' personalities and motivational styles to identify individuals who might be receptive to mentoring.

In many organizations, mentoring relationships work best as formal ones between, for example, a project manager and a person on another project team. Such a relationship enables both parties to focus more clearly on the developmental needs of the mentee, without the distractions associated with both parties working on the same project. Regardless, whenever mentoring takes place, its effectiveness should be evaluated by the mentor, the mentee, and others on the program or project using one-on-one interviews or surveys.

It is important to carefully select mentors. Typically, mentors volunteer for these assignments, but they must be evaluated to determine if they have the required interpersonal skills and competencies to assist team members or the entire team. It is recommended that specific criteria be developed for selecting a mentor. A training program for mentors in the organization is beneficial. Training in providing advice, listening skills, communication approaches, and problem solving may be needed.

Mentors must have enough time to adequately perform this role; they have to provide timely guidance and feedback for the relationship to be a successful one. Similarly, the mentee also must have sufficient time to work with the mentor.

A formal relationship between the mentor and the mentee, in which each person commits to specific goals and objectives and signs off on them, is recommended. The mentor and mentee usually document this relationship in their first meeting. The documentation describes the goals and objectives of the relationship, how often the mentor and mentee will meet, whether meetings will be held face to face or virtually, how they will discuss issues or concerns outside regularly scheduled meetings, areas in which improvement is sought, and how each party will evaluate the benefits of the relationship. This documented process can benefit the mentee by ensuring that he or she is receiving mentoring advice that is consistent with the organization's values. If not, the mentoring relationship should be changed to add value or terminated.

When a documented approach is in place, it is easier to evaluate the relationship and determine ways in which it could be improved. Later, the mentor and mentee can determine whether the documented mentoring objectives were achieved, especially with regard to improving interpersonal skills, as work on the program or project continues.

Some mentees describe the mentoring relationship as a positive one in which they can talk in confidence with a professional outside their program or project team about matters of professional growth and development. Mentors report positive feelings about the opportunity to give something back to the profession in terms of helping a junior colleague move along the career path.

Summary

Leadership challenges program and project managers face are more complex than those faced by the functional leader. The program and project managers must confront leadership hurdles in the areas of organizational structure, consistency and availability of human resources, and the motivation of team members. Many organizations recognize that program and project managers must become real leaders who handle strategic, operational, and human factors (Shenhar et al. 2007). The leadership role of program or project managers is multifaceted; they must simultaneously serve as leaders, managers, facilitators, and mentors.

The leadership role requires that program and project managers provide a vision to the team, or describe the desired end state of the program or project by defining the value that will be added by its completion and the benefits to be achieved. The manager role helps keep the focus on the customer in terms of performance, time, cost, and value. The facilitator role involves providing the emotional and logistical support that team members need to complete the program or project. Finally, the mentor role asks the program or project manager to artfully assist team members with issues of professional growth, development, and direction.

It is rare that a program or project manager excels equally in all four of these leadership roles. Managers need to be realistic regarding their own strengths and weaknesses in each role and proactively address weaknesses in their individual development plan (without criticizing themselves in the process). It is also important for program and project managers to develop the ability to recognize the situations in which a specific role is appropriate and when to move from one role to another.

Discussion Questions

A project manager working for an aerospace company in San Diego is placed in charge of a major project in her company, ranked number 10 on the list of 125 prioritized projects. Her team members are mostly junior-level professionals with little experience working in project management and also in working on their own without close supervision. This presents a problem for her because the bulk of the project work is to be conducted by this team, which is a virtual team operating in three locations in the United States, one location in Europe, and one location in Asia. She has limited funding for a face-to-face meeting with all of the team members and will need to rely on conference calls and emails for most communications among the team. The company does not have a standard project management methodology but is considering establishing an enterprise project management office.

While she has managed projects before, the project manager's teams were staffed with more senior professionals, many of whom were PMPs, each with a history of self-directed performance, and the teams were co-located, so it was easy to meet regularly and discuss issues of concern.

For this new project, she makes the false assumption that her laissez-faire management style, which was successful in the past, will still be appropriate. She believes she can leave much of the direction up to the team.

However, as the project evolves, problems surface because the laissez-faire approach is not working. The team members often have conflicts that she must resolve, and team members are often unsure about how to proceed effectively to do their assigned work. Some are not even certain what they are supposed to be doing on this project. These problems stemmed from a need for greater monitoring and structure for this team, their junior-level status, and the challenges associated with working in a virtual environment.

Consider the following questions:

1. How can this project manager establish a more structured managerial approach?
2. How can the project manager then communicate the need for the structured approach to the team?
3. How can the project manager mentor some of the junior-level team members?
4. How can this project manager ensure that all of the team members share the same concept of the project's vision, its goals, and the benefits that must be achieved?

Team-Building Strategies

2

Katzenbach and Smith (1993) define a team as a small number of people with complementary skills committed to a common purpose, performance goals, and approach, for which they hold themselves mutually accountable. Parker (1994) writes that a team is a group of people with a high degree of interdependence geared toward the achievement of a goal or the completion of a task. Stuckenbruck and Marshall (1985) define an effective project team as one in which the team members are interdependent, have a reason to work together, are committed to working together, are accountable as a functioning unit, and have a moderate level of competition and conflict.

Mayer (1998) defines a virtual team as one composed of people who are distributed across buildings, states, and countries. Delisle, Thomas, Jugdev, and Buckle (2001) write that a virtual team is a collection of task-driven members separated by geographic or temporal space.

Virtual teams are common in today's workforce, especially as more and more organizations move to a management-by-projects approach. They are also common in programs in which the program manager may be managing component projects located in other areas and in which team members on one project may support another project located in a different area. In portfolio management, the members of the portfolio review board also often work virtually. Virtual teams are no longer considered unique but instead are viewed as a routine way of working. Many virtual teams will never meet face to face on a project or program, or if they do have the luxury of a face-to-face meeting, typically it is held at the beginning of the project or program, and these meetings are not regular occurrences.

In a co-located setting, in which team meetings are the norm, it is easy to use each of these meetings as an opportunity for team building. Often, a special meeting is held just to focus on team building and the challenging people aspects of the program or project. Virtual teams do not provide these opportunities, so they must take different approaches to team building. This chapter presents strategies for effective team building.

What Is Team Building?

The Project Management Institute discusses eight key interpersonal skills for project managers, one of which is team building (PMI 2008a). It defines team building as "the process of helping a group of individuals, bound by a common sense of purpose, to work interdependently with each other, the leader, external stakeholders, and the organization" (p. 410). This is a far broader definition than PMI offered in the glossary of terms in the 1987 *PMBOK® Guide*, which defines team building as "the process of influencing a group of diverse individuals, each with their own goals, needs, and perspectives to work together effectively for the good of the project such that their team will accomplish more than the sum of their individual efforts could otherwise achieve."

Team-building activities involve establishing goals, defining and negotiating roles and procedures, and establishing processes, including an emphasis on communication, managing conflicts, motivating team members, and leadership (PMI 2008a). Team building is not a one-time exercise but is a continual process throughout the project life cycle.

Stuckenbruck and Marshall (1985) write that team building "can well be the most important aspect of the project manager's job" (p. 50). They say that the major focus of team building is "identifying and obtaining consensus on the project's goals and objectives" (p. 5). Many of the approaches Stuckenbruck and Marshall discuss, while designed for the co-located team, apply to any team (see Table 2-1).

The Growth of Virtual Teams

While program and project work has been done virtually for years, the teams themselves were rarely considered virtual in a literal sense. Instead, a lead organization performed and coordinated the work, using regional offices or other business units for support and integration activities. Beginning in the 1990s, the use of the term *virtual teams* became commonplace. It will only be used more in the future.

Table 2-1   Team-Building Approaches

Team-building approach from Stuckenbruck and Marshall (1985)	Applicable to co-located teams in 2010?	Applicable to virtual teams in 2010?
Incorporating team building into project activities	Yes	Yes
Project manager must be responsible for its effectiveness	Yes	Yes
Planning for team building	Yes	Yes
Negotiating with functional managers to recruit team members	Possibly (resources may be preassigned)	Possibly (resources may be preassigned)
Using a responsibility assignment matrix	Yes	Yes
Having a kickoff meeting	Yes	Yes
Obtaining team member commitments to the project	Yes	Yes
Building communications links	Yes	Yes
Conducting team-building exercises	Yes	Yes
Promoting team development throughout the project	Yes	Yes

Many people believe that virtual teams are contributing to the growth of management-by-projects and the consideration of programs and projects as strategic assets to an organization. Having a continuous stream of projects has emerged as the method to ensure the growth and survival of the organization. By using virtual teams that are planned and supported appropriately, programs and projects can be delivered in a more effective and efficient manner.

Benefits of Virtual Teams

The increasing globalization and complexity of work makes the use of virtual teams a necessity for many organizations. Through the use of communications and information technology, greater collaboration among people working in a virtual environment now is possible; organizations are not limited to working with people located in a single time zone, and people can work together without needing day-to-day interaction or socialization, and with fewer constraints on time and infrastructure.

While the effective use of resources is often the motivation for forming a virtual team, another key factor is a lower total cost for the program's or project's deliverable. If more than one country is a potential provider for the same resource, a resource in a country with a favorable exchange rate may be much less expensive. By building a virtual team, the program or project manager can select the most skilled resources, possibly at a lower cost, because the resource pool is much larger. Juhre (2001) notes that when skilled technical resources are in demand, global staffing becomes a critical success factor for enterprise projects.

Global virtual teams also may allow for around-the-clock work, even if the team has only one shift in operation at any given location. An effective configuration management system and attention to documentation management among all team members allow documents to be easily passed from one location to another. The receiving team can review and enhance what the previous team has done, then pass it on to the team in the next geographic area. Software, systems engineering, and information technology programs or projects especially benefit from this approach.

Challenges Associated with Virtual Teams

It is necessary, though, to recognize that virtual teams present challenges that are not present in traditional co-located teams. These include, but are not limited to, working with people in different time zones, the locations of the key stakeholders, the need to effectively use web-based technologies for collaboration and communication, the requirement for rigorous documentation control, contingencies for volatility in the exchange rate, regional and political risks, and possible differences in terminology even when using the same language.

There are challenges that particularly affect team building and communication:

- Often, there is increased pressure on a virtual team to develop into a cohesive group in less than optimal time.

- As noted by Mehrabian (1968), the rarity of verbal communication and the inability to observe team members' nonverbal cues present additional barriers. Body language may indicate nonverbally whether one feels positively or negatively about the project.

- Virtual team members rarely have opportunities to talk casually with each other, so they often are unaware of the work performed by others.

- It is easy for team members to be silent in a virtual environment, and this silence might be interpreted as their agreeing with program or project decisions when in fact they might be totally unaware of the decisions. Assumptions about agreement may result in groupthink.

Managing Virtual Teams

While clear communications are important on any team, they take on even greater importance on virtual teams. On a virtual team, many challenges may be avoided if everyone agrees to establish and follow clear communication channels. For example, a workable communications plan is critical if the team is located in different time zones throughout the globe. It is important to ensure that one individual on the team is not always inconvenienced when conference calls and team meetings are held.

Some ways to manage a virtual team include:

- The distributed approach
- The "pure" approach
- The joint-venture approach.

The Distributed Approach

Teams can follow a work breakdown structure and combine it with a resource breakdown structure (Rad and Levin, 2003). Each work package could be assigned to a separate team, which will design, plan, and implement the work and complete the deliverable. There is a separate project manager, or team lead, for each work package, who reports to the overall project manager. Following such an approach, the team responsible for a particular work package has no need to communicate with other members of the team. This approach has been used in the construction field for years and in other fields in which a corporate office or government agency might ask a business unit or regional office to handle certain program or work packages.

The "Pure" Approach

If the project is planned and implemented by a single team, a separate project manager for each work package is not required (Rad and Levin, 2003). Tasks are assigned to individual team members, as are resource allocations and schedule adjustments. The team works directly for one project manager, and team members must actively communicate and collaborate with others on the team because everyone is working as a cohesive unit.

The Joint-Venture Approach

As outsourcing and offshoring have become more common, so have joint ventures, even among companies that often are competitors. Drouin, Bourgault, and Sauders (2009) note that such joint ventures and alliances have become ways to enter markets that in the past a single company may not have pursued on its own. They found in their research that some of these joint ventures are more successful than others; often success is due to the implementation of effective human resource management processes. However, attention to human resource management occurs after the joint venture is established, rather than in the planning stage. Drouin, Bourgault, and Sauders' research includes work done by Frayne and Geringer, who estimated that only four percent of the entire time devoted for forming the joint venture was devoted to human resource management. This statistic is not given to imply that joint ventures will not be successful; rather, it shows that human resource management is often overlooked when joint ventures are established and planned.

Characteristics of the Virtual Environment

Though the approaches Stuckenbruck and Marshall (1985) discuss are applicable to any team, they must be handled differently in a virtual team than on a co-located team to ensure their effectiveness. Key characteristics of the virtual environment that differ from most co-located environments include:

- Personal flexibility
- More interactive communications, rather than ones that are "pushed" or "pulled"
- Greater use of collaborative tools and techniques
- A high-trust culture with defined team values

- Collaborative leadership

- Greater adaptability

- Dynamic team membership

- Less time for team members to learn to work together effectively

- Multicultural teams

- Less visibility in the organization

- Required knowledge, skills, and competencies

- Unknown conflict.

Personal Flexibility

Some people want to be on a virtual team because they think of such teams as a way they can actively contribute to a project with minimal administrative structure and bureaucracy. Once virtual team members commit to the project through a charter and understand their own roles and responsibilities, they can execute them according to the project's schedule and their own schedules. With fewer administrative processes and procedures to follow, virtual team members can instead focus on innovation and creativity in their work. They can be more task-oriented because they are not encumbered by frequent in-person interruptions. Communications with fellow team members are planned rather than impromptu, enabling more focused concentration on work. When team meetings are held, they tend to be more productive because they follow a set agenda.

Interactive Communications

On a virtual team, team members may receive extensive "pushed" communications such as letters, memos, or status reports, but ideally, virtual (and co-located) teams strive to engage in interactive communications, which PMI promotes as more efficient (2008a). Teams should have a communications plan specifying how and when communications will take place and should define methods for communication in the virtual team charter. The plan and the charter may specify, for example, how often team members should check their email and how quickly they must respond, when teleconferences will be held, and how portals, discussion forums, and blogs are to be used. The virtual team can collectively determine how to reduce "pushed" communications that may be interesting but not necessary and establish processes for accessing significant amounts of information from knowledge repositories or intranet sites at their convenience.

Greater Use of Collaborative Tools and Techniques

One reason that management by projects has become more prevalent globally is that today's advanced communications technologies facilitate virtual teamwork. It is no longer necessary for everyone to be co-located, nor is it necessary for program or project managers to practice "management by walking around." Instead, it is necessary for the program or project manager to ensure the same collaborative tools are available to all team members regardless of their location. Everyone must be able to access a portal, if one is to be used, use the same email system, have access to the same project management tools and techniques, and have the equipment to conduct video and audio teleconferences.

A High-Trust Culture with Defined Team Values

It is easy on a virtual team for members to have out-of-sight relationships and common for them to feel as if they are not really part of the team. It also is common for team members and the program or project manager not to trust someone who is new to the team. However, because the virtual environment allows teams to obtain the services and skills of subject matter experts, regardless of their location, teams frequently have to work with people they do not know. Teams must learn to practice *swift trust*, which Meyerson, Weick, and Kramer define as trust that is "conferred presumptively or ex ante" (1996, p. 177). (For a fuller discussion of swift trust, refer to Chapter 3.) Mishra (1996) explains that swift trust is necessary for work in temporary teams, particularly when there is pressure to achieve the goals of the project.

Trust facilitates collaborative and cooperative behavior. Virtual teams should assume everyone trusts one another until proven otherwise and should build a climate of trustworthiness from the start of the program or project until its closure by establishing and communicating defined values for the team.

Collaborative Leadership

Collaboration—the merging of diverse points of view to resolve conflicts—has long been recognized as a preferred problem-solving approach. It is an attempt to completely satisfy the needs of parties that have dissimilar goals (Mishra 1996).

Collaboration combines assertiveness and cooperativeness. It demands that team members consider the merits of each other's positions, and it emphasizes learning from others by testing one's own assumptions. Team members who demonstrate a willingness to work with others and to understand other perspectives will gain greater trust and support, which in turn will improve future communications within the team. Parker (1994) adds that team members who exercise collaboration are goal-oriented individuals who encourage the team to fulfill its mission by trying new ideas and enhanced processes.

On a virtual team, because people are in different locations, a collaborative leadership approach is a necessity; the program or project manager cannot be in each location to meet with each stakeholder. Each team member, therefore, assumes a leadership role whenever required, making sure he or she communicates with the program or project manager and other members of the team as needed. In this way, the team members share power while building greater trust and rapport.

The virtual team is the ideal mechanism for collaboration because people are usually viewed in terms of what they have to contribute instead of their position or stature in the organization's hierarchy. People are more likely to be considered equals than in a co-located setting, where everyone's status, age, and experience are apparent or already known.

Greater Adaptability

When working on programs and projects, the goal is to keep changes to a minimum to help avoid scope creep, ensure delivery dates are met, and ensure budgets are not exceeded. But continual changes in technology and the possibility of downsizing, mergers, and acquisitions mean that teams must embrace change as necessary to ensure that programs and projects continue to support the organization's goals and objectives.

It is incumbent on all virtual team members to keep others on the team informed about any internal or external changes that may affect the program or project so that each team member can readjust and reprioritize tasks to be performed as required.

Dynamic Team Membership

Virtual teams are made up of people with specific expertise who may join and leave the program and project at various times, which makes team building an even greater challenge. When new members join a team, they must be immediately informed about the team's operating protocols and commit to working on the program or project. Ideally, each time a team member joins the program or project, he or she should review and sign the team's charter, making suggestions for improvement as appropriate.

When a team member leaves the program or project, the manager should conduct a debriefing session to promote knowledge management and the transfer of knowledge assets. Typically, such sessions focus on technical aspects of the program or project, but it is equally important for the departing team member, manager, and remaining team members to take the opportunity to suggest changes in the team's operating procedures and ideas for improving team building.

Less Time to Learn to Work Together Effectively

Because people join virtual teams at the time their skills and expertise are required, there is less time to learn how to work with the other members of the team. Immediately, the purpose and vision of the program and project must be explained, and the team member must quickly make a commitment. Role and responsibility charts should be prepared and continually updated. New team members should be introduced to the team through conference calls, emails, and postings on discussion forums. Teams can thus create a spirit of cooperation from the beginning.

Multicultural Teams

On virtual projects, especially those that span the globe, it is likely that people will work with others from different cultures. It is necessary for team members to make a real effort to understand the nuances of the different cultures that are represented and to respect fellow team members' cultural differences. This means, for example, that teams should recognize different holidays team members observe; strive to understand team members' different styles of working and responding to communications, comments, and conflicts; and use a common team language, such as the 4,000-word standard English vocabulary suggested by Kolby (2000), which eliminates slang and other terms unfamiliar to nonnative English speakers.

Less Visibility in the Organization

Virtual team members may believe that there is a lack of recognition for superior work on virtual teams. When assigned to work on a virtual team, some people express concern that their individual contributions may not be recognized to the extent that they would be if they were on a co-located team. While every team should have a team-based reward and recognition system, individual contributions also must be recognized. A virtual team member's work should be included in his or her performance plan, with objectives and goals set to assess his or her work on the team.

Required Knowledge, Skills, and Competencies

Although virtual team members are selected because they have the desired knowledge, skills, and competencies to fill a particular position, all programs and projects are unique and may not really be a good fit for a given individual, even if he or she initially seems qualified. (This also applies to those working on co-located teams.) Team members, when they join a program or project, need information about its vision, mission, deliverables, and benefits to decide whether they can make a positive contribution. If a team member believes he or she cannot contribute effectively to the technical aspects of the program or project, he or she should discuss this concern with the program or project manager without fear of reprisal.

Unknown Conflict

Conflict may exist between virtual team members that are not apparent to others on the team. Another team member who is aware of the conflict should talk with the team members involved and escalate them to the program or project manager if a resolution cannot be reached in a timely manner. While conflicts can be positive—for example, they can foster creativity—the negative aspects of conflict, such as a decrease in morale or infighting between team members, must be minimized. Each team member may occasionally need to be a facilitator by helping other team members resolve negative conflicts and promoting the positive aspects of conflict.

Team-Building Approaches

In both virtual and co-located teams, there is a focus on team effectiveness, and there are many similarities in how both kinds of teams are managed. The following team-building techniques can be effective for all teams:

- Clarifying roles and responsibilities

- Understanding priorities and establishing the vision

- Setting the stage for success

- Implementing collaborative leadership

- Using a team-based reward and recognition system

- Involving the team in decision-making

- Using stress-management techniques

- Conducting a "people issues" audit.

Clarifying Roles and Responsibilities

PMI defines a *role* as "the portion of a project for which a person is accountable" and a *responsibility* as "the work that a project team member is expected to perform to complete the project's activities" (2008a, pp. 222–223). For any program or project, clarity in roles and responsibilities is necessary, though it is especially important for a virtual project. Each team member must understand his or her program or project duties so that the required work gets done in a timely manner and people do not do each other's work.

The team may work together to develop a resource assignment matrix (RAM), which should link to the work packages documented in the work breakdown structure (WBS) so that each team member can see how his or her deliverables support the entire project. A similar approach is suggested when preparing a program WBS. A team charter can clarify the operating procedures or ground rules by which the team will operate.

Understanding Priorities and Establishing the Vision

Organizations' priorities are continually changing as challenges affect their strategic goals, objectives, and plans. Ideally, everyone working on a program or project should know what its priority is in the organization's portfolio, what it contributes to overall corporate strategy, and what value it adds to the organization. Team members may devote more effort to their other work than to the new program or project if they do not know how important it is.

Either during the kickoff meeting or by email, the program or project manager should ask each team member about his or her vision of the program or project. The email approach will likely elicit more original responses; team members are less likely to be influenced by what others have said. The manager can share anonymous emailed responses at the meeting, and the team can discuss the various views of the vision and collectively determine the desired end state. This mutually agreed-upon vision then becomes the commitment statement for the program or project, as documented in the team charter. Through the WBS and RAM, each individual can see how his or her contributions support the overall vision for the program or project.

Setting the Stage for Success

Feelings of frustration, apprehension, or even lack of confidence are common when one is assigned to a new program or project, especially a virtual one. While to some people such an assignment represents an exciting challenge, to others the program or project may seem like a hindrance and a drain on motivation, especially if it is not a high-priority program or project. Further, team members, especially on a virtual team, may not feel any connection to their new teammates; they do not yet know if they have any common interests other than the program or project. The manager should strive to identify people who obviously do not want to be on the program or project early so their negative attitudes do not affect other team members. If the manager believes someone obviously does not want to be on the team, he or she should consult with the human resources department to see if another person with similar skills and competencies is available to work on the team. If no one else is available, the manager should meet with the dissatisfied team member and explain how vital his or her skills are to the team and then continue to emphasize this person's contributions as often as possible to enhance interest in being part of the team.

The program or project manager can set the stage for success by emphasizing the importance of reaching team agreement if at all possible on all major issues, promoting open communication (and confrontation when necessary), ensuring people have the tools and techniques they need to do their work effectively and efficiently, and fostering both team and individual career development. It is important to recognize, however, that the program or project manager can create an environment for success only by developing and executing a team-building plan; he or she on his or her own cannot complete the tasks or activities.

The following are other ways the manager and team can nurture success:

- The team can get off to a positive start by establishing and meeting a major milestone early in the project. Early successes, which are publicized throughout the organization, lead to later successes, and team members' motivation to be part of the team grows.

- Periodically throughout the program or project, the manager should assess the team's performance to help diagnose strengths and weaknesses in team effectiveness.

- To gather ideas from team members to further team development and commitment, the manager can hold brainstorming sessions with the team, schedule one-on-one interviews, or distribute surveys. The manager should express appreciation of innovative and creative ideas team members propose.

Implementing Collaborative Leadership

It is easy to say that a team will follow a collaborative leadership approach, but this is difficult to implement, especially in organizations that are set up as silos where people communicate vertically up the chain of command or if the program or project manager is motivated primarily by power. On a virtual team, however, collaborative leadership is a must, especially if a team member, not the manager, is in the same geographic area as the customer or a major stakeholder and will be the customer or stakeholder's principal point of contact. It is also essential on complex, technical programs and projects because a subject matter expert on the team may have to be the person who communicates directly with a comparable person on the customer's team. For the collaborative approach to work, team members must respect each other and realize that each person has been assigned to the team based on his or her knowledge, skills, and competencies.

Even with collaborative leadership and an empowered team, the manager must still be accessible to team members. He or she expedites communications and continually works to build unity among team members. The manager must also encourage open and honest discussion and work to integrate the efforts of all of the team members into a common solution. Team members must be able to trust the manager to keep his or her promises and to effectively work to obtain necessary additional resources if possible. If these resources cannot be acquired, the manager must explain the situation to the team so there is a common understanding.

Using a Team-Based Reward and Recognition System

PMI recommends rewarding "desirable behavior" with a team-based reward and recognition system (2008a, p. 234). It also notes the importance of considering cultural differences when rewards are given and stresses the need for public recognition of outstanding performance as a way to increase motivation on any team, virtual or co-located.

A team-based system is difficult to implement because performance plans usually assess individual performance, goals, and objectives, and often these objectives are set by functional managers and do not include work on a program or project team. Moving to a team reward and recognition system (while keeping individual performance plans) is a culture change for many organizations.

To establish this system, the best approach is for the program or project manager to collaborate with the team and the human resources department to set performance expectations. The system should take into account the expectations laid out in the charter and the deliverables to be prepared, and it should emphasize customer and stakeholder satisfaction. All team members should suggest ideas for the system.

Initially, the system may include rewards such as public recognition for teamwork, small monetary rewards, or gifts such as plaques noting accomplishments. Over time, the manager may be able to offer other rewards, especially during programs and projects of a longer duration.

Ideally, each team member should participate in the reward and recognition system by conducting a 360-degree evaluation of the performance of the other team members and his or her own performance. The team should collectively determine the elements to be evaluated during the kickoff meeting or at a separate team meeting. On a mature team, this evaluation can be done openly; on a new team, an anonymous approach may be more appropriate. The program or project manager reviews the results, then discusses them privately with each team member and summarizes them for the entire team. The purpose is to reward outstanding accomplishments, not to point out the shortcomings of a single individual.

Both the team reward and recognition system and individual performance plans are tied to the organization's strategic objectives, and the data that are collected to evaluate performance used to determine how performance contributes to benefits. Outstanding individual performance also must be recognized, but PMI (2008a) says that this must be done in a manner that does not affect team cohesiveness. The best practice to follow is to tie the individual performance plans to the team performance plan to create a team culture that is focused on success from the beginning.

Another best practice is to hold a meeting with the entire team to review its performance, discuss objectives, and decide collectively whether any changes to the reward system are possible and warranted. Alternatively, a member of the enterprise program management office (EPMO) could perform the review. This review should reveal whether changes to the reward system are needed or if the team could benefit from training or mentoring. The EPMO could also offer recommendations as to how to improve overall team competencies.

Involving the Team in Decision-Making

It is common for a team member who is located in the same geographic area as a stakeholder or customer to decide to resolve issues or problems affecting the stakeholder or customer on his or her own, but the best practice to follow is to engage the entire team, when needed, or key experts, regardless of their location, before a decision is made. The program or project manager may ask that he or she be involved in decisions or consulted before any decisions are made.

The team should follow the communications plan to make sure everyone on the team is aware of the problem and the decision. A RAM and regular, open communication will assist in this effort.

Using Stress-Management Techniques

Everyone experiences stress. It can be positive or negative, and different people on a team will react to stress in different ways, as discussed in Chapter 7. If someone on the team is experiencing an extremely high level of negative stress, the program or project manager might try to find a replacement with similar skills and competencies, enabling the other team member to return to a functional organization or to a less stressful project. This not only relieves the affected team member but also prevents his or her stress from hindering the productivity or morale of the entire team. Locating a new team member may be easier in a virtual environment because the pool of candidates is larger, and new people are regularly added throughout the life cycle when their expertise is required. Virtual teams are basically agile teams.

Many people, though, find virtual work more stressful than work on a co-located team, especially if they are affiliation motivated and enjoy day-to-day contact with others. They may feel isolated. Leaders and members of any type of team must be alert to situations that can be sources of stress and work together to see what can be done to help make the working conditions less stressful and more productive. One approach is to communicate more frequently with members of the virtual team, so they feel connected and that their work is significant to the organization. (Chapter 7 discusses additional stress-management techniques at length.)

Conducting a "People Issues" Audit

Program and project managers and team members often think of audits as assessments conducted for compliance purposes. The typical audits focus on the triple constraints and customer satisfaction, especially if metrics suggest that the program or project may be in trouble. While these audits certainly are needed and should be scheduled regularly to improve overall performance, teams should consider undergoing a people issues audit, too. After all, programs and projects are performed by people.

For a people issues audit to be effective, the team needs to support it and be willing to work to improve overall team effectiveness in ways the audit suggests. Typically, a people issues audit is conducted by someone outside the team, often a member of the EPMO or in program management by the governance board.

The auditors should review the team charter and any other guidelines or procedures in place. They also need access to the knowledge repository and the team's exit interviews with staff members who have left the program or project after their work has been completed. The auditors will interview team members, focusing on the interpersonal aspects of their work and trying to gain insight into the effectiveness of the existing team-building activities and how they might be improved.

Once the auditors complete their work, their report should include specific findings based on facts rather than on hearsay or their own opinions, along with recommendations. These findings and recommendations then should be shared with the team, and the team will determine whether the auditors' recommendations can help improve overall team working conditions and performance.

Summary

- *Emphasize the importance of the program or project vision.* The vision of a program or project is its desired end state (PMI 2008c). It reflects the program or project's goals and objectives, linking them to the overall organizational goals and objectives. Each team member's interpretation of the program or project's vision should support the team's collective vision. After it is discussed at the kickoff meeting, the vision should be reviewed frequently: during other meetings, when changes are made that affect the overall strategy of the performing organization or that of the project's customer, and when new members join the team.

- *Recognize individual differences, including personal styles and communication styles.* Each individual communicates differently. On a virtual team, these differences are less obvious because communication is primarily verbal (Mehrabian 1968) and the typical cues of body language are not apparent.

Communication will be more open if the team's manager and team members are aware of each team member's preferred style of communication.

- ***Tailor motivation strategies.*** Understanding team members' preferred motivational styles can help the project manager assign roles and responsibilities and inspire them to greater achievement. Chapter 3 discusses motivational sources and styles in depth.

- ***Use effective interpersonal communication skills.*** The importance of effective communications on a program or project team cannot be underestimated. Research has shown that project managers spend approximately 90 percent of their time communicating (Stuckenbruck and Marshall 1985). On a virtual team, good communication is even more essential; team members are dispersed, so communication must be more intentional. Also, team members located in the same geographic area as customers and stakeholders may be charged with communicating with them. See Chapter 4 for more information.

- ***Determine communications requirements.*** To avoid miscommunications that might create hard feelings, set communications ground rules. These might include establishing English as the common language for the project or guidelines for how quickly team members should respond to emails or postings in discussion forums, how to offer suggestions and provide feedback, when conference calls are required, when team meetings are to be held, and how to respond to any action items discussed in these meetings.

Other communication tips:

- Team members should help determine the situations in which each communication method—email, phone calls, meetings—will be used.

- Open communication should be the norm so that everyone feels comfortable contributing to discussions and debates.

- Faster and more frequent communication may be needed on virtual teams to connect people in separate locations.

- If a team member does not have time to provide an immediate response to an email, voice mail, or memo, he or she should acknowledge receiving it and tell the sender when he or she will respond.

- Private conversations should remain private unless they are relevant to the team.

- *Fulfill planned commitments.* The success of the team will depend on the effective execution of all program and project management processes. All team members should work to high standards. This means they must organize and manage time well to complete assigned tasks and help others finish their assigned work as needed. Teams should document work in action-item logs and problems in issue logs, and prepare and analyze regular status reports.

- *Establish a team-based recognition and reward system.* The primary purpose of a recognition and reward system is to improve the program or project team's work performance. The evaluations on which rewards are based will also alert the manager to performance issues or problems or the need for new tools and techniques to support performance.

- *Apply different conflict resolution techniques at different stages in the program or project life cycle.* Conflicts happen on all projects, and different types of conflicts occur at different stages in the project's life cycle (Thamhain and Wilemon 1975). Conflict is sometimes positive; different points of view can be merged for more effective solutions. Chapter 8 details several conflict resolution methods; teams should know when to employ each one.

- *Establish mutual accountability.* A desire for success is central to the culture of any team. In a collaborative culture, helping others succeed is as important as one's own victories. Team members should look for opportunities to celebrate individual and overall team successes (Skulmoski and Levin 2001). Team members should listen to and understand others' points of view, treating them as equal partners in the quest for program or project success. If personal problems arise, refocus on the process and context that caused the problem rather than on the personal conflict promotes productivity and trust among team members.

- *Regularly review work to keep performance at optimal levels.* Continual reviews of program and project effectiveness can reveal how to sustain optimal performance or whether sub-optimal performance still exists. Regardless, these reviews should be frequent enough to keep pace with changing conditions that affect the program or project and necessitate the revision of processes and procedures.

- *Promote continuous improvement.* Ensure team members, whether co-located or virtual, establish professional development goals. Ideally, each team member should have a personal learning agenda. Team members should be given opportunities to develop new skills and competencies and to take an active role in the program or project to develop further the skills they need for advancement.

Each team member should also make a commitment to improving the effectiveness and efficiency of the team's processes and procedures for completing the deliverables. A formal continuous improvement program can encourage individuals and teams as a whole to propose improvements in processes and procedures as part of the organization's commitment to knowledge management for future program and project work.

Discussion Questions

Assume you are managing a virtual team for the first time in your career. Your project is the fifth highest priority in the organization's portfolio management system, which has 55 different programs and projects, so it is receiving extensive attention from management. The project is launched to develop and deliver a new product within two years, and the schedule is urgent because management wants to ensure that the product makes it into the marketplace before the company's competitors release a similar product of their own.

To help ensure your project's success, management has appointed a senior-level governance board to oversee its progress. This board meets with you monthly, and you are expected to consult with its members between meetings if any significant issues or risks arise. Unfortunately, economic conditions prevent you from having direct interaction with your project team, which is made up of 25 members located on three different continents. Your company does not have a video conferencing system, and most communications will be asynchronous except for occasional conference calls held at pre-arranged times.

You want to ensure that your project is a success and that your team members are pleased and motivated by their work on the project. Therefore, you meet with your governance board to ask if you can implement a team-based reward and recognition system for the project. The board members agree that although other programs and projects in the organization do not have similar systems in place, implementing a reward and recognition system might be a good idea. If the system is ultimately deemed beneficial, it could then be applied to other programs and projects in the organization as well.

You are pleased the governance board is supportive of your idea, and you decide to conduct a teleconference with your team to explain the concept to them. During the teleconference, you use a nominal group technique by giving each team member an opportunity to respond with ideas about the reward and recognition system. You then ask your team to formulate a draft plan for the system. One team member volunteers to lead this effort.

Questions:

1. What criteria should be used to determine team effectiveness?
2. How should this team-based reward and recognition system be structured?
3. Who should determine how to administer the system—e.g., the team itself, the project manager, the project sponsor, the governance board? What are the advantages and disadvantages of involving each of groups listed?
4. If a team member disagrees with the approach, can he or she opt out of the system without fear of reprisal, or does everyone need to participate for the system to be effective?
5. How often would a review of the system be conducted to ensure it's effective? Who would conduct this review, and how would the review be done?
6. How would a subject matter expert who is part of the project for only two or three months be compensated by the reward and recognition system?
7. What other problems could influence the development and implementation of this system?

The Art of Motivation

3

Motivation is a concept that is difficult to define. PMI (2008a) defines it as "creating an environment to meet project objectives while offering maximum self-satisfaction related to what people value most" (p. 410). PMI further explains that values differ but can include satisfaction with one's job, challenging work, a sense of accomplishment and success in one's work, personal achievement and growth, financial compensation that is commensurate with the work to be done, and other recognition and rewards.

Kerzner and Salidis (2009) define motivation as "encouraging others to perform by fulfilling or appealing to their needs" (p. 193). Jack Welch, the former chief executive officer of General Electric, echoes this idea, saying that managers' role in motivating employees "is *not* to control people and stay 'on top' of things, but rather to guide, energize and excite" (Godin 1995, p. 88).

Motivating team members is more art than science. A good motivator can tailor an appropriate approach for each individual on the team. Because certain workplace trends may make motivating team members more challenging, the program or project manager must adopt specific approaches to motivating the team as a whole as well as each team member. This chapter discusses various trends affecting motivation; some motivation approaches to consider, based on some of the work of various theorists but tailored to program and project management; motivation mistakes to avoid; and a motivation checklist that will help the program or project manager work effectively with team members.

Schmid and Adams (2007) conducted a survey using PMI's online research network to gain insights into perceptions held by project professionals regarding team motivation. They also wanted to learn about motivation during different project stages. The results of this survey showed that scope changes (as opposed to time, cost, quality, and other constraints) had the most negative effect on team member motivation. Weak team motivation was attributable to lack of top management support and commitment to the project, but even if the organization's culture had a negative effect on motivation, more than 54 percent of the respondents felt the project manager could still motivate his or her team toward project success. They also found team motivation to be at the highest level at the start of a project and that rewards affecting motivation play an important role during the intermediate or executing stage.

Seventy-nine percent of the respondents felt the project manager was responsible for encouraging team motivation at the beginning of a project; this dropped to 58 percent for the closing stage. This survey shows the importance of the project manager's early involvement in motivating each team member to want to be part of the project and to work toward project success.

Trends Affecting Motivation

Three trends affect work in program and project management that make the task of motivating team members more difficult for managers:

- Reductions in force
- Increasing complexity
- Cross-cultural influences.

Reductions in Force

Ongoing reductions in force through downsizing, offshoring, and outsourcing are underway in many organizations. No longer is there an unspoken agreement that once a person joins an organization, he or she will remain with it for the duration of his or her career. The old assumption that good work will lead to job security no longer applies, given the world's economic condition and the changing nature of each organization's strategy in response.

When downsizing, offshoring, or outsourcing decisions are made, the organization's strategic goals and its approach to reach these goals typically changes, and if so, the situation requires a rebalancing of the organization's portfolio. The program or project manager is rarely consulted about how such decisions will affect his or her program or project, though there may be significant losses and changes. The program or project's resources may be needed elsewhere, or the people working on the programs or projects may lose their jobs entirely. Scope changes may result if the programs or projects are continued. Subject matter experts, who were considered critical to completion of the work, may be among those who are no longer employed, challenging program and project managers to find people to fill these gaps.

If employees do survive, they must do more with less. Motivating these team members is difficult. They may experience anger toward the organization's executives and guilt about surviving the cuts when colleagues were forced to leave the organization (Noer 1995). In organizations or industries that undergo repeated downsizings, it is not unusual to find pervasive cynicism, feelings of alienation, increased resistance to even small changes, and skepticism among the surviving employees. Some team members will lack the trust and commitment needed to perform their assigned work packages or activities efficiently, believing they may be next to lose their own jobs.

Helping team members overcome these feelings is a major challenge for program and project managers, and it requires that they have available time and leadership abilities. They also must spend more time in the facilitation role to make the work environment as positive as possible, given the economic situation and the possibility of additional job losses or reprioritization of the work to be done. One study (Strom 2009) noted that in such situations, the organization must redefine its own vision and make sure it is communicated to the remaining employees. This study also suggests that additional emphasis be placed on both individual and team rewards and recognition. Further, Strom says that the organization should recognize that employees' self-esteem will be affected.

What does this study mean for program and project management? It is incumbent on the manager to meet with his or her team, explain the circumstances, consider the restructuring to be a critical incident, and discuss everyone's feelings. He or she should work out a strategy to somehow turn the restructuring into an opportunity for those who remain, revisiting and revising the program or project management plans as required, as well as each individual's developmental plan and annual performance plan.

Increasing Complexity

The growing complexity of programs and projects is a key challenge and the subject of a PMI study (Cicmil, Cooke-Davies, Crawford, Richardson 2009). Why is program and project work so complex? The study points to the unpredictability of future events, the ambiguity of performance criteria, different understandings of what constitutes success, and the numerous interactions and processes in terms of relationships on projects.

In addition to the factors PMI cited, in many organizations, the enterprise tools and techniques used to assist in managing programs and projects are often so difficult to use that people must become specialists in them, or outsiders must be hired to manage the tools. The tools sometimes drive the process, rather than the process driving the tools. The selection of the tools becomes a project in itself—let alone their implementation and the assessment of their contribution to overall project success.

Also, organizations, business units, departments, and even programs often have program management offices (PMOs) at various levels. While PMOs have been shown to provide numerous strategic and tactical benefits in many areas, unless they are managed effectively, they can become bottlenecks, slowing down the processes of delivering program and project benefits and ensuring that the work to be done has value.

Finally, as noted by Kerzner and Salidis (2009), the time of relying on only the triple constraint—getting projects done on time, according to budget, and within specifications—is gone. Instead, there is a new imperative: to follow the triple constraint but to ensure value is provided even if the triple constraint is met. Kerzner and Salidis point out that the entire project environment has changed amid rising costs, competition, the global economy, and the lack of attention to project definition. They write that "the final value of a project may be a moving target rather than a stationary target" (p. 5), as it was in the past. Such an approach means that new definitions of metrics are required to assess program and project success, team success, and individual success.

Cross-Cultural Influences

The extensive cross-cultural influences that affect many programs and projects can complicate motivation for the manager. If teams take advantage of their diversity, they can make more effective decisions and come up with creative ways to resolve conflicts, but diversity also presents motivational challenges. It is too easy to treat people as stereotypes based on their specific culture and not to recognize the importance of individual differences. If mutual respect does not exist on a team, team members will lack trust in one another and will not respect others' contributions. Individual differences require the program or project manager to consider how best to motivate and work with team members with different cultural backgrounds, and the challenges are even greater when working with a geographically dispersed team in which face-to-face meetings are rarely if ever held.

Strategies for Motivating Team Members

You can consider a number of different motivation styles as you work with your program or project team, including:

- Motivating using personal styles

- Motivating using career stages

- Motivating using career values

- Motivating using situational considerations.

The guidelines that follow can help you find an approach for use on your program or project.

Motivating Using Personal Styles

The Myers-Briggs Type Indicator (MBTI) can be used to identify individual personality differences on a team and to determine the best sources of motivation for the various personality styles. Using either formal or informal knowledge of team members' MBTI styles, the program or project manager can motivate individuals more effectively.

Table 3-1 suggests strategies the program or project manager can use to motivate team members based on their personality styles. For example, for a team member has extraverted and sensing MBTI preferences, an appropriate motivational approach would be place to him or her in a group with many people that is assigned to solve tangible, real-world problems. By contrast, an

Table 3-1   Motivating Different MBTI Personality Styles (Flannes 1998)

Personality Style	Best Approach to Motivating
Extraverted (Outgoing, enjoys dealing with people)	Have this person focus on the relationship or social aspects of the project, such as interfacing with stakeholders or leading team meetings.
Introverted (Quiet, reflective, inner-directed)	Offer this person work that requires extended periods of concentration, possibly working alone.
Sensing (Pragmatic, practical, down to earth)	Give this person work that has a distinct completion point and can be measured in concrete terms.
Intuitive (Conceptual, big picture)	Put this person to work on the strategic and design portions of the project, relating the project's objectives to the organization's strategic objectives.
Thinking (Logical, analytical)	Present this individual with tasks requiring quantitative skills, in-depth analysis, or research.
Feeling (People-oriented)	Allow this person to be in roles involving nurturing, supporting, and customer relationship management.
Judging (Orderly, structured, timely)	Permit this individual to create schedules, budgets, and project closure systems.
Perceiving (Flexible, spontaneous)	Direct this person toward situations requiring troubleshooting.

introverted person with intuitive and thinking preferences would be better motivated by tasks that give him or her time to reflect individually on innovative possibilities, using an analytical and logical approach to decision-making.

When using a personality style system such as the MBTI, it is important not to take the system too literally. Systems like the MBTI are excellent for giving a manager an approach to consider when thinking about motivation, but the best way to motivate people is to ask them what motivates them—and to listen carefully to what they say.

Motivating Using Career Stages

People evolve through different stages in a career. Schein (1990) presents a career stage model consisting of ten distinct stages that a person goes through during his or her career. An understanding of Schein's model can give program and project managers insight into how to motivate team members.

- *Stage One* and *Stage Two* occur in a person's life before he or she enters the world of project work. These stages involve the early years of initial career exploration followed by formalized career preparation, such as college and specialized training.

- *Stage Three* involves formal entry into the workplace, where real-world skills are acquired. To motivate a team member in this stage, the program or project manager should give him or her an opportunity to demonstrate competency in a variety of tasks, which will allow the team member to show how he or she can contribute.

- In *Stage Four*, training in the concrete application of skills and professional socialization takes place. The identity of being a professional is becoming established. The most effective motivational approaches during this stage will focus on helping the team member master the subtle technical and professional nuances of his or her profession.

- During *Stage Five*, the team member has gained full admission into the profession based on demonstrated competency and performance. Program and project managers can use motivational methods that help team members perceive themselves as full-fledged, responsible contributors, such as assigning them to senior roles on the team.

- In *Stage Six*, the team member has a sense of having gained a more permanent membership in the profession. To motivate a professional in Stage Six, offer opportunities for professional visibility, such as being a member of a cross-functional team or serving as a team advocate with other stakeholders.

Team members functioning in the final four stages require the program or project manager to use more sophisticated motivational methods because the challenges and issues inherent in these stages are more complex and demanding.

- *Stage Seven* involves a natural mid-career assessment or crisis. The person in this stage asks questions about the value of his or her career, what he or she has accomplished, and whether he or she can identify a new career direction. The best way to motivate a person in Stage Seven is to focus on identifying new directions within the existing program or project that the team member could pursue, with the hope that the new direction creates a spark that translates into increased motivation.

- *Stage Eight* involves the challenge of maintaining momentum as a career starts to move toward the end. Motivation during this stage and *Stage Nine*, when the individual begins to disengage from the profession and the world of work, involves:

  - Helping the team member focus on a program or project task that he or she has yet to accomplish during his or her career

  - Helping the team member get excited about the legacy he or she will leave in the company or within the profession. A legacy could, for example, take the form of developing educational resources or coursework.

- During *Stage Ten*, the retirement or separation stage, the team member ends his or her employment with the organization or membership in the profession. Strategies during this stage should be based on:

  - Motivating the team member to retire on a positive note—for example, encouraging him or her to complete the last assignment at a high level of quality

  - Helping the transitioning person use his or her professional skills in a post-retirement consulting or coaching role, if that is of interest to the team member.

This approach works particularly well for program and project managers who know the age of their team members. If this is the case, the manager can use these stages, working openly in conjunction with the team member, to determine the most effective motivational approach. Consider this career stage model a starting point, and then use interpersonal communication skills to ascertain what specifically motivates each particular individual.

Motivating Using Career Values

Schein (1990) developed another approach to examining what work functions and work-related values motivate people. He believes that:

- The more we understand our own values in specific areas, the better we are able to achieve work satisfaction.

- Our motivation in the workplace will be greatest when we are pursuing tasks and functions that are consistent with our values.

Schein's research identified eight work-related values, which he describes as *career anchors*. The word *anchor* means a fundamental activity that an individual perceives is important when he or she considers the aggregate of his or her skills, motives, and values. Schein's eight anchors have important implications for motivation.

Technical-Functional Anchor

The professional with a strong interest in being a specialist in his or her profession is an example of someone who prioritizes the technical-functional anchor or value. This person has little interest in roles involving general management and takes great pride in being a skilled, expert practitioner of the trade. To motivate a technical-functional team member:

- Create opportunities for this person to learn specialized skills.

- Reward this person through a professional or technical advancement track, not a general management or leadership track.

- On a virtual team, recognize the technical expertise of this team member so that others are aware of his or her strongest areas, and make sure that everyone knows how to contact the team member should they need help.

General Management Anchor

The team member with a general management anchor is highly motivated by situations in which leadership roles are available. This person seeks to ascend to consistently higher levels of organizational control and leadership and has little interest in remaining a technical expert.

Motivate the team member with a general management anchor by:

- Providing opportunities to manage some aspect of the program or project

- Offering concrete forms of acknowledgment, such as monetary compensation, status and titles, and recognition by senior managers

- Creating opportunities for him or her to help develop the administrative structure for the program or project, such as helping set up a program management office, as appropriate, or helping to determine methodologies to follow and tools and techniques to use.

Autonomy and Independence Anchor

The autonomy-driven team member has a strong desire to do things his or her own way with little external influence. This person may create problems in a team environment and is often thought of as not a team player.

To motivate the team member with an autonomy-independence anchor:

- Assign this person work that emphasizes self-reliance. (On a virtual team, this person may excel because he or she does not need to interact with others on a daily basis.)

- Keep the person out of roles that involve repeated group decision-making or general managerial functions.

- During group meetings, encourage this individual to participate, perhaps by asking open-ended questions, to get his or her views on issues affecting the program or project.

Security and Stability Anchor

A team member with a security-stability anchor poses motivational challenges for the project manager because he or she seeks continuity, a steady work environment, and job tenure—qualities that are at odds with the project environment. Challenging and innovative project roles hold little interest for this professional.

Motivating someone with a security-stability anchor involves:

- Placing him or her in roles that are more traditional, such as that of the project control officer or project administrator. Recognize that the program environment may be a better fit for this individual because programs typically last longer than projects.

- Guiding this person toward program projects that tend to be of long duration.

- Encouraging him or her to engage stakeholders from customer and product-support units because these units later will be responsible for benefit sustainment, and this individual may be an ideal candidate to support these organizations once the program or project ends.

Entrepreneurial-Creativity Anchor

The entrepreneurially driven team member can be a source of pleasure or frustration for the program or project manager, depending on the nature of the program or project. This individual has the urge to use his or her own vision to develop new business ventures. If working on a program, he or she can be given opportunities to assist a new project manager in crafting a vision for the project as part of the program. This individual can also ensure that the program or project's vision remains in line with the organization's strategic goals and objectives as they change.

People with an entrepreneurial-creativity anchor work best when they can motivate and create. They often become restless when working on routine, administrative tasks that are predictable and lack challenges. Motivate the entrepreneurial team member by:

- Involving him or her in creating the program or project vision and getting the program or project started

- Keeping him or her away from roles with narrowly defined duties

- Quickly moving this person from programs and projects that are ending to new ones. Do not expect this team member to efficiently close a current program or project.

Service Anchor

A person with a service anchor wants to perform professional activities that are personally meaningful. In the world of technical project work, for example, a biologist with a service anchor may seek a position with a company conducting environmental cleanup activities. A service-oriented person is especially valuable on programs and projects that emphasize sustainability—recognizing the effects of the program or project on the environment, the community, and the organization.

To motivate a team member with a service anchor, place him or her in roles where he or she can:

- Provide "customer service" to other team members or to program or project stakeholders

- Troubleshoot situations in which customer or client complaints require someone with a desire to help

- When planning a program or project, provide opportunities for this individual to participate because he or she may have ideas about the program's or project's long-term effects and sustainability, especially regarding possible risks and opportunities

- Enable this individual to participate in decision-making sessions as appropriate to ensure that sustainability remains a key consideration.

Pure Challenge Anchor

Motivation is rarely a problem for the team member with a pure challenge anchor, assuming that he or she is engaged in tasks and duties that consistently provide chances for him or her to feel professionally stretched and challenged. This person is always looking for a new professional challenge to master. Managers can motivate the challenge-focused team member by:

- Meeting with him or her at the start of the program or project to identify challenging professional activities

- Asking him or her to help "save the day" if disaster strikes the program or project

- Tasking him or her with reducing the complexity that is characteristic of program work

- Encouraging him or her to help other team members embrace changes.

Lifestyle Anchor

A team member who seeks balance between work life and personal life, believing that his or her professional work is not the sole focus of his or her life, has a lifestyle anchor. This person may value the flexibility offered by flextime or telecommuting.

Motivate the lifestyle-oriented team member by providing opportunities for him or her to:

- Work on tasks that have clear starting and ending points and do not regularly expand into personal time

- Get involved in program or project functions that do not require a great deal of travel or relocation

- Assist in developing and maintaining the program or project's administrative structure.

Schein's career-anchor approach can be a helpful lens for the program or project manager, who can then craft appropriate motivational strategies that reflect each person's anchors.

Motivating Using Situational Considerations

Maslow (1954) devised a theory of motivation based on the premise that people are motivated to satisfy various needs according to a hierarchy, with the most basic needs at the bottom of a *needs pyramid*. When one need is satisfied, the individual is naturally motivated to move to the next higher need level to attempt to satisfy that need.

Maslow's hierarchy of needs encompasses seven levels:

Level 1: Basic physiological needs, such as food and nourishment

Level 2: Security and safety needs, such as stability and survival

Level 3: Belonging needs, exemplified by affiliation or love

Level 4: Esteem needs, including achievement and recognition

Level 5: Cognitive needs, such as the expansion of personal knowledge

Level 6: Aesthetic needs, exemplified by a search for beauty or order

Level 7: Self-actualization needs, illustrated by the realization of one's personal potential.

Maslow's hierarchy of needs can be applied in a program or project environment by addressing the immediate work challenges facing a team member. Flannes and Buell (1999) adapted Maslow's hierarchy and redefined the need levels using situations frequently encountered in project work. Their adapted hierarchy reflects the idea that the project manager must observe dynamic situational variables to motivate team members effectively. Their work has been updated here to apply to program management and for work on a virtual team.

Level 1: Job Survival Needs

Level 1 needs are the basic needs of the team member (similar to Maslow's level 1 need for food and water), such as keeping his or her job during organizational reductions in force. Little else is on the mind of the team member during this period of ensuring basic survival. The program or project manager can motivate an individual at the job survival level by providing the team member with tasks whose completion increases the chances of job survival.

Level 2: Job Safety Needs

At this level, the team member must develop the confidence that he or she can "survive" in the organization over time and that his or her project management career path extends past the current program or project. To motivate a team member whose situational focus is at the job safety level, the program or project manager should think out loud with the team member about long-term opportunities within the organization, involving his or her functional manager in this discussion as appropriate. If working on a virtual team, spend time with this person chatting one-on-one through instant messaging or comparable software and through periodic phone calls.

Level 3: Belonging and Affiliation Needs

The team member functioning at this situational level is motivated by a need for affiliation and feeling part of the organization. To motivate a team member who is seeking affiliation:

- Provide opportunities for him or her to create professional relationships and liaisons within the company so that the team member can feel he or she is part of the action.

- Encourage the team member to become involved in professional organizations.

- On a virtual team, encourage him or her to serve as a relationship manager, introducing new team members to the team's operating norms and helping facilitate team meetings and encourage participation.

Level 4: Esteem Needs

At this level, a team member may want to be recognized for professional accomplishments and have a high level of visibility within the professional community. An appropriate motivational approach is to place him or her in situations in which he or she can be center stage. Motivate the person operating at the esteem level by encouraging him or her to:

- Present papers, write articles, or give talks within the organization or at professional conferences

- Obtain certifications such as the certified associate in project management (CAPM), project management professional (PMP), or program management professional (PgMP)

- Present a webinar at a team meeting on a topic of interest.

Level 5: Intellectual Challenge Needs

Project team members who have mastered advanced professional competencies and are looking for something new to do are at this level, which is similar to Schein's stage seven, during which people often experience a mid-career lack of interest or motivation. Motivate the team member seeking intellectual stimulation by:

- Giving him or her opportunities to learn more about the program or project world on a macro level. He or she might become more involved with tasks that demonstrate how this program or project integrates with the organization's strategic initiatives.

- Encouraging the team member to volunteer to help with any updates of the organization's strategic plan.

- Asking him or her to serve as the program or project's liaison to the organization's portfolio review board or comparable committee.

- Allowing him or her to focus on external changes that may affect the program or project, such as the use of new technology or the need to implement a new regulation, and determine how best to handle those external changes with minimal disruption to the work of the rest of the team members.

Level 6: Aesthetic Needs

A team member at the aesthetic level may, for example, become interested in shifting from the hard skills of the profession to developing soft skills that can be applied in his or her work. A senior project manager who has "seen it all" and now wants to give something back to the profession might be at level 6.

Motivate the team member interested in developing soft skills by encouraging him or her to:

- Become an informal mentor to a junior team member

- Serve as an informal customer relationship manager over the course of the program or project

- Become a knowledge manager for the team to promote lessons learned and the sharing of knowledge assets.

Level 7: Self-Actualization Needs

A team member in this situational stage is one whose comfort and sense of security allow him or her to take a path that is personally rewarding and that allows the team member to live up to his or her full potential. For some team members, this could mean deciding to leave the technical side of the organization and, for example, taking a position within the organization's training department designing training curricula for entry-level technical staff.

There are few concrete steps a program or project manager can take to motivate a team member at this level because the activities that motivate individuals are often less tangible than the day-to-day tasks. Nevertheless, the manager can:

- Encourage the team member to identify aspects of the program or project where he or she can give back or leave behind a personally meaningful achievement

- Ask the team member to serve as a consultant to the team on various issues, both interpersonal and technical.

Within this model, a team member may move in a fluid manner, up and down, from one level to another, based upon the external, situational variables that he or she encounters during the course of a program or project. For example, a team member may be operating within the esteem level (working to expand his or her professional network within the organization), but then may quickly drop to the survival level upon learning that company layoffs are planned and his or her job is at risk. Consequently, when using this adapted model for motivating team members, it is crucial for the program or project manager to remember that people and their needs are dynamic. External, situational variables such as downsizing, transfers, and project problems alter a person's immediate source of motivation.

McClelland's Achievement, Affiliation, and Power Theory

McClelland (1961) set forth a theory that people are motivated in different ways based on their needs for achievement, affiliation, and power. Rad and Levin (2003) adapted McClelland's work to project management and to work on the virtual team. This section expands their work as appropriate to also cover program management.

Achievement Orientation

A person who is motivated by achievement is driven by the challenge of success, especially in the technical aspects of the program or project work. This individual will take risks, but only if they are ones for which he or she feels the response to the risk is appropriate, and the risk will not unduly affect the work. The achievement-oriented team member is driven by setting goals that are attainable. In addition, he or she desires feedback on his or her work, but at a technical level, not on interpersonal issues.

When working with the achievement-oriented team member, the program or project manager can best motivate this individual by:

- Providing opportunities to work in an environment that allows autonomy and flexibility in performing assigned work packages and activities

- Encouraging the team member to seek identity in the work he or she is performing on the program or project

- Enabling the individual to set personal goals that complement the program or project's goals.

Because an achievement-oriented person likes an environment that provides challenges and that facilitates working alone, he or she tends to find work on a virtual team appealing. He or she does not need the daily interaction that would occur in a co-located environment and is comfortable using technology to communicate as needed. The program or project manager must ensure that when virtual meetings are held, this team member participates in them, asking open-ended questions to make sure the person is engaged in the team meeting and is not doing other work while the meeting is underway.

Affiliation Orientation

The affiliation-oriented team member may not find virtual work challenging and may resist being assigned to virtual teams. These team members enjoy the camaraderie of the co-located team, making friends with team members and getting together with them outside the work environment. In motivating the affiliation-oriented team member, whether on a co-located team or a virtual team, the following approaches are suggested:

- Provide an opportunity for this team member to serve as a relationship manager for the team, introducing new team members to one another, informing team members of the team's operating procedures and team charter, and ensuring that people on the team are comfortable with how the team works together to resolve issues and conflicts.

- Ask the individual if he or she is interested in becoming a mentor to others on the team, especially members who are new to the organization, to help others learn how the informal organization operates and which interpersonal skills are best to use in various day-to-day situations.

- Enable this team member to facilitate team meetings, encouraging active participation by everyone who is in attendance.

- Ask him or her to work with stakeholders to make sure they are receiving the information they need about the program or project in a timely way and find out if they need additional information.

Power Orientation

Often, the person motivated by power dislikes any role on a team unless he or she is its manager. This person then tends to dominate team meetings and wants others on the team to recognize him or her for accomplishments that may be team accomplishments rather than individual ones. The power-oriented team member can present challenges for the program or project manager but also can work effectively with customers and other key stakeholders. This team member may find being part of a virtual team difficult—he or she may lack the visibility he or she desires with the program or project manager, the program sponsor, the customer, or other key stakeholders.

The following are suggestions for motivating the power-oriented team member:

- Ask him or her to make sure the team's practices conform with the overall goals and objectives of the program, project, and the organization.

- Enable this team member to work with stakeholders as much as possible and especially to determine the best strategy to use to engage stakeholders so that they will have positive feelings toward the program or project.

- Ask this person to lead program or project team meetings from time to time to provide leadership opportunities.

- Encourage the team member to engage in problem-solving situations with others on the team to help the team close out issues and conflicts.

Rad and Levin (2003) present an example of how achievement-, affiliation-, and power-oriented people can work together to develop a project team charter. The achievement-oriented person should work independently to develop the charter; then, when the project begins, the power-oriented person can call meetings to discuss the charter and determine if changes to it are warranted. Throughout the process, the affiliation-oriented team member can work to ensure that others are comfortable with the contents of the charter, listening to any concerns people have about it and introducing new people to the team's operating norms. Additionally, when someone leaves the team, the affiliation-oriented team member can ask this person whether he or she felt the team charter was effective and can ask him or her for suggestions for improvement.

Systemic Approaches to Motivating the Team

In addition to pursuing strategies to motivate individual team members, the program and project manager should implement macro-level methods aimed at motivating the team as a whole. These systemic methods include:

- Creating an empowered team
- Applying force field analysis.

Creating an Empowered Team

Meredith and Mantel (2009) explain how a group motivation strategy in which team members experience a strong sense of empowerment through participatory management can be applied to project management. Empowerment, for Meredith and Mantel, is a participatory management approach that stresses:

- Individual initiative, as team members design their own methods, usually with some constraints, for doing their work
- Responsibility and accountability for project deliverables
- Synergistic solutions through team interactions
- Enabling teams to harness the ability of their members to manipulate tasks so project objectives are met and the team finds better ways to do things.

The authors further point out that project success is associated with teamwork, while project failure is almost guaranteed if the people on the project do not wish to work as a team.

This empowered approach complements the People Capability Maturity Model (P-CMMM®). The P-CMMM® states that empowered teams are ones that have the responsibility and authority to conduct their work effectively (Curtis, Hefley, and Miller 2001). These teams are characterized by team management, not management of individuals. Members of these empowered workgroups accept increasing responsibility for performance. They have a sponsor to whom the team is accountable and who represents the organization's interest to the team. In the P-CMMM® approach, the sponsor is the program or project manager. He or she acts as a liaison to other stakeholders, provides organizational resources, reviews progress and performance, clarifies the team's mission and responsibilities, provides guidance, and resolves problems and issues as escalated. According to the P-CMMM®, empowered workgroups or teams are responsible for:

- Recruiting and selection of team members
- Performance management
- Recognition and rewards
- Training and development
- Compensation activities.

The program or project manager who takes an empowered team approach may need guidance in facilitation and participatory management approaches, assigning responsibility and delegating authority, shifting some of his or her own responsibilities to the team, and guiding the growth of empowerment in these teams.

The challenge for the program or project manager who wants to lead an empowered team is enabling the team to make decisions and resolve issues while still retaining the needed leadership controls and monitoring the program's or project's delivery of benefits and overall performance. Such an approach requires the manager to focus on his or her role as facilitator. It also shows the importance of having a team charter that each team member supports and signs.

A team charter is different from a program or project charter and other planning documents. Its purpose, according to Levin and Green (2009), is to lay out the team members' roles and responsibilities and establish guidelines for how the team will operate throughout the program's or project's life cycle. It describes actions the team can take on its own and those that require escalation. It also explains how to escalate an issue if the team cannot resolve it on its own. Levin and Green (2009) recommend the charter include:

- *A commitment statement.* Describe the objectives the team plans to achieve and the benefits it expects to deliver.

- *A description of the program or project manager's role.* List the program or project manager's name and describe how the team plans to interact with him or her during the life cycle. Recognize that some team members will have more extensive interaction with the manager than others.

- *A description of the sponsor's role.* List the program/project sponsor's name and describe how the team will interact with the sponsor.

- *A description of the customers' roles.* List the customer(s) and explain how the team will interact with them during the program or project.

- *A list of other key stakeholders.* Describe team members' level of involvement with other key program or project stakeholders and the specific level of interaction. Consider using a responsibility assignment matrix.

- *Team performance objectives.* Describe performance objectives at the team level during the life cycle and link them to the program or project objectives.

- *Success measures.* Describe metrics that will be used to measure overall team performance.

- *The scope/boundaries of the team's work.* Build on the scope statement, which describes what work is within or outside the boundaries of the program or project, as well as assumptions and constraints that could affect the teams' work.

- *A description of the deliverables.* Using the program or project work breakdown structure, list the program packages or project work packages and include a resource assignment matrix to show roles and responsibilities for the deliverables.

- *The conflict management approach to be used.* Describe the process the team will use to resolve internal conflicts without involving the program or project manager, as well as the method the team will follow to escalate the problem to the program or project manager if necessary. Also, explain how resolutions will be communicated: If a conflict involves only a few team members, should the entire team be included in the resolution?

- *The decision-making process.* Describe the process the team will follow in making decisions, and list the types of decisions the team can make on its own without involving the program or project manager. Explain how the team will communicate decisions, e.g., informally or formally, to the program or project manager, and whether the team will use a decision log or register to track all decisions.

- *A description of the administrative activities.* State the roles and responsibilities team members will perform, such as preparing meeting agendas, taking minutes, updating plans, preparing reports, updating the knowledge-management repository, and performing closeout tasks. Consider using a responsibility assignment matrix.

- *The issue escalation process.* Explain the process the team will use to resolve issues on its own and list the types of issues that should be escalated to the program or project manager.

- *Charter updates.* State the frequency with which the charter will be reviewed to determine if updates are needed and how these reviews will be conducted.

- *Approvals.* Here, the program or project manager, sponsor, and team members sign the charter. When new people join the team, ensure that they also sign it.

Another key factor in building an empowered team is the need for trust. The program or project manager and team members must work to earn and assume trust. Because of the time constraints associated with program and project work, managers and team members must assume trust; i.e., the team members will not have enough time initially to earn the trust of their manager. Empowered teams are facilitated by a culture based on *swift trust*.

Swift trust is the willingness to rely on team members, who may have not met previously and may never meet, to perform their roles effectively, both informal and formal, in a quickly formed team. It also involves establishing and communicating clear roles and responsibilities among team members.

Swift trust is not accidental. Environmental factors act as preconditions, either enabling and encouraging trust and its effective use or blocking trust.

Teams must have processes for knowledge management, collaboration, and communication. Collaborative tools can help build relationships and forge connections within a team so that it will not have to rely on proximity alone. People must have access to each other, regardless of title, position in the organization, or location.

For overall success in virtual teams, and in any management-by-projects environment, there really is insufficient time to build trust in the normal way; teams must quickly form, and members must assume their teammates have a similar commitment to the project's vision, mission, and values. Handy (1995) writes, "If we are to enjoy the efficiencies and other benefits of the virtual organization, we will have to rediscover how to run organizations based more on trust than on control. Virtuality requires trust to make it work: Technology on its own is not enough." This means that for effective collaboration, the formation of swift trust among team members is essential. Trust facilitates collaborative and cooperative behavior. But in the majority of virtual teams, the conditions required to develop trust simply do not exist because physical proximity, daily informal and unplanned interactions, and face-to-face meetings are lacking. Including team members in conference calls, decisions, and activities as often as possible is one way to promote trust within a virtual team.

Verma (1997) states that trust is a basic condition for the achievement of highly functioning project teams. By implication, the establishment of trust becomes a basic component of any successful project leader's strategy for motivating team members Verma suggests that trust is developed in part by:

- Modeling desired behaviors, such as respect and the discussion of sensitive issues
- Helping create an atmosphere of interaction and friendly relationships
- Developing win-win strategies for individual and group goals.

Verma believes that team motivation is likely to flourish in groups that emphasize, and have, the following qualities:

- Pride, loyalty, and teamwork
- Self-discipline and accountability
- Dedication, credibility, trust, and dependability.

Applying Force Field Analysis

Lewin (1948) explored forces within groups that support change and forces that inhibit change. He believed that in any system or group, both kinds of forces exist simultaneously to different degrees, depending on the unique conditions of the particular group. His model, force field analysis, has been elaborated and modified to apply to team motivation. It can be a positive tool for program and project managers to use in examining the forces influencing motivation within a team. Packard (1995), for example, describes force field analysis as an effective tool for managers to use when instituting changes within a group or team.

When defining the forces that hinder motivation, the program or project manager is actually dealing with individual and systemic forces that can be described as *resistances*. Resistance to change, action, or motivation is to be expected, and managers should not overreact to it. In reality, some resistance is often warranted—for example, when a project manager is trying to motivate team members to take an action that may not make sense or may even be wrong. When a program or project manager encounters resistance, it is important for him or her to:

- Question whether the resistance is grounded in a valid and accurate assessment of the current facts

- Make certain that the vision, goals, and benefits of the program or project have been clearly communicated to the team members

- Examine whether individual differences (such as a personality clash) is obstructing cooperation.

A force field analysis has five general steps:

1. The program or project manager states the problem so the team understands it and why it is being discussed. For example: "Our program is considering adding a new project that has an approved business case. If this project is added, we may be able to complete the program earlier than planned, but we also will need some additional resources. It may require us to reallocate resources from an existing project to this new project."

2. With the team, brainstorm the positive and negative forces against the proposed change.

3. Then clarify the background of each force to show why it exists and also how it may affect the change. Determine whether any of the forces can be changed or modified.

4. Next, determine how strong the resisting forces are versus the forces in favor of the change. Look at the causes of the resisting forces and talk about how they might be overcome.

5. Prepare a plan to address the areas of resistance.

Ideally, force field analysis is best conducted in a face-to-face setting, but it can be effective for virtual teams, especially if these teams have access to conferencing tools. Regardless, it can be effective if everyone on the team is involved in discussing the positive aspects of the change as well as the resistance forces. This approach can be used to help teams reach consensus on a decision and prepare a plan to implement the decision.

Force field analysis can also be effective in portfolio management, which in turn affects both program and project management. Each time there is a change in the portfolio—for example, when a new project is added to it—this means the portfolio must be rebalanced. Often, other programs or projects will be canceled or deferred because the new project needs resources. Through the use of force field analysis, the portfolio manager can meet with program and project manager and use this approach to overcome resistance to the new project and the changes it may bring to the current work that is underway.

The portfolio manager also can use force field analysis to determine whether the proposed program or project is one that will support the organization's goals, objectives, and overall risk tolerance or whether including this proposed project in the portfolio may also engender too much resistance for it to be successful.

Motivational Mistakes

The program or project manager should experiment with different approaches to motivating team members. He or she should pay close attention to whether motivational efforts are working. Here are some examples of well-intentioned but questionable motivation strategies and beliefs:

- *"Whatever motivates me will motivate others."* This belief is an extension of the assumption that others want to be treated the way we would like to be treated. People are often motivated by the same approaches, but not always. Do not make assumptions about what will motivate someone—ask him or her!

- *"People are motivated primarily by money."* Although it is obviously valid to an extent, this belief does not explain the full range of human motivation. People are also highly motivated by personal acknowledgment from their managers, meaningful recognition from peers, and the opportunity to work in a setting in which they can keep developing marketable skills.

- *"Team members love to receive formal awards."* Many people do value the opportunity to receive a formal award noting a special achievement. Frequently, however, formal awards are presented in a way that may actually cause employee cynicism, such as a situation where employees believe that the recipient of the award is chosen for reasons other than accomplishment, such as company politics or political correctness. Formal awards are likely to be motivating forces when team members themselves vote for the recipient and when the award is not given to mask some other issue.

- *"Give them a rally slogan."* Initially, slogans can help win team members' focus and give them a sense of purpose, but if they are overused, they can quickly backfire on the program or project manager. Slogans can make the message behind the slogan seem like a sham. Many self-directed professionals feel that the overuse of slogans is patronizing.

- *"The best project leader is a strong cheerleader."* Cheerleading is an important part of managing people, but the program or project manager needs to be careful not to overdo it. Cheerleading comments can be positive, but they need to be used carefully. Often, the best way to motivate people is to let them come up with the inspiration and energy for their own actions, free from outside cheerleading.

- *"These people are professionals. They don't need motivating!"* Project professionals are generally self-motivating, following an inner drive that leads to achievement and productivity. However, nearly everyone profits from occasional outside sources of motivation, particularly on programs that are lengthy or projects that are frustrating.

- *"I'll motivate them when there is a problem."* This approach to motivation takes the old adage that says "No news is good news" to an extreme. Unfortunately, people tend not to tell others when their motivation is starting to lag;

their level of motivation usually needs to get seriously low before most people speak up and address the issue. The skilled motivator takes a proactive approach to motivating the team, not waiting for motivation issues to surface.

- *"I'll treat everyone the same. People like that, and it will be motivating for them."* It is safe to assume that it is important to treat everyone the same on issues of basic fairness and job performance standards. But it is also important to recognize team members as individuals, especially when creating strategies to motivate each of the individuals on a team. Different things motivate people at different points in their lives.

Motivational Checklist for the Program or Project Manager

Here are seven suggestions to follow when considering how to motivate a team member:

1. Determine the team member's personal style (using the MBTI system or another framework for describing individual differences).

2. Assess the member's career stage (as described by Schein).

3. Identify the team member's career anchors (the work-related values described by Schein).

4. Identify the team member's primary need: achievement, affiliation, or power (as described by McClelland).

5. Determine the team member's particular level of need according to the Flannes and Buell model based on Maslow's hierarchy of needs.

6. Use force field analysis as appropriate.

7. Remember to be proactive in motivating others, and try to avoid making the common motivational mistakes discussed above.

Summary

Motivating team members is one of the most challenging and sophisticated interpersonal tasks required of the program or project manager. In developing and implementing motivation strategies, the program or project manager should consider macro-level factors such as downsizing and sociological forces such as the increase in cross-cultural influences and virtual teams. Motivational approaches must also consider individual variables, such as each team member's personality style, personal values, and career development stage, as well as situational variables.

The program or project manager should remember that all sources of motivation are fluid and dynamic. Keep in touch with team members to determine what is currently motivating for them. The best approach to use when deciding what is motivating for any particular team member is to ask that person. That may sound simplistic, but it will provide the manager with a wealth of current, specific information that cannot be obtained through any other method.

Discussion Questions

Angelica is the project manager for a software development project. When she was chosen as project manager, her manager told her that her team comprised some highly skilled professionals representing diverse backgrounds and professional goals. These team members, the manager explained, would need to be skillfully motivated to get the work completed on time.

As Angelica left the initial meeting with her manager, she began reflecting on how she would motivate these people, particularly given the rumor of impending company layoffs. She knew what was motivating for her, and she assumed that these same things would also motivate her team members.

However, as she learned more about her team members' backgrounds during her next meeting with her manager, she began to have second thoughts about what motivating approaches she could use successfully with them. One of the members, for example, was an introvert and a long-term employee 14 months from retirement. Another team member was a new employee who recently arrived in this country after completing his degree in another country. Two others were technical contractors on loan to the project for undetermined lengths of time. There was a disgruntled mid-career engineer who believed that he should have been selected as project manager. Finally, two other team members were young, fast-track engineers who were noted for their technical innovation but were often perceived to be short on task follow-through and closure.

Reviewing the composition of her team, Angelica realized that she would be significantly challenged to motivate each of these individuals given their unique situations and professional needs.

1. If you were this project manager, how would you motivate each of these different individuals?
2. What would be your first step in the motivation process?
3. How would you assess your effectiveness as a motivator?

Interpersonal Communication Tools | 4

While program and project managers have a variety of technical tools to aid them in their work, such as information technology, project management methodologies, and earned value, one tool that is rarely considered in detail is interpersonal communication. Portfolio, program and project managers can make effective use of this tool to improve their teams' performance. Key interpersonal communication skills include the ability to:

- Use concrete communication skills, which can serve as the "nuts and bolts" of an effective discussion

- Identify and appreciate individual differences among stakeholders

- Pay attention to the tone and texture of the communication

- Recognize communication stoppers.

The Importance of Communications in Portfolio, Program, and Project Management

Stuckenbruck and Marshall (1985) write that effective communication within a team and between team members and other stakeholders is necessary if a team is to be effective. But the project manager, primarily, is responsible for communication. The authors note that 90 percent of the project manager's job is communication and that he or she spends approximately 50 percent of his or her time communicating with the project team. Hollingworth says, "Communications is much like a game, and those who know its rules—those who have a command of good skills, play it better than those who don't"

(1987, p. H-1). She further notes that "the quality of one's communications skills is probably the most important of all traits."

Communications became more important in project management in the 1990s (Chiocchio 2007) because of increasing emphasis on the project team and the growing complexity and globalization of the business world. The way people communicate also changed. In the 1990s, new technologies became widely available. These have influenced performance by enabling people to think in different ways and to communicate and work together differently.

Shenhar, Levi, Dvir, and Maltz (2001) points out that traditional forms of communication are not always appropriate. He notes, for example, that projects with low uncertainty can rely on existing technology, while highly uncertain projects may require new or different types of technology that do not even exist for richer, less formal communications. In other words, these highly uncertain projects may require new and different forms of communications to ensure that everyone involved can use the same type of communications methods regardless of their location.

PMI (2007) recognizes the importance of communications as a key personal competency for the project manager. Communication, for the project manager, has four key elements: actively listening, understanding, and responding to stakeholders; maintaining lines of communication; ensuring the quality of information; and tailoring communications to the audience (pp. 26–27). Further, PMI (2008a) says that communication is one of the major reasons a project either succeeds or fails. Openness in communication is essential for teamwork and strong performance.

The *PMBOK® Guide* explains several dimensions of communications (p. 245), with examples tailored to portfolio, program, and project management.

- Internal and external

  - Internal: A project team member communicates via email with others on the team.

  - External: The program manager communicates with his or her customers.

- Formal and informal

  - Formal: The program manager regularly conducts stage-gate reviews with the program's governance board to determine whether the program should move to the next phase of the program life cycle. Stage-gate reviews can also involve deciding whether additional work is required before moving on to the next life cycle phase; whether circumstances have changed; whether the program is delivering its planned benefits; and whether the program still fits appropriately within the organization's portfolio.

- Informal: A project team member telephones another team member to brainstorm an idea.

- Vertical and horizontal

  - Vertical: When working on a program, a project manager escalates an issue to the program manager; if the program manager cannot resolve it, he or she escalates it to the sponsor or to the governance board.

  - Horizontal: The organization establishes a community of practice (CoP) for its project managers to meet regularly to discuss best practices, to learn about new trends from internal and external speakers, and to interact with other project managers when needed—for example, to prepare for certifications or to discuss lessons learned.

- Official and unofficial

  - Official: A program manager working in the pharmaceutical industry prepares a press release announcing the availability of a new drug after approval by the Food and Drug Administration.

  - Unofficial: Two project team members have an off-the-record conversation about whether they think the project will succeed.

- Written and oral

  - Written: A project team member prepares a weekly status report regarding his work package for his project manager.

  - Oral: A project manager gives an oral presentation to the portfolio review board about why her project should continue to be part of the organization's top five projects in terms of resource availability in the upcoming year.

- Verbal and nonverbal

  - Verbal: Co-located team members meet informally to discuss project status.

  - Nonverbal: During an informal meeting, one team member evidently does not share the same views as the others: he shows absolutely no interest in the discussion even though it involves his specific work. It is unclear why he is not participating; he could be preoccupied or bored, or he might disagree with the comments others are making. In any case he decides not to engage the team members as he is under pressure to complete his work as quickly as possible and wants to avoid conflict at this time.

Program managers spend even more time on communications than do project managers (PMI 2008c), given the larger number of stakeholders, communications channels, and technology and tools involved (and their complexity), as well as the length of programs.

The portfolio manager deals with stakeholders at many levels, but especially those at the highest level of the organization. He or she therefore must be adept at reaching out to various people and must have extremely well-developed communication skills. These skills are especially important because the portfolio manager helps make the business case to the portfolio review board or similar group for a new project or program, may have to inform a sponsor if a program is not selected, and also may need to inform a program or project manager if the portfolio review board decides to cancel the manager's program.

Communications on Virtual Teams

Certain considerations uniquely affect virtual teams. These include:

- Considering different time zones so that one team member is not always inconvenienced when conference calls or virtual team meetings are held

- Using comparable technology for the most effective communications

- Being aware of team members' cultural norms to prevent misunderstandings—for example, knowing whether a team member's silence represents concurrence or respect.

Even if a team is not geographically dispersed, it will likely rely on communications technology of some kind, such as email, discussion forums, and blogs, to a greater extent than in the past when team members would hold more informal meetings and discussions with others to talk about issues of concern as required.

Language differences are another consideration. Many programs and projects, especially in the virtual environment, adopt English as a common language even if there are team members who are native speakers of Mandarin Chinese or Spanish [Note: The number of people in the world who speak these two languages is far greater than the number of native speakers of English.] Adopting English as the official language of a program or project can be done by following a formal English approach—one in which dialects, accents, slang, and colloquialisms are eliminated. Charles Ogden in 1930, was an early proponent of such an approach; he developed *Basic English*, intended to be an international language with 850 words that could be used to communicate about day-to-day processes. More recently, Kolby (2000) developed a dictionary containing the 4,000 words he asserts are essential for an educated vocabulary and success in business, education, and life. This dictionary is an excellent tool for multilingual teams to use to avoid common misunderstandings by eliminating slang and other daily expressions used by native English speakers, which may not be familiar to other members of the team.

Developing Concrete Communication Skills

A number of concrete communications skills can foster effective communications on both virtual and co-located program and project teams, including:

- Sending "I" messages
- Listening actively
- Asking open-ended questions
- Tracking the message
- Reframing a point.

Sending "I" Messages

"I" messages, such as "I believe there is a key issue on the Richards project that we need to discuss," are effective because the speaker is clearly taking responsibility for his or her point of view and at the same time is giving the other person the opportunity to consider whether he or she shares that opinion. This accountability is especially important for program or project managers. For example, in a meeting the program governance board discusses a problem that will cause the program to miss a key milestone. If the program manager can say to the board, "I want you to know we are going to miss our upcoming milestone to deliver the software to the customer on time because we encountered a testing issue," he or she takes accountability for the problem. Another approach would be to say, "Our team is not working well together, and one team member is extremely late with his work package so I want you to know this means we cannot deliver the software to our customer on the planned date." The "I" message shows the program manager takes responsibility for the team's work and for the overall success of the program. This approach also demonstrates that the program manager is aware of the various issues affecting the program and is willing to openly communicate them to the board.

Taking responsibility for one's own point of view is a great way to identify and clarify individual points in a discussion. If there is a downside to frequent use of "I" messages, it is the possibility that the speaker may come across as overly self-referencing or egocentric, and listeners may feel that the speaker is not team oriented.

Listening Actively

Typically, we focus on improving our abilities to speak and write effectively, with little time devoted to listening actively to speakers, whether they are key stakeholders, outsiders to the program or project, or peer or team members. Listening is not just hearing. It is a skill that takes time to develop and perfect.

Hollingsworth (1987) defines *active listening* as paying close attention to what is said, asking the other party to spell out carefully and clearly what he or she means, and asking the speaker to repeat him- or herself if the listener is not sure what was said. This definition is applicable to our work in program and project management.

Some program or project problems can be attributed to someone's failure to actively listen:

• Perhaps a team member made a mistake because he misunderstood his assignment—which happened because he did not listen or heard only what he wanted to hear.

• When working with customers, it is easy to assume that we understand their requirements and that our proposed solution will meet or exceed them, but instead, we often have not listened to their concerns and have not developed a joint understanding of what must be done for mutual success.

- It is easy in meetings or on conference calls to just tune out and do or think about something else and thus miss something that is critical to one's work on a program or project.

Active listening gives the speaker the message that the listener hears what he or she is saying, even if the listener does not necessarily agree with the point. The active listener gives feedback—for example, "Carl, I hear that you strongly believe that the project is not going to be done on time unless you get two additional engineers on the project." This response lets Carl know that you have heard his message; this is crucial to effective communication but does not commit you to agreeing with his point.

Active listening is an effective tool to use when the speaker has very strong feelings about something and needs to get it off his or her chest before continuing with the conversation. Active listening keeps the conversation moving, allows your partner to be heard and understood, and buys you some time if you are uncertain about how you want to respond to the issues being discussed.

Such active listening is especially important when working on a virtual or a culturally diverse team. For example, assume you are on a conference call with your virtual team. A word in English—for example, *resent*—may mean "I have re-sent you the email you did not receive," or it may mean "I resent what you are saying and disagree with it totally." If you are unclear as to the meaning of the speaker's words, you should ask the speaker for clarification to avoid misunderstandings. If overused, however, active listening can have the negative effect of making you appear wishy-washy, patronizing, or perhaps unable to make a decision. According to PMI (2007), listening is a core personal competency, one in which self-improvement is critical.

You can demonstrate active listening skills by:

- Confirming that you understand another person's point of view, even if it differs from your own

- Telling and showing team members that their views do count, are important, and that you consider them when you are making decisions regarding the program or the project

- Responding verbally to issues raised by others to show you have listened to their concerns (and showing your commitment to action by keeping a log, accessible to the team, to track progress toward resolving those issues)

- Letting others know that you heard their suggestions but needed to go in a different direction because, for example, of a change in the organization's strategic objectives, a merger or downsizing, or a risk to the program or project

- Confirming that you have received someone's message, even if you cannot respond to it immediately, letting the sender know when you will respond, and responding as planned, without another delay.

You can seek feedback about your progress in improving your listening skills by:

- Surveying stakeholders on the program or project to determine whether they feel as if you, the program or project manager, have really heard them and understand their key concerns and issues

- Asking a peer to observe a conversation you have with your program board or during a team meeting and offer feedback and suggestions.

Asking Open-Ended Questions

Open-ended questions give the answering party the chance to expand on a point without feeling forced to respond with a terse yes-or-no answer. Open-ended questions work well in situations in which answers are not necessarily clear-cut. Open-ended questions also are "friendlier" than a yes-or-no questions—they show the other person that you are truly interested in his or her point of view.

Even when you ask a yes-or-no question, you can follow it up with an open-ended question beginning with "why" or "how" to elicit more information. For example, if you want to find out how a certain team member is handling a key aspect of the project, an open-ended question such as "Phil, would you please lead me through a description of what you have done recently on the project?" will elicit this type of information. This question offers Phil latitude in responding, which will likely reduce his defensiveness and allow him to speak with a degree of comfort because he is setting the direction. This style of questioning allows you to sit back and listen for the information you're interested in.

If Phil fails to address one of your areas of interest, you can ask a follow-up question such as, "Sounds good, but can you please tell me a little more about how you are covering the administrative details?" Open-ended questions help create an expansive tone in the conversation, encouraging your partner to volunteer more information.

What is the risk of using open-ended questions? Risks include coming across as indirect and unfocused, possibly having a hidden agenda or a concern that is not verbalized. To a more concrete person, open-ended questions may seem nebulous.

Tracking the Message

All of us have had the frustrating experience of suddenly realizing that we are talking with someone about four different subjects at once and have no idea how we got off the original topic. This often occurs when both parties are not tracking the content or purpose of the discussion and are inserting new topics into the discussion. Insertion of a new topic can occur for a number of reasons, including a failure to listen to the other party's key message, a strong emotional reaction from one of the parties, or a tendency to avoid closure on one subject before moving on to a new one. A conversation can be brought back on topic with a tracking statement such as: "Bob, I think we are going off topic. Can we please back up to the point where you were mentioning the cost for the software package? I think that is when I started to lose you."

Conversations during meetings are quite vulnerable to going off track. Virtual teams frequently communicate via conference calls, and it is easy for one team member to become so interested in the first item discussed that he or she places the call on mute and does some research to adequately respond to this issue. But when this team member goes back to the call, everyone else on the call has moved on to other items on the agenda. The team member who has gotten behind often interrupts the conversation to explain to the rest of the team what he or she has learned from research. While the information may be of interest, the team may have already reached consensus on the issue at hand or may have determined that it was not appropriate for further discussion at the time.

If you find yourself in such a situation, you may consider raising the issue again at the end of the call. Apologize to the group for leaving the call, then explain that you have learned something new on the topic, and ask them if it is all right to tell them what you have learned.

Reframing a Point

At times, discussions reach a point where communication is faltering or has become negative. Unless some change takes place, the discussion is headed for failure. In these situations, a valuable communication tool is reframing. Just as a picture framer can change the appearance of a painting by putting a new frame around it, you can put a new frame around a failing discussion and create a new sense of optimism or achievement.

For example, assume that your team has been talking for 45 minutes about a shortage of engineers needed to complete the software project on time and within budget. The tone in the room is one of frustration, with some sense of hopelessness and resignation. Reframing this discussion would put a different spin on the conversation. It would allow the team to see the issues from a different perspective—one that offers more optimism. A reframing comment at this point of the discussion might be something like: "We need to consider if the discussion keeps going in this direction, we are not going to get anything done. What if we look at this situation as an opportunity to build a bridge between the engineering group in the other division and our group? We have said for a long time that a bridge like that would be good for us to have."

Reframing the issue, which can be done by any person in the conversation, involves creative thinking and a willingness to take a chance by offering a new perspective. When offering a reframing comment, be prepared for some people to remain stuck in the negative and to resist these creative alternatives. Be persistent. It may be necessary to state the same reframing message in different ways before success is achieved.

To work effectively with those who still may be negative toward the new approach, suggest forming a small group to work together to come up with a possible solution to discuss with the rest of the group. Set a time to do so quickly so the issue can be resolved. Include a member who is reacting negatively in this small group to help to gain some type of consensus for the new approach. Crafting a different approach may still take some time because it does require ingenuity.

Identifying and Appreciating Individual Differences in Communications

It is easy for us to assume that everyone will communicate in similar ways, especially if they are working on the same work packages and activities and therefore have comparable technical interests. However, each person will approach his or her work assignments in different ways and will also communicate using a variety of styles. Each person will require different kinds of communication about the program or project, and you, as the program or project manager, should avoid overloading team members and other stakeholders with information. They will have preferences for how they want to receive information and also how they want to provide it to others. Some people overcommunicate; others undercommunicate or do not communicate at all. Once you are aware of a stakeholder's preferred communication style, you will be better able communicate with him or her. Here, we discuss a few methods for interacting with various stakeholders based on their individual styles.

The MBTI Approach

There are many ways to assess the style and personality of project team members. One conceptual framework that can be useful when considering individual differences is the Myers-Briggs Type Indicator (MBTI). Based on the work of Carl Jung (1971), the MBTI describes various components of personal styles. Jung believed that individuals vary in how they approach and perceive the world. In today's world of work, the MBTI is used extensively with teams, both as a team-building instrument and as a method for discovering the different communication styles of team members (Hammer 1996).

The MBTI may be administered in a number of formats by certified practitioners. Some teams prefer to take the instrument via various online assessment forms; other teams prefer to take it in a shortened, hard-copy form during team meetings.

In essence, the MBTI measures an individual's preferences among four pairs of qualities or preferences:

- ***Extravert or introvert.*** Extraverted people are energized by a significant amount of interaction with the outside world. This type of individual is action oriented and becomes bored if things move too slowly. In contrast, the introverted individual is energized by reflective activities away from lots of outside stimulation. This type of person enjoys being involved in tasks where he or she can really immerse him- or herself in the depth and the details of the issue.

- *Sensing or intuition.* A person with a sensing preference looks at the world from a pragmatic, concrete, and immediate point of view. The sensing person prefers to use the five senses to attend to the world and has a present-tense focus aimed at solving problems that can be scored, measured, or quantified. The intuitive person, on the other hand, prefers to look at a problem with more of a big-picture focus, eyeing future possibilities and trends. This person enjoys insights and abstract-based activities and has less interest in the concrete present than the sensing person does.

- *Thinking or feeling.* The individual with a thinking-based decision-making style likes to look at the logical and rational components of an issue and make a decision that is supported by facts, analysis, and numbers. The feeling-based decision maker, by contrast, makes decisions with the "heart." The feeling person prefers to consider values, beliefs, and personal feelings—types of "information" that are much more subjective in nature.

- *Judging or perceiving.* The person with a judging orientation prefers to use an orderly approach to plan and structure activities and events. The judging person seeks to achieve closure on tasks and is generally quite goal-oriented. The perceiving person, conversely, wants to approach the world in a less structured manner, leaving things more to chance. This person is comfortable with flexibility and responding to whatever comes up in the moment. Perceivers are often viewed as curious and may engage in many activities simultaneously.

Communication Tips: Using the MBTI Ideas to Deliver Your Message

Using the ideas on individual differences suggested by the MBTI, you can tailor your message to reach each person on your team in a way that suits his or her unique style. By customizing your message, you increase the chances of successful communication and team cooperation. Table 4-1 suggests ways of communicating with team members based on their MBTI type.

Communicating with the Extraverted Team Member

The extraverted team member is one who is interactive, who focuses attention and energy outside him- or herself, who enjoys mixing with people, and who generally has a great deal of verbal contact with others. The extravert wants to be involved and to be at the center of the action.

Table 4-1   Communication Tips Using the Myers-Briggs Preferences

Personality Style	Compatible Type of Communication
Extraverted	Get together personally to think out loud.
Introverted	Help draw out this person, then give him or her some time to privately reflect on your message.
Sensing	Present tangible facts, examples, data, and real-world experiences to make your point.
Intuitive	Offer a "big picture" overview, presenting concepts that are crucial for your discussion.
Thinking	Present arguments that appeal to a rational analysis of the facts; appeal to the "head."
Feeling	Talk more from the "heart," using statements that address values and gut-level decision-making.
Judging	Be orderly in presenting your message, and keep the discussion moving toward resolution and closure.
Perceiving	Allow for an open-ended discussion, staying flexible about the agenda.

To communicate effectively with an extravert:

- Think out loud with this person; the extravert enjoys brainstorming.

- Communicate in a personal, face-to-face manner if possible, and minimize written, email, or other types of communication that the extravert may view as too impersonal.

- Place the extravert in settings where group communication is needed, such as brainstorming sessions; this type of milieu will stimulate the extravert and will get the creative juices flowing.

- Because extraverts can be verbally outgoing, they can dominate group meetings, particularly when dealing with more introverted team members. Work to keep the extravert's output in such settings at an acceptable level.

- If you are working virtually, use computer-mediated technology, such as instant messaging, to communicate directly with this team member.

- On the virtual team, occasionally phone this person if possible, recognizing his or her need to communicate by other than asynchronous means.

In these calls, ask him or her for his or her points of view on issues facing the program or project.

- Enable the extraverted team member to lead discussions if working in either a virtual or co-located team; if on a virtual team, ask this person to become familiar with computer-mediated technology to facilitate group meetings.

- Set up situations on a virtual team, if possible, that will allow the extravert to be able to interact with the sponsors or customer(s). This will put his or her enjoyment of working with others to good use.

- Suggest to other team members who may have difficulty speaking up that they might contact this extraverted team member for suggestions. (Of course, ask the extraverted team member first if he or she is willing to do this, and ask him or her to be as encouraging as possible should he or she be contacted by others on the team).

Communicating with the Introverted Team Member

Introverts are known for keeping a lower profile within group discussions, and they tend to be more thoughtful and reflective than expressive. They often appear deep in thought and may need some supportive prodding before they will offer an opinion. When communicating with an introvert, consider the following:

- One-on-one settings often allow the introvert to be more disclosing and communicative. Within group settings, the introvert may remain quiet or be less involved.

- Introverts do not particularly enjoy thinking out loud. Rather, they usually prefer to have some time to think issues through before responding.

- Introverts may prefer more impersonal methods of communicating, such as email or written documents. Such written messages give them the privacy they prefer to reflect and think ideas through until they are ready to respond.

- Consider using nominal group type techniques, in which everyone is required to participate without interruption, to get this individual engaged in brainstorming sessions without fear of criticism of his or her ideas.

- Provide an agenda for team meetings in advance so the introverted team member can think through what is to be discussed and can be prepared to offer suggestions.

Introverted people are especially suited for work on virtual teams, in which they have solitude to do their work and are not constantly interrupted by other team members, because people cannot drop by and chat. However, on virtual teams it is too easy to forget these team members and the contributions they can offer, especially if there are changes in the organization's strategic direction that affect the program or project, a key issue to resolve, a decision that must be made, or a risk that requires resolution. If you feel the introvert needs to be involved but is not participating, contact the introvert directly and ask him or her to comment. Determine approaches to involve these team members in such important discussions, giving them time, if possible, before they must respond.

Communicating with the Sensing Team Member

The sensing person approaches the world with a pragmatic, tangible, and immediate focus, paying close attention to details while working at a steady pace. This person wants to deal with tasks in ways that can be quantified and measured. When communicating with a sensing team member:

- Give the sensing person details, facts, examples, and concrete points. He or she has little use for theory or "the big picture."

- Stay in the present when delivering your message. Explain the current importance of your message.

- Stick to the business at hand. The sensing person thinks extra communication about tangential matters is a distraction.

- Provide an agenda in advance of all team meetings, especially if working in a virtual environment, and stick to the agenda so the sensing team member does not find the meeting a waste of his or her time. If topics that are not on the agenda come up, note them and plan to discuss them at a later time.

Communicating with the Intuitive Team Member

The opposite of the sensing person is the person who approaches the world intuitively. The intuitive person likes to develop a vision and is good at synthesizing future possibilities and trends. Routine tasks are boring for this individual; he or she is always looking for better ways to do things. When communicating with someone who has an intuitive style, consider the following:

- Provide context for the issues and an overview of where you envision the discussion may take you. During work on the program or project, discuss the goals and how the program or project supports the organization's vision.

- Remember that an intuitive person likes to theorize and follow different tangents during a conversation. You may need patience as this person brings up a number of other areas that may seem unrelated to the problem at hand.

- In meetings, the intuitive person will often communicate with peers by assuming the role of devil's advocate, expressing ideas and messages that seem outside the box or tangential to the current point.

- If the program or project manager believes that people on the team do not understand how the program or project fits into the overall strategy of the organization, ask the intuitive team member before a team meeting to relate the program or project's vision to the organization's overall strategy to refocus the team.

Communicating with the Thinking Team Member

The person with a thinking style prefers to interact with the world using logic and reason. His or her communication is often concise and to the point, focusing on a logical presentation of the facts. This person adopts a rational mode of addressing a situation; the thinking person frequently works "from the head" when solving problems. The best way to make your point with a thinking person is to:

- Present a logical argument, focusing on an analysis of the situation that is grounded in an assessment of the facts.

- Get to the point; the thinking person has little interest in casual conversation.

- Not take it personally if you encounter a thinking person with little need for small talk. The thinking team member is ideally suited to a virtual team, where small talk is not a major concern.

- Ask the thinking person an open-ended question to draw him or her in if he or she is not participating in a meeting. This will help him or her take the meeting seriously and find it a valuable use of time.

- Encourage this team member to state his or her opinions in a way that can help others not only understand the situation but also persuade them to adopt a proposed solution.

Communicating with the Feeling Team Member

The feeling person uses a significantly different approach from the thinking person when dealing with the world. The feeling person places emphasis on the subjective aspects of the situation, such as personal values, how people feel about the issue, and what his or her "gut" says is the correct thing to do.

Try these methods when communicating with the individual with a feeling style:

- Appeal to this person's values when making your argument.

- Expect this person to talk a great deal about feelings; he or she may put less emphasis or credence on the logical facts of a situation.

- Consider that this person may need to talk feelings through, or "get it off their chest," before they are able to move to verbal communication geared to tangible problem solving.

- When managing a virtual program or project, the feeling team member may be the person who raises a conflict or an issue to you for resolution, even if he or she is not involved directly in the situation. If this happens, give the feeling team member time to explain the details to you so that you can better understand the situation, involve the appropriate members of the team, and make a decision.

- Ask the feeling team member to encourage others to express their points of view during team meetings.

Communicating with the Judging Team Member

The judging approach is one in which the individual uses an orderly method to structure activities and endeavors. Judging people like to have a project plan, a detailed work breakdown structure, or an agenda for each project meeting. They are motivated toward gaining closure on an event and moving forward. Because the person with the judging preference seeks order and structure, consider trying these approaches:

- Present your message in an orderly manner, using agendas and outlines to define the purpose of the discussion.

- Stay on point and try to avoid drifting into other topics or tangential points.

- Remember that this person works toward closure; keep the conversation moving toward a conclusion. Set both time and topic parameters before beginning.

- Involve this team member in a gatekeeper-type role during team meetings in case a meeting is diverting too much from the agenda. This is especially important when working in a virtual environment because the lack of shared physical space to hold the team's attention might cause individual team members to get off track more easily. The "gatekeeper" team member can help the team move toward closure, and he or she can make a list of other issues to address later as necessary.

- Ask the judging team member to summarize what has been said during a meeting to ensure everyone understands and supports the decisions made.

Communicating with the Perceiving Team Member

The perceiving person prefers flexibility and spontaneity. For the most part, perceiving people like to keep their options open and prefer not to work from a schedule or plan. Talking with this type of person will be a free-flowing experience, and there will be little need for structure and closure.

Consider these suggestions when working with a perceiving team member:

- Stay flexible and avoid using a rigid agenda for your meeting.

- Remember that this person will want to let the communication take its natural direction; expect him or her to mention many topics. Also, when meeting with a perceiving person, he or she may not worry about time and so continue to discuss an issue longer than planned. A judging person might have a hard time working with a perceiving person in this type of situation, because a judging person might be anxious to come to closure on tasks rather than letting communications drift to other topics outside of the planned agenda.

- Gently help this person stay on track when necessary; offer comments that acknowledge his or her ideas but still help maintain focus.

On a mature team, especially one in which people have worked together as a team before or on a program that has been underway for some time, it is often appropriate for people to share the results of their MBTI assessments or talk about their results on other personality instruments discussed in Chapter 3, such as Schein's career anchors or McClelland's needs for achievement, affiliation, or power. This open sharing should be encouraged so that people recognize one another's preferred style and can then better communicate with one another. Sharing also indicates an empowered team in which people trust one another and want to collectively work toward team success in all aspects of the program or project. On such teams, people can openly discuss any concerns or problems and recognize the importance of consistent, open, and honest communication among team members and with stakeholders.

Paying Attention to the Tone and Texture of Communications

Just as important as considering the individual styles and preferences of your team members as you craft your communications is having a keen awareness of the texture and tone of any communication. This awareness involves:

- Being present during the discussion
- Listening to the "music behind the words"
- Considering the alliance and the context
- Keeping the communication reciprocal
- Being aware of content and process.

Being Present during the Discussion

Being in the present when communicating means paying attention to the thoughts, ideas, feelings, and beliefs you are experiencing during a specific moment in the conversation. It means being aware of your mood, energy level, and emotions. For example, are you having a good day? Feeling angry? Having this awareness does not mean that you have to disclose or act on these feelings when you are communicating. Rather, the goal is to have a healthy awareness about what is going on with you now so you can use that awareness to communicate more effectively with your team members.

How can a program or project manager work on being present during a conversation? Here are two approaches to consider:

- *Reflect on your immediate feelings.* Your goal should be to develop an awareness of what you are feeling at that moment. Such an awareness will help you avoid stepping into metaphorical potholes as you communicate with the other person.

- *Reflect on what your body is telling you.* This physical level of awareness often reveals what is going on with us emotionally. Other people may also be able to tell how we are feeling from our body language. Most people have their own set of body cues that signal important information about their feelings. While these body cues may be apparent during face-to-face conversations, people are obviously unaware of them in virtual environments. During virtual communications, verbal explanations can substitute for body language. If, for example, you are having a bad day and you think your tone of voice (or the tone of an email or message you are writing) reflects your negative mood, you might briefly explain how you are feeling to the virtual team member with whom you are communicating.

An awareness of your feelings and your body cues will enable you to do the following when you are communicating with your stakeholders:

- *Really hear what the other person is saying to you.* If you are communicating with a virtual team member, unless it is on a teleconference or video conference, obviously you cannot hear the person talking to you or see his or her body cues. Likewise, the person you are communicating with cannot hear you or see your body cues, either, and may not understand the message you are trying to convey. Often, in these settings, you may wish to ask an open-ended question for some additional clarification.

- *Demonstrate more respect and consideration for the other person.* This approach also coveys your trust for the other person, which can foster the impression of being empowered as a team. Keep your body cues in mind when demonstrating respect, consideration, and trust. For example, you may be stressed or displeased about something else going on in your life—something unrelated to this team member—and if your body cues indicate this displeasure, you might confuse the other person.

Listening to the Music behind the Words

Flannes and Buell (1999) encourage people to "listen to the music behind the words." Doing so means listening to the message that is rarely verbalized or that indicates mood and emotions. The obvious message, which often masks the "music," is the content of the message and applies to the subject of the discussion. The music behind the message is the subtle affective level of the communication. It tells you so much more about what is happening. Consider this example of listening to the music behind the words:

> Judith told her project manager that the project was meeting specifications, was under budget, and would be completed on time. The project manager heard these words, registered that Judith was saying that everything was in good shape, and then allowed the conversation to end.
>
> However, if the manager had listened to the "music behind the words," he might have noticed her tone of voice, facial expressions, and body gestures. These indicators would have said, "I'm bored with this project, it is not challenging me, and I am frustrated that you do not find something for me that suits my skill level!"

By listening on this deeper level, the project manager would have picked up important cues suggesting that things were actually not going well on the project. It could also be that the project is progressing satisfactorily, but Judith is dissatisfied with this project and feels she cannot continue to contribute at a high level. She may wish to be reassigned to another project in the organization or to return to her functional unit.

Considering the Alliance and the Context

It is not possible to describe the "right" thing to say in any given situation. Figuring out the right thing to say is always a function of the nature of the alliance or relationship between the people who are interacting, plus an awareness of the context in which the communication is taking place.

Bugental (1990) developed the concepts of alliance and context. *Alliance* refers to the nature and quality of a specific relationship. Alliances differ in degrees of history, trust, openness, formality, and role. Different types of alliances exist between people on a team who are already friends before the project begins; between project team members and the project or program manager; between the team and the sponsor, the customer, and other key stakeholders; and between outside vendors. Thinking about the nature of an alliance offers the chance to tailor communications to the intricacies and the specifics of the immediate relationship.

Examples of types of alliances include the following relationships:

- Two friends who have worked together in the organization for 12 years and now are assigned to work on the same project
- Two programmers, each new to the company, assigned to work for the first time with each other
- Two virtual team members from different cultures working together.

There is no ideal alliance. Each alliance needs to be seen as a living thing, requiring nurturing and attention. Alliances must show sensitivity to specific needs of each party, and mutual respect is required for the alliance to strengthen and grow. Be careful not to take any alliance for granted.

Remember that every alliance is dynamic. Each alliance also is different, which makes it special and unique in its own way. There is no ideal alliance, and over time, alliances will shift as people move to other teams or other positions in the organization or leave the organization.

Bugental's (1990) view of context addresses the idea that an effective interaction is a function of an awareness of current circumstances. For example, in deciding how to tailor a message to a team member, the project manager should consider a number of context variables. These variables may include the current mood of the other person, the amount of pressure on the project team, or the fact that the organization may have recently undergone a reduction in force. A context variable will also include the setting—whether the message is being delivered in front of a formal group of stakeholders or over lunch at a neighborhood cafe.

By being aware of the context in which you are speaking, you can craft messages that are conducive to the current surroundings, thus helping put the person you are talking with at ease and increasing the odds of delivering your message effectively. On a virtual team, such face-to-face interaction is rare, but the context in which a message is delivered remains critical. Sometimes email is appropriate, while at other times the message is better delivered through a phone call or video conference.

When considering how to use the concept of context in communicating, be aware of these variables:

- Degree of formality or informality of the surroundings

- Current atmosphere in the workplace (e.g., anxiety, stress, pressing deadlines, recent reductions in force)

- Level of intimacy of the setting—whether it is an individual or a group setting.

Many of the ideas behind the concepts of alliance and context are obviously grounded in common sense. However, it is precisely because these ideas do appear to be commonsense that we often overlook them or give them minimal consideration when we are communicating. If we keep the concepts of alliance and context in mind, and we slow down and take time to apply them sensibly, we can achieve greater success in communication.

Keeping the Communication Reciprocal

Another important but subtle aspect of communication is the ability to create an atmosphere in which people on the team are treated with mutual respect and dignity, regardless of each team member's seniority or level of expertise (Buber 1970).

Buber discusses the importance of reciprocal, meaningful interactions. People must understand and hear what others say and are able to respond accordingly. Buber also focuses on the importance of the community of others and shared principles. A community focus and shared principles are essential in program and project management because of the sheer number of stakeholders on each program or project. The creation of shared principles must be intentional; a group of people are unlikely to all have the same principles. This points to the importance of the program or project team developing a charter in which they state the principles they will follow for overall team success. Determining the team's principles in concert is one step toward ensuring that managers and team members communicate as equals.

Here are some ways you can apply the idea of reciprocal communication in the day-to-day program or project environment.

- When looking at your communications partner, try to visualize this person as an equal, whether you are a project sponsor who has been with the organization for more than 30 years and are talking with a new project team member who just joined the company or you are a new team member talking with the sponsor.

- Situations in which you are talking about solving a problem can help you think of your communications partner as an equal. For example, assume you are a new team member and you are talking with the project sponsor. You have an idea based on a software integration you did in graduate school for applying a new software tool to the project. In such a situation, you are speaking to the sponsor about a possible way to improve the overall operations of the project, so you can communicate equally because improving operations is something that both of you view as essential for success.

- Watch out for the natural tendency to treat people as stereotypes; such an approach locks one into rigid ways of seeing others and creates long-term barriers to improved communications.

Rad and Levin (2003) write that the virtual environment is ideal for fostering reciprocal communications. On virtual teams, people are often unaware of the age or seniority level of each individual team member. People who might normally not speak up at a team meeting because they lack seniority or are new to the organization may offer ideas using asynchronous methods (such as email) or in teleconferences, where it is not obvious that they are, for example, younger than the rest of the team. Consider the following example.

> Cynthia was new to a database project. She brought subject matter expertise to her role as database administrator and had some excellent ideas, which she shared with the team in emails. People appreciated her suggestions and the new perspectives she brought to the team.
>
> Later, Joe joined the team. He was used to working in a functional, hierarchical environment. Technically, he was her supervisor, but the team was working as an empowered team and was small, so everyone essentially worked for the project manager.
>
> The project manager, Greg, eventually noted that Cynthia was sending fewer emails and asked her why she no longer was actively communicating with the rest

of the group. Greg learned that Joe told Cynthia that all communications should go through him, and Joe would then decide what would be escalated to Greg. The team no longer benefited from her ideas because Joe was the filter.

When Greg realized what was happening, he talked with Joe by phone to review the team's norms, which had been successful for several years, and informed him that the team operated in a manner that stressed open communications and was not based on a hierarchical, silo-type structure. He reminded Joe that the team consisted of senior-level people in their own fields of expertise and told him that the team was used to working in a self-directed manner and that he wished to continue to work in this way.

Unfortunately, this example does not have a happy ending. Joe found such a self-directed approach uncomfortable; he could not adapt to the team's norms and as a result had to leave the project.

Being Aware of the Content and the Process

Any communication can also be viewed through the filters of content and process. *Content* refers to the subject being discussed, such as the results of the project review meeting, what someone had for lunch on Tuesday, or the hardware items in next year's budget. Content items are the obvious parts of a communication and are the aspects that people can usually track most easily.

The more complex aspect of a communication is the *process*, which refers to the manner, style, and methods in which the content is presented. It often hints at underlying feelings or emotional responses that are not being expressed directly. You can look at your team's communication process by asking questions such as:

- Is one person dominating the team's discussion? In a virtual environment, is one person inundating others with emails and instant messages or taking over discussion forums, wikis, or blogs?

- Are people's comments coming across as critical or cynical?

- Does one person continually interrupt when a particular person is talking in a team meeting or teleconference?

- Does one person get very quiet when another team member is speaking in a team meeting or teleconference or if a conflict or sensitive issue is being discussed?

- Is one person continually playing the role of devil's advocate, questioning decisions so often that other team members tune him or her out and do not take him or her seriously?

- Are the project team members following the communications management plan, and were they involved in its development?

- Does the structure of the team (e.g., in a functional organization, in a projectized organization) affect the nature of the communications between team members, with the program and project managers, and with other stakeholders?

- Is the team charter effective, or is it too structured, hindering communications among the team?

By paying attention to the process level of communication within the team, the program or project manager can identify unspoken issues, problems, or areas of resistance that are hindering the progress of the project. Attending to process communication issues often takes some nerve and courage. Be active, assertive, and willing to speak your mind.

Recognizing Communication Stoppers

We all have communication shortcomings. Four behaviors—denial, projection, displacement, and objectification—plague us from time to time, particularly when we are fatigued or when we feel emotionally threatened. Which of the four is your biggest risk area?

Denial

A little denial in life is not bad and can sometimes help us get through a tough time. However, denial works against us when we stubbornly maintain a view or position even when those around us continue to make strong arguments to the contrary. (For example, we may continue to deny team members' messages that we are too controlling during team meetings, even after hearing this message four or five times.) As program or project managers, we need to be cognizant of the negative aspects of denial, especially if we are in a situation in which we need to solve a problem or assist a team member and instead we consciously elect to ignore the importance of the situation. This can affect not only our own productivity but also that of the team. We may choose to avoid the problem, believing someone else will fix it even if we are the person who is accountable for the program, project, work package, or activity.

Because programs and projects are time-bound, if we ignore or deny problems too often, we run the risk of being overscheduled and needing to add resources or use methods such as fast tracking to keep on schedule.

To monitor your risk of falling into the trap of denial, consider the following suggestions:

- When communication falters, ask an open-ended question, such as, "Am I missing something here that you are trying to tell me?"

- Stay receptive and non-defensive to feedback from such an open-ended question.

- Try to avoid conveying an attitude that says, "I do not care" or "Nothing ever changes here anyway, so why should I make an effort to do something in a different way?"

Projection

Projection is defined as attributing to others a feeling or belief that, in actuality, we hold ourselves. It is not beneficial to attribute a belief or attitude to another member of the team without confirming the reality of the projection for that team member. For example, if a project manager believes that all others on the team must share his or her specific view about how to approach a project design process, this project manager is projecting his or her belief upon others.

Projection is especially easy to do on a virtual team, in which meetings with everyone on the team are rare or may not happen at all. One person's frame of reference may be entirely different from another's.

Here are some ways to keep projection under control:

- If you think that others believe, think, or feel as you do about an issue, confirm this belief with them before you move forward, particularly on key issues.

- Use an "I" statement, followed by a question of inquiry. For example: "I believe very strongly that the specifications for this project need to be reevaluated and probably changed. Am I correct in assuming that you feel the same way?"

- Use discussion forums to post items on which you believe there is agreement by your team and ask team members for feedback before implementing a solution. Let them know how much time you have before the decision must be made.

Displacement

Who has not had a fight with a family member one morning, then come to work and bitten off the head of the first coworker who said something to him or her? Displacement occurs when some emotion or strong feeling that has been generated in one setting (in this case, the fight at home) is passed on to someone (in this case, the coworker) who has done nothing to warrant such treatment. The innocent coworker has no idea where this emotion originated and usually feels confused and distrustful of the person who delivered the blow.

Strong feelings are often generated in the complex world of program and project management, where the manager has many relationships to monitor and must navigate the tricky waters of matrix management and conflicting stakeholder agendas. Under these circumstances, it is easy to displace feelings upon innocent third parties. However, there are steps a program or project manager can take to reduce the risk of displacement.

- After an argument (or any interaction where negative feelings have been created), stop and take notice of what you are feeling.

- Before getting involved in another interaction (such as a meeting or discussion), take some time to let the negative feelings subside.

- As you begin the next interaction, do your best to initiate some discussion with yourself, such as, "I am still angry from the last meeting, but my anger is not about Joe, with whom I will be meeting, so I need to go slow in our discussion."

These approaches to minimizing displacement can be surprisingly effective and can have profound influence on keeping communication succinct and straightforward. In a sense, these approaches to managing displacement are an evolution of the old advice to count to ten before speaking.

Objectification

Program and project work is difficult and is becoming even more complex. Most programs and projects are facing greater numbers of stakeholders, a lack of sufficient resources to complete the work effectively, and pressure to complete the work faster and more efficiently given the increase in competition. This increase in the number of stakeholders means we have even more relationships to manage than in the past. Some of these stakeholders may be ones we never see or hear from during the program or project, but they are still important to manage to ensure success.

After a certain amount of experience and time spent struggling with different types of relationships, we can slip into the potentially risky habit of developing a shorthand approach to explain these different relationships to ourselves. Consequently, we create labels and categories such as "sponsoring executive," "project auditor," "outside vendor," and "project numbers guy." These shorthand terms allow us to put people into categories so that we can relate to them more readily. We create assumptions about the nature of each of these categories, which helps us plan how to deal with the categories; in essence, these assumptions give us a blueprint for explaining how these people operate.

Viewed from a negative perspective, however, these categories can become stereotypes. When we use these stereotypes in dealing with others, we run the risk of turning people into static categories or objects. When this takes place, objectification of the other person occurs. Objectification of a team member generally happens slowly. At some point, however, the objectification becomes solidified, and it becomes difficult to see people as they really are: dynamic, changing human beings who rarely conform to the boxes into which we often place them. When working in a virtual team, objectification may be even easier: Some people join the team only to contribute specific technical knowledge at a certain time in the project. These individuals then may be known as subject matter experts who only fit in one small box in the project but in reality could contribute in other areas if allowed to do so.

Guarding against the tendency to objectify is difficult. The best approach to reducing the risk is to be aware of your assumptions about a specific person or group. Here are some objectifying assumptions held by one project manager:

- Project auditors care only about the numbers.

- Auditors never listen to what I have to say concerning project budget over-runs.

- They always start meetings with the rudest comment they can make.

If you notice that your list of assumptions contains words such as "only," "never," "they," and "always," you can assume that you are starting to turn auditors into objects—entities with fixed and rigid qualities. Once the objectification begins, communication becomes problematic. Your messages to the auditors may become more stylized and rote, emanating from your stereotype of what constitutes an "auditor." Eventually, you start wearing a set of blinders that will not allow you to see any communication and behavior from an auditor that does not conform to your preconceived categories or expectations.

The following suggestions may help you avoid objectifying others:

- ***Pay attention to individual differences.*** Team members will respond differently to your communication efforts, and for each individual, some tools will be more effective than others. Using a system such as the MBTI can help you determine how to tailor messages to particular team members.

- ***Consider the issues of alliance (the nature of the relationship) and context (the setting in which the communication is taking place)*** as you work to craft the most effective message.

- ***Practice the "nuts and bolts" techniques of communication.*** Experiment. Find the most effective tools for you. Get feedback from others about whether these tools have been successful.

- ***Stay open to feedback about your blind spots.*** Everyone has them, so try to receive constructive criticism without becoming defensive. This is not easy to do, but give yourself credit when you try.

- ***Observe those who communicate well,*** and adopt approaches from them that you think would work for you. Successful interpersonal communication is more art than science.

On a project to assess an organization's level of maturity in program management, the organization decided to bring in an outside person who had been certified in PMI's Organizational Project Management Maturity Model (*OPM3*). The head of the business unit had requested this assessment to improve the program management practices the organization was using, but people in the organization felt as if the assessment was an audit and believed they would be blamed if they were not using the organization's program management methodology, tools, and templates. They viewed the *OPM3* assessor not as someone who was coming in to suggest improvements, but instead as someone who was checking for compliance with existing processes and procedures. They labeled him—incorrectly—as an auditor and tried to avoid answering his questions. Further, in preparation for their interview with the assessor, they worked hard to prepare documents that showed they were in compliance with the standard methodology, though they actually did not follow the methodology at all in their day-to-day work.

This led the assessor to prepare a report showing that the organization had achieved about 90 percent of the program management best practices, when in reality, the level of achievement was far lower. The head of the business unit then questioned the assessor's ability to understand the situation and the *OPM3* tool the assessor used to assist in the process. The business unit director decided not to share the assessor's report with the people who had participated in the assessment. As a result, the entire process was seen as a waste of time and resources, and no improvement came of it.

Summary

Communications is a key competency for all project professionals—whether at the portfolio, program, or project level. It is easy to just maintain your current communications style, but keep in mind that your style may not be the most appropriate in certain situations. To improve your overall communication skills when managing portfolios, programs, and projects and interacting with stakeholders, consider all the approaches suggested in this chapter and try to use the most appropriate approach for each unique situation.

Discussion Questions

You have been the project manager on a telecommunications project for only four weeks, and already you have experienced a number of communication problems on your team. Your frustration is mounting as you review what has happened to date:

1. Two of your senior engineers keep calling you into meetings because they cannot seem to communicate with each other, and they want you to help them make a decision. What approach would you take in trying to figure out why these people are not communicating effectively with each other?

2. You ask one of your team members to attend a meeting with a group of external stakeholders. After the meeting, you get a call from your counterpart on the stakeholder's team complaining about your team member's performance in the meeting. The other project manager yells, "This guy did not hear a thing we said today!" What communication skill does your team member seem to lack? How might you handle this situation?

3. You are puzzled that two of your most competent technicians never seem to say anything during project meetings, although they have many good ideas to contribute. What might be contributing to these people's silence during the meetings? What could you do to help them be more communicative during team meetings?

Building and Managing Relationships with Stakeholders

5

Maintaining effective and positive relationships with stakeholders at all levels is essential for success in portfolio, program, and project management. These relationships can either positively or negatively affect the program or project. In a study of management of large capital projects in the United Kingdom, Baker (1962) points out, "You cannot get large projects carried out without persuading large numbers of extremely different sorts of people to understand the importance of what is being done and to work together" (p. 328). This assertion supports later research (de Abreu and Conrath 1993) showing that defining stakeholders' expectations based on their perception of the project's objectives and then determining the extent to which they are (or are not) fulfilled can predict the success of a project. McElroy and Mills (2003) also underscore the importance of "the continuing development of relationships with stakeholders for the purpose of achieving a successful project outcome" (p. 103).

First, it is incumbent on the manager and the team to identify all of the key stakeholders who will be involved and then determine how best to work with each one. This is not an easy task. While some stakeholders are obvious, such as the program sponsor or the customer, others are not. These people still may have a direct interest in or impact on the portfolio, the program, or the project. Once the stakeholders have been identified, it is necessary to build a relationship with each one to ensure his or her concerns are heard and addressed in an effective and timely way.

Connecting with stakeholders is even more difficult in complex, global programs and projects performed by virtual teams. In such situations, there are many more stakeholders, and they are more likely to represent different cultural and political views. A stakeholder management plan and a stakeholder strategy, along with strong interpersonal skills that include influencing and relationship building, can help.

You can use a number of methods to identify stakeholders, as described in PMI (2008a), Milosevic (2003), Smith (2000), Jepsen and Eskerod (2009), and elsewhere. It is not the purpose of this chapter to detail these identification approaches. Rather, this chapter discusses how a portfolio, program, or project manager can best work with various stakeholders, as well as the key interpersonal skills required for success.

Identifying Stakeholders

PMI (2008a) defines stakeholders as the people or organizations who are actively involved in a project or whose interests may be affected, either negatively or positively, by the project. It notes that stakeholders may influence the project, the deliverables, and the team, and emphasizes the importance of stakeholder identification throughout the project because different stakeholders may have interests at different times in the project. Freeman (1984) is credited with setting the stage for this definition. He states that "a stakeholder in an organization is any group or individual who can affect or is affected by the achievement of the organization's objectives" (p. 4).

PMI (2008a) notes the following categories of stakeholders:

- Customers or users

- Sponsors

- Portfolio managers and the portfolio review board

- Program managers

- Project management office

- Project managers

- Project team

- Functional managers

- Operational managers

- Sellers/business partners.

The project manager is responsible for stakeholder identification, and he or she must work with each stakeholder through a defined strategy. However, Mitchell, Bradley, and Wood (1997) point out that anyone who is affected or could be affected by the organization is a stakeholder—making the job of the portfolio, program, or project manager even more difficult. The authors emphasize how important it is to understand the stakeholder's ability to influence and recognize the legitimacy of each stakeholder's concerns. The authors also note that some stakeholders will have urgent demands for information; when this is the case, the portfolio, program or project manager must actively engage this stakeholder to ensure he or she maintains a positive attitude about the program or project. Baccarini (1999) suggests focusing attention on the important stakeholders to ensure project success. The task then is determining which stakeholders are the most important, at what times during the project their role will be most prominent, and how best to interact with each one.

It is important to recognize that on programs and projects, we are acutely aware of some key stakeholders; others may know of our plans but may not be involved, but they still could influence or impact our products, services, or results in either a positive or negative way. We may need to convince most every stakeholder that our work has benefits and value. As Armstrong and Beecham (2008) state, conflicts occur if one stakeholder perceives that his or her interests are not taken seriously, are being opposed, or are affected by another stakeholder. These stakeholders may have different goals for the program or project, different values or beliefs, ambiguous roles, and communication problems with others who are involved. If there is not agreement on goals and objectives, for example, this disagreement will lead to later risks and issues for program and project managers. Jepsen and Eskerod (2009) note that the proactive project manager views stakeholder identification and analysis as a route to ongoing learning and an opportunity to talk with stakeholders to consider their ideas early in the project, which contributes to overall project success.

Communicating with Stakeholders

In a matrix environment, the project manager must communicate with team members and their functional managers to ensure that there is a clear understanding of the role each team member will play, when the team member will be needed, and how the team member's work will be evaluated. If the functional manager is reluctant to let the team member join the project, the project manager should point out any common areas of interest and how the project can help the team member develop new skills that then will be useful to his or her functional team when he or she completes the specific assignment. Focus on building a partnership with the functional manager based on mutual trust, and involve the functional manager and his or her staff in key decisions involving the project beyond the need for resources.

As the project manager, you should recognize that the functional manager may think that you are encroaching on his or her assigned resources. If you have not built a positive relationship with the functional manager, he or she may act as an obstacle—for example, by mandating complete compliance with all technical requirements. This factor alone makes the functional manager a critical stakeholder. Establishing a long-term relationship with him or her is vital.

Karlsen (2002) notes that certain stakeholders control needed resources for the program or project and explains that each stakeholder has different ideas about what constitutes the success of a program or project because each stakeholder's interests are different. Frooman (1999) says that stakeholders may withhold resources or attach constraints to what the resources are allowed to do to exert their influence or even change the overall intent of the program, the project, or the organization.

If the project has only one customer, serve as the liaison to the customer and provide regular information. Actively listen to understand the customer's point of view, and point out any opportunities that the project team has noticed for the customer to improve its processes, even if they do not apply directly to the project. Obviously, these suggestions must be subtle. You do not want the customer to think that you are telling it how to do its work. You simply want to explain that you see an area in which the customer might be able to make a small improvement that will enable it to excel in its field. If the customer is receptive, you have set the stage for a closer relationship, one in which you as the project manager are viewed as a valued partner, rather than just the person who is responsible for the current project.

If there are multiple customers, consider making a team member responsible for interacting regularly with each one. Make sure to communicate directly with each one; do not expect them to communicate among themselves, even if they are in the same organization.

Show each stakeholder that you are interested in compromising as much as possible when decisions are required on key project issues, and regularly solicit ideas from stakeholders about ways you can foster continuous improvement on your project.

A project sponsor at the agency administrator level was working for a federal regulatory agency on an organizational restructuring project. The organizational restructuring project was for one unit in the agency, though this unit interfaced with several others. When the project manager began communicating and building a relationship with the administrator's point of contact, the head of the unit that was the focus of the project felt left out of the daily interaction and communication, even though his organization was the object of the study. He quickly became a negative stakeholder, tried many times to curtail the project, and met regularly with the administrator to insist that the project was unnecessary because he had everything under control. He also solicited others in other parts of the agency to support his point of view.

It became evident to the project manager that she needed to work closely with the organizational unit head for success and to avoid being seen as part of the "administrator's group." Knowing that the senior staff in the organizational unit worked on Saturdays, she asked if she could come in then, when they had more time to talk about the project. They were surprised that she was willing to meet with them on a non-workday. There was a more informal atmosphere at their Saturday meeting, and it set the stage for more open discussions. Because the meeting was a positive one, the unit's senior staff invited her to meet with them the following Saturday. Over time, the staff came to feel as if they were the owners of the project, and they took an active role. While building this relationship took time, it was essential to the success of the project to gain their buy-in to its objectives.

Communicate actively and often with sponsors, especially concerning resource use, requirements, and progress, so that the sponsor learns about any issues firsthand from the project manager rather than from others in the organization. Recognize, though, that the sponsor has time constraints. Make sure you are providing the information needed, not information overload. If there is a problem you think you can solve on your own, you can suggest a solution to the sponsor to gain his or her support, but do not surprise the sponsor with a request for help. Some problems cannot be anticipated and may suddenly affect the project. When such problems do occur, immediately inform the sponsor and maintain a policy of no surprises in your relationship with him or her. Keep in mind the organization's goals as well as those of your project. Ask the sponsor questions about how your project can better meet the organization's goals and what you can do to foster improvement in both financial and enterprise measures of success.

Remember that the sponsor is the champion of the project and will be involved throughout the life cycle, so you need to establish a winning relationship with him or her. The sponsor can influence decision-making, facilitate problem-solving, and assist in stakeholder identification, especially because the sponsor probably prepared the initial business case for the project. Open and consistent communications with the sponsor must be the norm.

The sponsor may provide feedback to you as the project manager, so you must be an active listener, appreciate the sponsor's advice even if he or she is critical of a decision you have made or an action you have taken, and strive to improve your skills.

When working with team members, the project manager acts as a facilitator; it is up to the team to actually complete the product, service, or result. In the facilitator role, the project manager:

- Works with team members to promote shared values so that everyone has a sense of the overall vision and direction and does so in a manner that stresses the importance of teamwork to overall success.

- Focuses on setting up an atmosphere of trust for a strong, positive, and success-focused team culture.

- Shows the team that he or she is willing to commit the time to make the team a highly productive one, with a culture that considers team members' views and promotes their inclusion in as many decisions, problem-solving sessions, and meetings with customers and sponsors as possible.

- Routinely helps team members as needed to enable them to best perform their specific responsibilities.

- Helps interested team members work toward development of a career path in project management, or promotes this career path if it already is in existence in the organization.

- Shows a genuine interest in the well-being of each team member and demonstrates consideration if anyone is undergoing a personal crisis.

- Promotes an environment in which team members are comfortable with working with one another.

In short, your team should be one on which membership is coveted by others in the organization.

In an interview with *PM Network* in 2008, General Colin L. Powell noted the importance of turning to lower-level staff for information. He said that while he was chairman of the Joint Chiefs of Staff and then later as secretary of defense, "I would force [people] to talk with me even if they were scared to death. I wouldn't just listen. I would debate with them to force them to argue their points" (p. 63). At the end of these discussions, he would thank the people involved and would seriously consider their points of view. This approach let people know that he was accessible and wanted to hear diverse points of view on key issues.

Communicating with External Stakeholders

Because outsourcing as a cost- and risk-cutting method has become more common, suppliers, subcontractors, and vendors are often key stakeholders on programs and projects. To encourage positive interactions with these people, the project manager should show that he or she understands and appreciates their unique competencies and contributions to the project and should be familiar with the supply chain management process. The project manager should bring these stakeholders into the decision-making process on key issues, especially if their contributions are essential in certain phases of the life cycle, such as in new product development.

As the project manager, you should focus on creating a partnership based on trust. It may be helpful to set up a partnering agreement that details how you and your team will work with the supplier's team. Through such a partnering relationship, you can openly discuss problems and issues and work to jointly resolve them, which will help you avoid extensive change requests and contract disputes later. The supplier is seen as a valued partner to the project team—a win-win situation.

The public is a stakeholder in many external projects. When working with the community, the project manager must provide up-to-date information on the project's status and must explain to the public why the project is important and desirable, especially in terms of environmental sustainability or economic or social development, if applicable. Sharing information, especially when public support is necessary and regulatory hurdles are involved, is one way to foster positive public opinion of the project and to improve the end result.

Communicating with Key Program Stakeholders

As in project management, in program management stakeholders are critical in the implementation of successful organizational change. At the program level, program managers can best communicate with critical stakeholders by:

- Sincerely understanding and respecting their key concerns about the program.

- Talking with them, either face-to-face if co-located or on the phone or by instant message, about the importance of the program to the organization and its customers, emphasizing the need for change and the benefits the program will provide.

- Continually interacting with stakeholders to discuss progress and to find out if their concerns have been addressed successfully; if not, determining what the program manager and the team can do to make sure their needs are met.

- Providing up-to-date information to stakeholders about the program, especially about their specific areas of interest.

- Working with team members to create an atmosphere of open communication and to encourage the delivery of consistent messages in both directions.

- Serving as the lead with customers, showing a genuine interest in immediately resolving any problems or issues that may surface, and creating solutions that both the customer and the program team see as a win-win. To maintain a successful relationship that endures over the years, program managers must actively communicate with customers, sometimes as often as daily but at least several times each month, not only to inform them of program status but also to enhance these relationships.

- Recognizing the long-term nature of most programs and working with stakeholders to help prepare for the future once the program is complete and the benefits have been transitioned by building new skills and competencies at a variety of levels.

- Talking with the customer after the program is complete to see if there are ways in which both the end products and the interpersonal processes could have been more successful, which will help foster future relationships and broaden business opportunities.

Considering the complexity and length of programs, it is likely that issues will remain, and not all of them will be solved easily. The program manager must recognize that people still may not totally accept the changes from the program and should openly and actively listen to their concerns. If there are points of disagreement, the program manager must look for some areas in which there is agreement and then move to solve remaining issues in a way that benefits both parties. The program manager then focuses on continuing to build relationships with stakeholders.

Communicating with Key Portfolio Stakeholders

At the portfolio level, PMI (2008b) again stresses the importance of stakeholder identification and reiterates that stakeholders' level of involvement may vary. PMI notes the following key stakeholders:

- Executive review board
- Portfolio review board
- Portfolio managers
- Sponsors
- Program managers
- Project managers
- Program/project management office
- Project team
- Marketing management
- Operations management
- Engineering management
- Legal management

- Human resources management
- Functional managers
- Finance managers
- Customers
- Vendors/business partners.

This list shows there are even more stakeholders for portfolio managers to consider than there are for program or project managers, and the stakeholders' involvement is at a different level. The organization's portfolio manager must use different approaches to communicate with each kind of stakeholder.

The portfolio manager is charged with linking corporate goals and objectives to specific programs and projects, sharing the success criteria proposed for each program and project, and discussing programs' and projects' progress with the executives and members of the portfolio review board or comparable group. Further, the portfolio manager must work with each stakeholder or stakeholder group regularly to build a relationship based on trust. Trust cannot be assumed and must be developed.

Executive Review Board

The portfolio manager should keep members of the executive review board apprised of any internal or external changes that will have a major effect on the organization's portfolio by providing timely information in an easy-to-read format. He or she should, if possible, make suggestions for capitalizing on external forces that may impact the organization. Embracing change and adapting quickly to the effects of the change are key.

The portfolio manager must recognize the executives' desire to improve the organization's competencies in program and project management. When working with these executives, the portfolio manager should stress how program and project management can best support organizational transformation and innovation.

Portfolio Review Board

The portfolio manager should provide members of the portfolio review board with timely information about changes involving resources that may affect the current portfolio mix, as well as updates on the progress of the current portfolio components.

Portfolio Managers

The overall portfolio manager must work with portfolio managers in different areas of the organization because these managers need information on strategic changes that may affect the priority of their programs, projects, or other work. They also must be notified when the business rules involving the portfolio process change or the priorities in the portfolio are rebalanced. The key role of the portfolio managers when working with the executives and the members of the portfolio review board is striving to achieve balance as the organization's priorities change. Portfolio managers must show a willingness to adapt to constant change and to use the changes to benefit the organization. They also must be skilled in communicating with people at all levels about why a change has occurred and the effects it will have on the programs and projects within the portfolio.

Sponsors

Each program or project will have a sponsor. For a new program or project, the portfolio manager must first meet with the sponsor to find out if the business case for the program or project is complete and then must provide timely information to the sponsor about the portfolio review board's decision to accept or reject the program or project. If the program is accepted, the portfolio manager must work with the sponsor to provide information to the portfolio review board concerning the program's status.

The best approach when working with the sponsor is to recognize that the sponsor is interested in overall success. Because many programs and projects involve organizational change, the sponsor becomes a critical stakeholder because he or she has ultimate responsibility for the program's or project's success. The sponsor must ensure that the organization is ready to accept the program's benefits and deliverables. Often this is a difficult process because people tend to resist change. Patton and Shechet (2007) say that the relationship between the portfolio manager and the sponsor should be a partnership, and they suggest that the parties prepare a sponsor agreement that shows each person's roles and responsibilities during the various phases of the life cycle.

Customers

Customers are the critical stakeholders. The portfolio manager should strive to improve communications with all customers to boost customer satisfaction. Working with the marketing staff, the portfolio manager can help cultivate customer support and future relationships.

Program and Project Managers and Team Members

The portfolio manager may elect to communicate directly with program and project managers or may leave communication up to the sponsor. Program and project managers need to be informed about the business rules to be followed as priorities are established by the portfolio review board. The portfolio manager focuses on coordinating any interfaces between programs and projects underway to overcome any barriers to following the portfolio process or to offer proactive solutions to risks and issues. He or she also must help assess how well the programs and projects are preparing the organization for future success. By working to build long-term relationships with program and project managers, the portfolio manager can maintain better communication with them, which in turn will encourage the program and project managers to offer updates when requested, even if the program or project is struggling.

Marketing Management

Because the portfolio manager is charged with assessing changes in the marketplace that may affect the organization's strategic goals and objectives and the programs, projects, and operational management work in the portfolio, he or she must forge a relationship with the marketing staff and work closely with them to identify changes and new markets to pursue. Thinking of marketing as separate from program and project management is inappropriate in this era of rapid, continual change and frequent adjustments to portfolios because of environmental changes. Marketing must be integrated with program and project activities.

Active involvement with the marketing staff is necessary in the early stages as the program or project is initiated and at the end when the deliverables are complete and the benefits have been realized and are being transitioned. Resources from the marketing staff must be involved throughout each program and project to offer strategic and innovative ideas for deliverables. Marketing people can present different insights that the teams might not otherwise consider.

Portfolio managers should talk with marketing staff about ways to broaden the business by focusing on opportunities that can lead to increased benefits. Program and project managers should leverage the expertise of marketing staff to promote more creativity and innovation in deliverables and to learn how the deliverables can further benefit current or future customers.

Finance Management

The finance department is a major stakeholder for each program or project and especially at the portfolio level, because it is a critical partner in investment decisions and overall investment strategies. When communicating and working with people in finance, the portfolio manager must demonstrate an understanding of business skills and competencies. He or she cannot make choices based only on technical considerations and must involve the finance staff as appropriate, especially when new programs and projects are proposed for consideration as components in the organization's portfolio.

The portfolio manager must work with the finance staff to help prepare the business case for a proposed portfolio component and to ensure that resources are available to support it if it is selected to be part of the portfolio. He or she must convey a desire to use programs and projects as a way to increase overall revenue.

The program or project manager must recognize that the finance department may constantly be looking for ways to reallocate funds, even those that have been officially designated for the program or project. Continual communication and involvement with the finance staff is essential to ensure that funds are not reallocated to a program or project that is, for example, new or struggling.

Legal Management

The legal staff is a critical stakeholder in decisions made by the portfolio team about program and project selection. It also is involved if the organization works with labor unions. In dealing with the legal staff, portfolio managers should bring up any issues regarding confidentiality agreements and intellectual property issues. Further, it is necessary for all managers to comply with regulations and standards, including codes, inspections, and approvals.

Building Stakeholder Relationships

Parker (1994) suggests that a worksheet is helpful in building relationships, or "bridges," as he calls them, with stakeholders. Teams can complete a bridge-building worksheet for each stakeholder. The sheet lists:

- Who the stakeholder is

- What kind of help the team needs from this stakeholder

- What guidance the stakeholder needs from the team to determine what the team can do for the stakeholder

- Common objectives and outcomes the team and the stakeholder share

- Potential barriers (such as past problems, competition, lack of respect, or lack of support) that might prevent the team and the stakeholder from working together in a positive way

- Ways to overcome these barriers

- Which team member will work with the stakeholder

- The steps the program or project manager can take to develop a positive relationship with the stakeholder.

Uniting the Team

To succeed as a portfolio, program, or project manager, the manager must have an orientation toward people, not just toward tools and techniques. (Applying tools and techniques is the responsibility of team members.) The manager is the one who pulls everyone together to work effectively and who takes the high road even, for example, when a stakeholder makes negative comments about the project or program.

To unite team members with diverse views, the portfolio, program, or project manager must:

- Be able to sense stakeholders' attitudes toward the portfolio process, especially negative attitudes, and to identify their needs. Negative attitudes are sometimes characterized by stakeholders who do not buy into the portfolio process or have negative opinions about the program or project.

- Keep stakeholders' needs in mind while making realistic determinations about what actually can be achieved

- Look at issues from the other person's point of view

- Have a positive attitude and respect for and genuine sensitivity toward the views of others, even if they are different from his or her own point of view

- Actively listen when meeting with stakeholders at all levels

- Speak clearly and concisely in terms each stakeholder can understand, rather than relying on project management jargon, which may be too confusing or limiting to stakeholders who are not team members

- Be willing to provide extra help and assistance when required

- Not expect any special recognition or rewards for offering help

- Respect people at all levels, not just those who are in upper management positions

- Recognize that everyone's contributions are important

- Be able to balance the demands of stakeholders, recognizing that over time, their interests may change, which means their expectations regarding the portfolio, program, or project may change

- Continually communicate the vision and mission of the program or project or, if he or she is a portfolio manager, communicate the strategic objectives of the organization and the organization's culture

- View change positively, but recognize people's resistance to change and work with them to overcome this resistance and support the program or project by explaining the benefits of the change and why it is important

- Understand that relationship building takes time, and the more stakeholders involved, the longer it takes.

Explaining Decisions

Even if the manager is sensitive to the needs of everyone involved, he or she will make decisions that some will not totally support. No one really likes change, and often it is difficult to accept, but it is constant in today's environment, especially on programs and projects. The manager must meet individually, if in a co-located environment, with anyone who does not support a decision to explain why the manager has chosen that course of action. (In a virtual environment, the manager should have a one-on-one conversation with the person on the phone or electronically.) Such an approach may not always work, but it does show that the manager has a genuine concern for the other person's point of view, that he or she has taken this point of view into consideration, and that the manager has thought about the decision and made it in an objective, systematic way.

Once the decision has been made, the manager then must introduce it to the stakeholders. If the decision leads to change, the program or project manager must show that he or she embraces the change and must explain how the change will benefit the program or project. The manager should then convey information concerning the decision to the stakeholders through consistent messages. Everyone must hear about the decision in the same way. On a virtual team, the decision can be posted on the home page of a portal, and an email can be sent to everyone on the team to tell them to check the portal. On a co-located team, the manager can call a meeting to explain the decision and also issue written information about it to everyone involved in case a key stakeholder cannot attend.

Summary

Building relationships with stakeholders at all levels is an ongoing key process for portfolio, program, and project managers. Consider using a variety of approaches in working with stakeholders at all levels and preparing a stakeholder management plan and stakeholder management strategy to help ensure successful relationships. It also is important to recognize that various stakeholders will have different requirements at different points of the program or project life cycle. Sometimes people who were not identified as stakeholders initially may turn out to have an interest in the program or project, and new stakeholders may join the organization and require information about the portfolio management process or a specific program or project of interest to them.

Discussion Questions

Imagine that you managed an internal improvement project. Your company is on the customer's qualified supplier list, but it had never worked directly for this customer's representative before. The customer asked you to hire a subcontractor who has special expertise in the kind of work being performed in the internal improvement project. It soon became apparent that the customer really wanted to work directly with this subcontractor, but it was not on the qualified vendor list. At the kickoff meeting, you could tell that the customer's representative and the subcontractor's representative not only respected one another but also were personal friends. Soon after, you learned that the customer was talking directly to the subcontractor without telling you or your team about it. You and your team became less and less involved with the project; in fact, it seemed as if you were just a pass-through to the subcontractor. However, your company was still responsible for the project.

The customer's representative immediately accepted the first deliverable and made few changes. The second deliverable also was well received.

You realized that there was another area in which your firm had specialized expertise that it could contribute, and you asked to meet with the customer. The customer informed you that your firm would not get any additional work from the organization. You were surprised; the first two deliverables were accepted with almost no changes. You then learned that the subcontractor was now on the qualified supplier list. Next, you found out that your contract was being terminated for convenience.

1. What should you have done to prevent this situation from occurring in the first place?
2. What specific interpersonal skills should you have used so that the customer worked through you, not directly with the subcontractor?
3. How could you have better worked with the subcontractor so that its representatives included you and your team in its work with the customer?
4. How should you have created an atmosphere that was conducive to project success from all three perspectives—the customer's, your organization's, and the subcontractor's?

Decision-Making

6

The project manager is responsible for resource allocation and use, as well as cost and schedule tradeoffs and changes in terms of the project's scope, direction, or characteristics (Adams, Barndt, and Martin 1979). These responsibilities obviously require strong decision-making skills. Though decision-making is not the domain of the project manager alone, it is certainly an important role because each decision has consequences that affect the overall direction of the project. Project managers must work constantly to build consensus or confidence in decisions about critical aspects of the project (PMI 1987).

PMI (2008a) describes four common decision-making styles: command, consultation, consensus, and coin flip (random). Each style is appropriate in certain situations. According to PMI, decision by consensus is optimal; the effective project manager is one who can lead others through the decision-making process. The project manager should work to balance the triple constraints of the project and trust his or her team to ensure the quality of the project's deliverables in conjunction with the customer's acceptance criteria.

PMI suggests a decision-making model consisting of the following stages:

- *Problem definition.* Make sure you understand the problem before making a decision.

- *Problem solution generation.* Brainstorm various solutions.

- *Ideas to action.* Determine criteria to use in making the decision, assess advantages and disadvantages of each possible solution, and then select the best solution and make the decision.

- *Solution action planning.* Involve those who will be affected by the decision to gain their commitment and buy-in to it.

- *Solution evaluation.* Analyze what happened after the decision was made. What lessons were learned? Was the decision appropriate?

- *Evaluation of the outcome and the process.* Assess how well the problem was solved and how it affected the project's goals and objectives. Were the team's goals and objectives advanced by the decision?

The program manager has a broader focus: the program's objectives and the organization's culture and processes. He or she must make decisions about, and affecting, resource use across the program (PMI 2008c). The program manager has to take into account how decisions will affect other program components.

At the portfolio level, there are even more decisions to be made as the portfolio components are selected and prioritized (PMI 2008b). The portfolio manager, working with stakeholders, typically establishes the portfolio decision-making process and guides the selection, prioritization, and balancing process. He or she also supports senior-level decision-making and ensures timely and consistent communication on the progress of components in the portfolio, their progress, and any changes to them.

PMI (2006) describes two types of decisions. Decisions made in an emergency situation, when something must be done immediately—for example, in a fire—are *naturalistic* or *qualitative*. Decisions that are based on quantitative data—those that depend on information—are called *rationalistic*. PMI says that a blend of both types is ideal in the project environment.

Decisions are critical at each stage of the program and project life cycle and throughout the portfolio management process. This chapter examines the types of decisions program and project managers must make and approaches that will help them make ones that are effective and beneficial. It also describes the role of the portfolio manager in his or her work with senior executives in the decision-making process. It concludes with a decision-making checklist that the portfolio, program, or project manager can use.

The Importance of Team Cohesiveness in Decision-Making

It is wonderful to be on a team in which everyone enjoys working together and is pleased to begin each workday. One project manager was part of such a team early in his career and thought that this was the norm. (Unfortunately, this team was the only one he was on in which it was a pleasure to work.) Everyone on the team felt that working together was rewarding. Its projects required collaboration at various levels, and everyone performed their assigned roles and stepped in as required to help others with their tasks. To this day, almost 40 years later, members of that team have maintained their close camaraderie, respect for one another, and personal ties. The manager is still grateful for this experience.

However, few teams are like the one described above. Most lack sufficient time to develop close relationships and trust; bickering among team members, boredom, and a lack of commitment or pride are all too common. People often miss team meetings, or if they attend, they read and write emails during the meeting rather than focusing on the problem at hand. On virtual teams, they "participate" in conference calls by pressing the mute button and doing other things.

On these teams, the cohesiveness needed for effective decision-making and program and project accomplishment is lacking. Even if teams like these complete their deliverables on time, their members are pleased when the program or project is over and they can return to their functional team or start another program or project. They have no desire to work together again on another program or project.

Cohesiveness, as defined by Fisher (1974), is "the ability of group members to get along, the feeling of loyalty, pride, and commitment of members toward the group" (p. 31). He further notes that cohesiveness may be viewed as an output of the social dimension of a team or a group; it is therefore not so much a process but a state of being. While all teams have some degree of cohesiveness, it varies widely.

Fisher emphasizes the importance of tension in teams to help hold them together. The presence of tension implies that there is work to be done. Tension will vary over the life cycle of a program or project, but it is typically high when the program and project begins, starts to drop off once the program or project is underway, then rises as the program or project reaches the closing stage.

It is a difficult but important challenge for program and project managers to get their teams focused around cohesiveness and productivity and an even greater challenge when working in a virtual environment. This focus is especially essential when key decisions that affect the planned benefits and deliverables of the program or project must be made. More ideas can be generated by a team than by a single individual working alone, and the cohesive team can critically evaluate the ideas generated as the decision is made. It is also more likely to buy into the decision and wish to implement it.

The Decision-Making Process

Decision-making is more complex on larger programs or projects because more stakeholders, at a variety of levels, are involved. These stakeholders may be internal or external to the organization and may include the general public and the media. When many stakeholders are involved, the decision-making process tends to take longer. On virtual teams, cultural considerations may add another dimension to the decision-making process, and while diversity can help teams make better decisions, it also sometimes prolongs the process. Procrastination can slow down decision-making as well. Program and project managers often gravitate to solving routine problems rather than proactively tackling complex decisions.

Fisher (1970) describes four key phases in the process of team decision-making, here tailored slightly to the program and project management environment:

- *Orientation phase.* In this phase, team members are beginning to understand the overall purpose of the program or project and why it is being done. They are getting acquainted and often express opinions tentatively. A solution may be obvious to a particular team member, but he or she may elect to remain silent for a while to see if others come to the same decision. Program and project managers must create an environment in which people feel free to openly communicate and make suggestions.

   Team members are unsure about their position on the team and their key roles and responsibilities, and they tend to agree more often in this early stage. For example, if the client suggests a new requirement, even though it may affect the project's deliverables, team members are more likely to accept it and move on to actually completing the work, rather than analyzing it in detail and determining whether a change order is required.

- *Conflict phase.* At this point, the team members are involved in the program or project and are familiar with one another's roles and responsibilities. A work breakdown structure (WBS) has been prepared; teams usually have a resource breakdown structure (RBS) and a resource assignment matrix (RAM) or responsible, accountable, consult, and inform (RACI) chart as well. If subject matter experts will be called upon during specific phases, people recognize why they will be required and are willing to accept them as temporary team members. When a decision must be made, people feel able to express their points of view, positive or negative, even if they conflict with others on the team. People back up their views with specific data to support them, and they do not express opinions in a tentative or ambiguous manner.

- *Emergence phase.* During this phase, team members express fewer negative opinions. The program or project direction is better defined, and debates are less frequent; people understand the vision and mission of the program or project. People are more willing to confront and resolve problems when they occur, rather than waiting until later. They are familiar with their teammates' points of view and know where they stand on key issues. Teams more easily reach compromises. If teams cannot reach agreement, they are likely to follow the procedures set forth in the team charter and escalate the decision to the program manager or project manager, or even higher, until a decision can be made. As Fisher writes (1974), in this phase "the eventual outcome of group interaction becomes increasingly more apparent" (p. 143).

- *Reinforcement phase.* This final phase is the one in which the team achieves consensus. People continue to provide data to support their views on key issues. Team members make fewer arguments against the proposed decisions because there is greater unity within the team. Team members may re-propose suggestions that they withdrew earlier because the team is now ready to work toward consensus.

The Decision-Making Process on Virtual Teams

Is the decision-making process different on virtual teams? Hedlund, Ilgen, and Hollenbeck (1998) found that on virtual teams, members have varying levels of expertise, so the project manager must coordinate the team members' suggested solutions into the final decision. Consensus may not even be desirable in the virtual team. These authors suggest that in the initial phases of the project, the project manager must initiate a flow of information that is helpful for individual decision-making, but when decisions depend on the contributions of other team members, social pressure to conform to team norms and to respect the expertise of other team members, especially in highly specialized projects, often prevents virtual teams from being efficient. These teams must rely on electronic communications rather than face-to-face inter-action, often making the entire process more challenging. The program or project manager must pay more attention and be more involved if the decision-making process is to be effective.

Bourgault, Drouin, and Hamel (2008) studied the decision-making pro-cess within a virtual team, exploring the relationship between team autonomy and formalization of the process and the quality of the decisions and overall effectiveness of the team's work. Their work showed that it is essential for virtual teams to have a quality process to guide decision-making that helps avert or proactively address obstacles. They noted that while it is difficult to implement such a process, it is the project manager's responsibility to do so. Another important factor contributing to successful decision-making was an emphasis on team members' autonomy and on building an empowered team that can make its own decisions and escalate them to the project manager when required.

Creating and Implementing a Decision-Making Process

Of course, a quality decision-making process can benefit a co-located team as well. How can program or project managers best put such a process in place? Here are some guidelines:

- Review the types of decision-making processes other teams have used suc-cessfully in the organization, either through a knowledge management repository, if one exists, or through interviews with program and project managers whose work was considered successful.

- Draft a decision-making process, then ask the team to comment on it before it is implemented to gain their buy-in and support for it. In a co-located or a virtual team, set up a way for people to comment anonymously, quickly, and easily.

- Make sure people understand their specific roles and responsibilities and the degree of autonomy they have to make decisions on their own; describe the escalation process people should follow if a decision cannot be made without the involvement of others.

- Depending on the length of the program or project, survey team members and other key stakeholders about the effectiveness of the decision-making process. Ask people for specific feedback, using open-ended questions as much as possible. Make clear that you are willing to change the process as necessary.

The Power Bases

When making decisions, sources of power are a key consideration. Etzioni (1961) was one of the first of many authors to discuss this dimension. He described the differences between position power and personal power and how each type of power influences decisions. In a program or project context, *position power* refers to a person's ability to influence another to do a certain work package or activity because of his or her position in the organization. For example, assume the sponsor of a project is the chief information officer (CIO) in the company. One project team member is reluctant to be on the team because she is close to making a breakthrough innovation in her functional department. She constantly complains to the project manager about her role on the team and asks to be reassigned back to her functional unit. The project manager knows he needs her expertise on a critical part of the project and also wants her to be involved in other areas of the project, so he asks the CIO to meet with her. She has never met the CIO before and is amazed that the CIO would spend valuable time with her. He acknowledges her work in her functional unit but asks her to put this work aside until the project is successfully completed because the project is so important to the company. The CIO's ability to influence this team member to be an enthusiastic and active contributor stems from his position in the organization.

By contrast, a person with *personal power* uses it to encourage others to support him or her on a program or project. Personal power typically is earned, and people who are noted for it are respected in the organization. For example, assume a project team member was working on testing software modules as they were completed. He believed his expertise would be better used in development than in testing, and he was new to work in the testing world. He asked the project manager if he could be reassigned to development. The project manager explained that he had sufficient resources in development and really wanted the team member to work in testing. Still, the team member was dissatisfied, and the project manager recognized that his poor morale might be affecting others working in testing. He asked the CIO to meet with this team member. Though the team member had never met the CIO before, he respected him because of his credentials and the various responsibilities he had in the company before becoming the CIO. He had read various articles the CIO had written for technical journals and believed the CIO understood not only the technical aspects of the work to be done but also the overall importance of the work to the organization.

When the team member met with the CIO, the CIO used personal power to gain this disgruntled team member's commitment to the project. The CIO told him that working in testing would enable him to broaden his skills, contributing to his own individual development and overall worth to the organization. The team member returned to the testing unit with some enthusiasm for the work to be done. He complained less and instead offered constructive criticism and feedback.

Etzioni's concepts of personal and positional power influenced French and Bell's concept of sources of power (1973). They describe five sources of power managers may claim: reward power, coercive power, legitimate power, referent power, and expert power.

Reward Power

A manager with reward power is able to give team members rewards, such as money, recognition within the organization, and security. It is usually easier for program managers to apply this type of power than it is for project managers because programs tend to last longer, and core team members may stay with the program for some time. Any projects operate in a weak matrix, not a strong matrix or projectized structure, and project managers are rarely even able to participate in team members' performance reviews.

However, everyone appreciates recognition, especially if it is sincerely and appropriately given. PMI (2008a) asserts that a team-based reward and recognition system is appropriate. People are motivated if they feel the organization values their work; rewards can demonstrate that people are valued (p. 234). The program or project manager should do his or her best to find rewards that he or she can give for outstanding individual or team accomplishments. For example, the manager might place a notice in an organizational newsletter or post on a portal that a team member did exemplary work, offer an extra day off for a long weekend if team members worked overtime to complete a critical milestone, or allow a team member to attend a seminar for personal development.

Managers must realize that this source of power is to be respected; "only desirable behavior should be rewarded" (PMI 2008a). For maximum effectiveness, program and project managers should give rewards throughout the life cycle, rather than just at the end of the program or project. When other team members see that people are being rewarded for good work, they may contribute more than they otherwise would.

Coercive Power

A leader who wields this type of power makes clear that if team members do not comply with the organization's or its leaders' mandates, there will be major negative repercussions. For example, one project manager who used coercive power mandated that everyone arrive at work no later than 7:45. If someone arrived late, this manager made the person take an hour of personal leave. Exceptions were not allowed even if there was bad weather. This manager abused coercive power, and it led to an atmosphere of fear that overshadowed the project. In an economic climate noted by downsizing, outsourcing, or offshoring, the power of such coercive tactics cannot be understated. People often accept assignments they do not really want so that they can keep their jobs. They also believe that they must follow the organization's program and project management procedures explicitly and should not make suggestions for improvement to avoid rocking the boat; they want to be considered "ideal" team members. This approach ensures compliance but stifles new ideas that actually could benefit not only the program or project but also the entire organization.

Legitimate Power

A leader who claims this type of power asserts that he or she has a legitimate right to influence others and expects everyone to follow his or her approach to the program or project. Team members may show respect for the leader, but teams led by a manager who emphasizes his or her legitimate power often fail to show continuous improvement and do not develop breakthrough approaches that could provide the organization, program, and projects with additional benefits. Under such circumstances, team members often believe that they cannot live up to their manager's standards and that they lack the needed skills and competencies to contribute.

The manager for a project to develop a plan for the transportation infrastructure of the nation for the next 20 years was new to the organization and was noted for her willingness to explore new ideas. The sponsor for this project was pleased by his stature in the organization and how quickly he had attained it, and he relied on his legitimate power. He believed new ideas were not appropriate and insisted that the organization's standard project management methodology be followed explicitly. The team members and project manager believed that the traditional methodology would be detrimental and limiting to the project if it were followed without tailoring because this project was different from the organization's typical types of projects. But the project sponsor discouraged any innovative approaches when they were presented to him. The project team's morale steadily decreased, and many members found other jobs; some even left the agency.

Referent Power

Referent power is based on people's identification with a leader and what the leader symbolizes. People admire the leader, value his or her charisma, want to follow him or her, and seek his or her approval and appreciation. The leader may not consciously promote this power.

Assume you have been assigned to work on a project. The project manager is a well-recognized thought leader in the field and speaks regularly at the local PMI chapter and occasionally at PMI congresses. She has PgMP (Program Management Professional) and PMP credentials, she holds a master's degree in project management, and she is now in a doctoral program. You feel honored to be on her team.

The project is a complex one involving the development of a new food additive. More than 150 people are working on the project; they are divided into core teams based on specific work packages. You wish you were a core team leader, and you think that you might be chosen if you grab the project manager's attention, but you rarely see her except in large group meetings.

When your core team leader says he believes an approach other than the one the project manager proposed will enable your sub-team to complete its work package more effectively and quickly, you are concerned because your sub-team is not following the project manager's original suggestions. You want the project manager to admire the work you are doing and worry this will be impossible to achieve if you do not do the work the way she suggested. You decide, then, to ask for an individual meeting with her. Of course, she contacts the core team leader before the meeting to find out why you wish to meet with her. When you meet with her, you learn that the core team leader has already briefed the project manager on the new approach. Your desire for the project manager's admiration has led you to go over the core team leader's head and assume she was not informed of the change in direction. Your core team leader then meets with you and indicates that you need to follow the chain of command in the future and first meet with him or at least ask him to accompany you to meetings with the project manager.

Expert Power

A leader with expert power uses his or her experience or knowledge to influence others. For example, assume you are on a team with the project manager described above, who is noted for her expertise in the field. Your teammates respect this project manager because they believe her leadership will guide them in their work. Her approach is more persuasive; she does not use the command and control approach used by leaders who favor coercive power. She requires status updates and meetings with team members in order to better influence the team and guide it toward success. This leader realizes she cannot stand totally on her credentials and must continually show she is focusing on her own continuous development in the project management field and expects team members to do the same.

Table 6-1 presents some approaches you might consider if you are a team member working for a program or project manager who has a dominant source of power.

While Table 6-1 focuses on ways a team member might best interact with a program or project manager who claims or is endowed by others with a certain source of power, Table 6-2 offers suggestions that you as a manager can use if you notice that you tend to exhibit a dominant source of power over others. The table explains how the manager can use each of the five sources of power to gain team members' support and avoid making the team atmosphere one that is considered hostile or undesirable.

Table 6-1   Working with Managers Who Hold One of the Five Power Sources

Source of Power	Suggestions for Effective Work with the Manager Who Holds This Power
Reward power	While the team charter is being developed, discuss the inclusion of a section on rewards and recognition and decide when individual, as opposed to team, rewards and recognition are appropriate.
	If you are evaluated by your functional manager but have been working for the program or project manager for the majority of the evaluation period, ask your functional manager if the program or project manager can participate in the performance evaluation.
	If you know you will be continuing with the program or project into the next evaluation period, include specific performance objectives in your performance plan relative to the program or project.
	Encourage the program or project manager to conduct team-based assessments on a periodic basis and to provide feedback on how the team can better perform for overall program or project success, which in turn could lead to greater rewards and recognition.
Coercive power	While job security is important, realize that at times, you may need to challenge the program or project manager and his or her approach.
	However, do so in a careful and respectful manner. Ask the program or project manager if it is a good time to talk to make sure you are not interrupting him or her at an inappropriate time or when he or she is under stress.
	When meeting with the program or project manager, present your ideas in a way that does not appear to be in complete opposition to the manager but instead complements the manager's approach.
Legitimate power	Recognize that the manager has worked diligently to attain his or her position in the organization, so treat him or her with respect.
	If you have a suggestion that you believe is beneficial, first share it with others on the team before approaching the manager directly.

If others on the team believe your idea has merit, work with them to develop a way to present it to the manager. You should introduce the idea in a nonthreatening way, showing that it is not totally different from the manager's approach and is designed to enhance it, not replace it.

Make sure that when you present the idea, the manager is not in the midst of a crisis and has the time to listen. Thank the manager for taking time to listen to your ideas.

Referent power   Show respect for this program or project manager's accomplishments, but do not constantly seek his or her attention.

Ask the manager for advice, or ask him or her to suggest a mentor who can help you enhance your own knowledge, skills, and competencies.

Seek out opportunities to show your own value to the organization and to the project management profession by writing articles on your own time and submitting them for publication by journals, volunteering at the local PMI chapter, or attending prerecorded webinars that do not take time away from the project but do help you develop as a project professional.

Point out your accomplishments in a subtle way, especially when it is time for your own performance review. You should avoid seeming egotistical when you do so, but you do not want your work to go unnoticed. When you speak with the manager, convey in an understated way your desire to follow a similar career path.

Expert power   Recognize this person's accomplishments and demonstrate from the beginning that you are pleased to be a member of his or her team.

Be willing to present your own ideas if you feel they can lead to a breakthrough.

Approach the manager cautiously and confidently when he or she has time available.

Without undermining the manager's expertise, show that your idea can benefit the program or project and the organization, and ask the manager to review it at his or her convenience. Later, meet with the leader again to obtain feedback. Do not take criticism personally; the criticism may help you enhance your suggestion and enable you present it again to the manager.

Table 6-2: Effective Ways to Use the Five Sources of Power

Program or Project Manager's Type of Power	Effective Use on the Program or Project
Reward power	Point out during the kickoff meeting that because the program or project's resources are matrixed, as the manager you are not able to give the typical rewards a functional manager can. Strive to work with the governance board, the sponsor, or other critical stakeholders to see what types of rewards you can give to the team. Motivate team members and show them that their work on the program or project is valuable by discussing with them the rewards you are able to give. Find out if it is possible to contribute, even verbally, to performance appraisals conducted by the team members' functional managers. Continually reinforce the importance of the program or project to the organization's strategic goals.
Coercive power	Realize this type of power can alienate certain team members, but if it is used judiciously, it can also help the team complete the program or project quickly and do quality work, leaving behind a positive legacy. Explain the importance of the program or project to the team at each meeting and why an accelerated schedule or adherence to a specific methodology is required—for example, you need to ensure that your product is first to market, or resources are constrained, so people can work on the program or project only for a limited time. Note that while you expect team members to follow your guidance, you will listen to new approaches. Tell them the best way to communicate with you—for example, in writing, in a one-on-one meeting, or by email. Also specify whether you would like team members to work alone or collaborate to develop new ideas.
Legitimate Power	Recognize that you have this type of power as a result of your position in the organization, but your team also knows about your areas of expertise and the contributions you make to the organization.

Explain to the team that you value your role in the organization, but you are also pleased they are on your team, and you are dedicated to their success as a team. Tell the team you realize you cannot succeed unless the team succeeds, so you want to establish an atmosphere focused on success from the very beginning.

To foster high morale, structure project milestones so the team can easily accomplish one early in the project and so you demonstrate an understanding of what each team member must do for the group as a whole to succeed.

Referent power   Do not overemphasize your credentials to your team; they are already aware of them and admire you for your success. Encourage team members, as appropriate, to seek you out if they are uncertain about whether project management is the right career path for them or for suggestions about how they can advance in the project management career path in the organization.

At team meetings, or through discussion forums or blogs, point out any new ideas in the field that you think may be of value to the team. Encourage the team to use discussion forums to exchange ideas and talk about how they might be applied on the program or project.

Expert power   Recognize that team members are aware of your expertise. Use your expertise, especially if you believe the program or project is in trouble for whatever reason—for example, stakeholders seem to be raising objections, milestones are being missed, or key performance indicators show the project is not proceeding on schedule.

When meeting with the team, suggest ways problems can be overcome and what each person can do to help.

Encourage team members, as appropriate, to advance in their own careers, either on the technical side or on the managerial side, and offer suggestions.

Making a Decision

First, it is necessary to determine who is responsible for the decision. Is it one that:

- A team member is empowered to make on his or her own without consulting the project manager or others on the team?

- The team can make on its own without consulting the project manager?

- The program project manager can make on his or her own?

- Must be escalated to the sponsor, the governance board, a steering committee, or another group?

It may be helpful during the preparation of the change management plan to classify the types of changes that may occur and link them to the specific roles and responsibilities, perhaps using a RACI chart to show who is responsible for making decisions, who needs to be consulted, who needs to be informed, and who is accountable for its implementation.

Sometimes the decision-making process can be inclusive, while at other times, decisiveness is required. Wellman (2007) presents an analysis of a case study of an organization within a Fortune 100 company that has used matrix management since the 1950s. There were three key conditions in the organization that influenced decision-making: an open environment in which it was acceptable to disagree with senior executives; a need for program team members, program managers, and executives to make decisions quickly; and an emphasis on rational decision-making based on clear thinking, rather than an expectation of always getting good answers. One participant noted, "Even if the decision wasn't total agreement with my way of thinking, I had good rationale … it wasn't a matter about saving face and egos … it was about let's talk about it in the open, make a decision and make some consensus if at all possible" (p. 68).

In this organization, sometimes there was enough time to wait for additional information before making a decision, and delaying the decision was beneficial. Other times the decision had to be made immediately or with little time for additional interaction with others involved. Portfolio, program, and project managers must determine how much time is available and whether sufficient information must be gathered before a decision can be made.

Consider the following questions if you are working in an environment in which time is of the essence:

- If I could ask the opinion of only one or two team members, who would I select, and are they available?

- If I could obtain one other piece of information before making this decision, what would I want to see, and how long would it take to generate it?

- If the organization has up-to-date information on the knowledge, skills, and competencies of its resources, can I easily and quickly locate someone with the expertise to assist me, even if he or she is not on my team?

- Once I make the decision, if others feel I have made the wrong choice, is it possible later to reverse it or change it in any way? What will the ramifications be?

Escalating the Decision

Ideally, one should not make a decision unless he or she is completely confident that all the information needed to make the decision is available and that the decision will not affect other aspects of the program or project or other work underway in the organization. At times, however, all the necessary information may not be available and it may not be possible to get that information before a decision is required. If you have doubts about your authority to make the change, the best approach to follow is to escalate it. Escalation can help promote executives' buy-in to the ultimate decision and may make it easier to implement. The escalation process can be described in the team's charter and in the charters for the program and project managers. However, if you believe you are empowered to make the decision, do so if you have the needed information and expertise, keeping in mind any time constraints.

Communicating and Documenting the Decision

Once the decision is made, follow the program or project's information distribution process to share it with stakeholders. PMI (2008b) suggests using a decision log (sometimes called a memorandum for record) to document decisions. Levin and Green's (2009) decision-log template offers one approach to describing the decision and relevant background information and noting the decisionmakers, the implementation date, the person responsible for implementation, and the actual implementation date. The template also links the decision to the program work breakdown structure. The decision log should be part of the program's knowledge repository system and placed on the portal or shared drive for reference during program work. It also can be used for future programs and projects as a source of lessons learned.

Making Decisions and Accepting Change

Once a decision is made, it will lead to a change in the portfolio, program, or project. At the portfolio level, for example, different business units or departments may propose activities to pursue that will advance the strategy, and resources may have to be allocated or reallocated accordingly. Ideally, the stakeholders will buy into the changes and accept them, but this is unusual. Even if certain stakeholders had active involvement in the decision-making process, they may still have to work to accept it. Lewin (1947) described a three-phase change acceptance process:

1. *Unfreezing:* In this phase, the goal is to prepare stakeholders for the change. The objective is for each person to see the need for the change, even if they do not support it.
2. *Changing:* During this phase, the stakeholder is motivated to change; identifies a way of changing; tries to make the change meaningful for the stakeholder; or internalizes the change into his or her approach to the work.
3. *Refreezing:* At this time, the change has been accepted, new ways of working are in place, and stakeholders are following them. The change is reinforced and ingrained.

Applying this approach to portfolio, program, and project management, PMI (2008a, 2008b, and 2008c), notes distinctions in how each type of manager approaches change. The project manager tries to keep changes to a minimum and to control and monitor them, while recognizing that change is inevitable (2008a). The program manager embraces change and expects it to occur both internally and externally to the program, so he or she must have skills in managing change across the program (PMI 2008c). And the portfolio manager monitors changes in the organization's environment that might affect the portfolio at a strategic level and shares these changes with members of the portfolio review board or a comparable group (PMI 2008b).

For example, assume you are managing a large program that is scheduled to last six years. There are nine different projects in the program management plan; three are already underway. It also has nonproject work. A large virtual team is working on this program; its members are located in various areas on three different continents. When changes occur and decisions are made, you want to be able to easily implement them without disruption to the team. Levin and Green (2009) suggest:

• Preparing a change management plan early in the program, as part of the planning process, that describes the processes and procedures that the team will use to manage program changes

• Recognizing that certain types of changes are mandatory, while others are optional but may benefit the program

• Realizing that some changes are more risky

• Describing the process to follow to submit a change request and listing the people who will need to sign off on it

• Determining how the change is to be communicated and how its status is to be tracked.

Decision-Making Checklist

The following decision-making checklist is for use by portfolio, program, and project mangers.

• Who makes the decision?
    • Sponsor, portfolio manager, program manager, project manager, team member

• What alternatives are considered before the decision is made?
    • How is information obtained before making the decision?
    • Who provides the information?
    • Is the source considered credible, or are experts required to evaluate the information?
    • Is the person with the greatest access to the information able to make the decision? This gives a sense of ownership to the decision.
    • How are priorities determined?
        • Are different categories of decisions made at different levels?
        • When is escalation required?
        • Is a team charter or program or project manager charter followed?

- Have all available resources been considered and used?

  - Were subject matter experts consulted, or does the program or project manager lack the time to consult others?

  - Were the necessary internal and external stakeholders consulted?

- Are any additional problem-solving skills needed before the decision is made?

  - Should the decisionmaker use focus groups (to obtain information on attitudes), brainstorming (to obtain a variety of ideas in a random way), the Delphi technique (to obtain consensus using a facilitated approach anonymously), the nominal group technique (to obtain ideas by asking only one person at a time to share his or her ideas), or interviews?

  - Should decision matrices and decision trees be used?

- Are people satisfied with the process that is being followed?

  - How often is the process evaluated?

  - Does the team charter help the team determine if a decision requires escalation?

- Is a log of all decisions made on the program or project maintained for future lessons learned and for the archives?

- Are the decisions effective?

  - What criteria are used to make the decision?

  - Are prevailing organizational values or standard approaches to making decisions followed?

  - Are people committed to implementing the decision?

Discussion Questions

Fisher (1974) lists a number of inaccurate myths about group decision-making:

- Members of a group discussion do not focus on argumentative positions but maintain an open mind and a spirit of free inquiry.

- If there is too much interpersonal criticism, communications break down.

- Effective groups strive to achieve nearly equal participation among their members.

- Each member must perform certain duties.

- Making decisions is more important than getting along with one another.

- A group must follow an orderly agenda that directs it to its goal for effective decision-making.

- Some people are natural leaders.

- The group members' personalities exert the most significant influence on group decision-making.

- In the long run, the group will achieve more effective results through using democratic processes than if it achieved results in other ways.

- Almost any job can be done by a group rather than an individual.

Consider the above list. Are any of these myths true for your program or project? If so, how can you prevent their occurrence? For example, what would you do if your team felt everyone had to be involved in each of the work packages; if a team member believed he was such a natural leader he tried to usurp your authority; if your team consisted of all extraverts except for one introvert, and the introvert rarely contributed in team meetings?

If your team has not experienced any of the problems listed by Fisher, why do you think this is the case?

Managing Stress

7

The work of portfolio, program, and project managers involves a large number of stakeholders across a variety of organizational boundaries. The tasks performed by these managers are complex and involve interactions with many people who have different points of view. In addition, portfolio, program, and project managers are often expected to produce results within limited periods of time and with less than optimal resources. And because global, virtual teams, on which around-the-clock work is possible if it is planned and managed effectively, have become more common, there is an even greater emphasis on quickly completing programs and projects.

Both managers and team members experience stress to varying degrees when working on a program or project. Turner, Huemann, and Keegan (2008) write that additional pressures are created each time a new program or project starts or an old one finishes, as the configuration of human resources in the organization changes. People in project-based organizations feel stress for several reasons:

- The peak in workloads at unpredictable times makes it difficult for people on programs and projects to achieve a workload balance.

- Uncertainty about future assignments: Will there be a future assignment, and if so, where will it be located, and what will the role and responsibilities entail?

- Will the new assignment be in line with my career objectives?

The authors conclude that it is a challenge for people on programs and projects to manage these pressures; both the individuals themselves and organizational leaders need to take positive action.

What causes stress for you in your role as a portfolio, program, or project manager?

What do you notice when you answer this question? Maybe an event begins to surface from your memory, something that was upsetting for you. Possibly a feeling begins to emerge, such as anger or anxiety. As you formulate your answer to this question, consider these "truths" about stress:

- What is stressful for you is not necessarily stressful for someone else.

- Stress is neither good nor bad; all events that are perceived as stressful can have positive components.

The best approach to handling stress is to develop a strong sense of your personal style, your own sources of stress, and the most adaptive methods you use to reduce stress. As Aitken and Crawford write, "Understanding how project managers cope with stressful situations is the first step to being able to manage their outcomes, both positive and negative" (2007, p. 667).

Inherent Sources of Stress in Project Management

A number of challenges inherent in project management create a stressful work environment for the project manager. These include the intrinsic stress of being a project leader, the matrix management style of leading, the challenge of solving singular problems, project ramp-up and ramp-down (Table 7-1), and virtual teamwork.

Being a Project Leader

A project manager faces two types of inherent stressors in the role of leader:

- The pressure to create a culture or "container" in which the team functions

- The tendency for team members to project numerous feelings, motives, and attributes onto the team leader.

The notion of a leader creating a positive culture for the team suggests that the leader must expend personal energy and resources to create an atmosphere in which the team will operate successfully. This kind of team atmosphere does not simply happen; the project leader must strive on a personal level to

Table 7-1   Inherent Stress in Project Management

Source of Stress	Type of Stress Placed on Project Manager	Optimal Stress-Management Approach for Project Manager
Intrinsic stress of being a project leader	Creating a positive atmosphere for teamwork	Enlist team members to develop a team culture.
Matrix management systems	Pressure to build a team quickly and efficiently	Develop the skills of influencing others, clear communication, and conflict resolution.
Singular problem-solving	Challenge of solving unique problems for the first time	Develop an ability to embrace problems and stress on a day-at-a-time basis.
Project ramp-up and ramp-down	Demands energizing oneself on intellectual and emotional levels and an ability to function in an atmosphere noted for a lack of continuity, stability, and predictability	Develop the ability to intellectually and emotionally pace oneself through positive self-talk, diet, and relaxation strategies.

create an approach that holds the team together. Individuals do not coalesce into a team without the leader exerting energy to create a bond within the group.

A project manager applies a positive atmosphere to bring his or her team together when he or she:

- Stays late on a Friday afternoon to meet with team members to help them work through a personal disagreement

- Publicly acknowledges the hard work and achievements of all team members

- Finds the personal strength to motivate the team after a frustrating period of project delays and setbacks.

The project manager should remember that these efforts require physical, emotional, and intellectual energies. Do not overextend yourself by trying to develop a team culture solely on your own. Enlist team members to help you create the glue that bonds the team together.

The second general component of leadership that can prove stressful for the project manager is team members' tendency to project their own feelings, attributes, or beliefs onto the project manager. In essence, team members assume that the project manager has certain qualities—either positive or negative.

Project managers enjoy being the target of projections that are positive—for example, if a team member projects the belief that the team leader is a fair person, possibly because the team leader physically resembles a fair person from the team member's past. But negative projections, such as when a team member attributes bad motives to the project leader because the leader reminds him or her of a previous manager with whom he or she had a conflictual relationship, are a source of stress for the project manager. Examples of problematic projections that team members may direct toward the project manager include:

- Treating him or her like a parent (which may have a positive or negative tone)

- Making assumptions about his or her attributes based on gender, race, religion, or age.

If you believe that you are the target of a team member's inaccurate projections, it is helpful to:

- Schedule time to speak privately with the team member, gently exploring his or her perceptions of you without immediately challenging his or her observations.

- Attempt to redefine for the team who you are as a person, telling members about your management style, your beliefs, and how you like to operate.

Managing in a Matrix Organization

Many projects are staffed by individuals who are on loan to the project from other functional areas within the organization. This is the core of matrix management. The project manager may encounter a number of issues and events arising from matrix systems that will be stressful. The biggest challenge for the project manager is influencing people to get the job done while knowing that the working relationship is temporary, lasting only for the duration of the project.

Because the project manager within a matrix system must use influence to obtain results, he or she may experience a feeling of powerlessness when the influencing behavior fails to work. Project managers often report that this feeling of helplessness accounts for a tremendous amount of stress in leading projects.

When a project manager experiences these feelings of helplessness, stress quickly develops. Internal pressure mounts, and if the helpless feeling continues unchecked, the project leader loses motivation and initiative. Some thoughts to keep in mind when trying to manage stress in matrix systems:

- Matrix organizations are known for their ability to create a sense of powerlessness, even for the best managers. Do not take the situation personally.

- When influencing is not effective, use more subtle forms of personal empowerment, such as making arguments that appeal to the self-interests of the various stakeholders.

Solving Singular Problems

Each project is unique, designed to solve a singular problem. Singular problem-solving represents both the best and the worst of project work. It gives team members a chance to work on something new and different, unlike anything they have done in the past. But solving singular problems can also pose many stressful challenges for the project manager. By definition, a singular problem is one that a team has never faced, so there may be no readily available solutions, software, or technology to apply to building the finished product or to deliver the promised service or result. Everything has to be invented, from the conceptualization and design of the solution to the manufacture of the tools for doing the work.

All of these factors place great demands on the project leader. Team members are looking for direction and support and may need guidance on how best to proceed. Their emotions may be running high, and they may feel anxious and uncertain, not wanting to take a step and risk making a mistake.

Project managers can handle the stress that comes from solving singular problems by considering the following suggestions:

- Keep motivated by focusing on the positive aspects (e.g., novelty, challenge) of solving a problem for the first time.

- Remember that it is understandable to feel uncomfortable when attempting something new. Avoid self-critical comments such as, "There must be something wrong with me because I cannot figure out how to get this solution started."

- Keep in touch with other professionals. They may be able to suggest problem-solving approaches that may not have been considered.

- Use the organization's knowledge management system to research whether other programs or projects had similar difficulties. If the organization lacks a commitment to knowledge management, suggest that it set up such a capability.

Ramping the Project Up and Down

The periods of project ramp-up and ramp-down may cause pressure and stress for the project manager. Some individuals react more positively than others to the emotional and physiological ramping up at the start of a project. In fact, some people thrive in these settings, enjoying the rush of energy and the exhilaration that come from starting something new and demanding. These individuals can be considered sensation-seeking people who need to have their physical and emotional systems regularly exposed to this type of emotional and physiological activation. During these periods of arousal, sensation-seeking people feel more alive and creative and are often operating in their most positive mood state.

However, not everyone is a sensation-seeking individual, and project managers should not underestimate the demands that ramping up and ramping down can have on the emotional and physiological well-being of their team members as well as themselves. The project life cycle is demanding and requires that the individual operate in an environment that is intense and constantly changing.

Project managers who repeatedly experience discomfort during this life cycle need to take a serious look at whether the role of project manager is the most appropriate one for them to play. Some people, regardless of length of service and best intentions, do not function well as leaders during these demanding periods. For these individuals, taking another role on the team may be a healthier career decision.

Project managers can attempt to take care of their emotional and physiological reactions during project ramp-up by considering these ideas:

- Place avocational pursuits off to the side during this period.

- Take the steps of the ramp-up process one at a time. Stress and discomfort increase when the project manager experiences anticipatory anxiety, which is caused by excessive focus on future events over which one has little current control.

During project ramp-down, the project manager can manage personal stress by remembering that:

- Endings involve a sense of loss and frequently a melancholy mood, even when the ending brings great success and achievement. Occasionally, team members may find it difficult to complete the project and finish all the necessary closeout tasks.

- Endings also involve saying good-bye to team members, which can cause natural but unexpected sadness.

As ramping down is concluding, it is crucial to take stock of how one is feeling emotionally, intellectually, and physically. Some recharging of the batteries may be necessary, such as a weekend away or time with friends.

Remember, the savvy project manager has a strong self-awareness of how he or she functions during the ramp-up and ramp-down stages and crafts coping strategies to address individual problems that may surface at both ends of the cycle.

Research by Turner, Huemann, and Keegan (2008) concludes that people experience more stress when working on a typical small or medium-sized project that can be completed in a short time than on a program or on a project that is of longer duration. Typically, programs last longer than projects, and on a program, it tends to be easier to plan each person's work. People also are less concerned about the next assignment or whether they will even have a next assignment.

On many projects of small to medium size, stress is a greater concern. These projects tend to last between three to nine months, which means that it is challenging to pace the work. Customers have key milestones, and time is the dominant of the triple constraints. It is difficult on these projects for people to take vacations or personal days to pursue other interests. It also is hard to plan how many people, and what kinds of people, will be needed to do the work, which puts pressure on the project manager when he or she tries to coordinate with people from the human resources department. Additionally, it is rare for a person to be assigned to work on only one project, and this then presents other time-management challenges. Consider the following situation.

Assume you are working for a consulting company that primarily bids on work from the U.S. federal government. The government makes many awards just before the end of the fiscal year so that agencies can use any unspent or end-of-year money. Your organization tends to work hard in the spring and summer to submit as many proposals as possible for its consulting work in project management. This year, the company won 90 percent of the bids it submitted and is extremely pleased that its proposals were accepted.

However, last year, its win rate was only 40 percent, and its capture ratio was even lower. As a result, the company downsized. Now it does not have enough people to do all the work it has won. This means there is excessive stress on the project managers and team members until additional staff with the necessary competencies can be hired and can learn the organization's project management procedures and about the work to be done for the various customers.

On top of this problem, your company has never worked with many of the customers before. Additional sources of stress for project managers include working to understand the customers' culture, gaining their confidence and trust, and identifying the key stakeholders with whom they will work. Project managers become overwhelmed with the work they must do and the many projects they must manage. They have less time to spend one-on-one with their team members, developing personal relationships and ensuring their well-being.

To cope in this environment, explain the situation to your team and let them know the organization is working hard to hire additional staff or contractors until full-time staff are available. Hold weekly meetings or conference calls if you are working in a virtual team, thank people for their hard work thus far, and inform them of progress in hiring new team members to support the project. Work actively with the human resource department to prepare needed job descriptions and other materials to accelerate the hiring process, and let your team know that you are actively involved in this way.

Working on a Virtual Team

People new to a virtual environment may find that they are taking on a different type of assignment outside their usual comfort zone. They are interfacing with different stakeholders at different levels, most of whom they have not worked with previously or even known about at all. They may feel lonely because they are not able to regularly interact with team members. Cultural differences, the use of a language on the program or project that is not one's native language, and a lack of solid understanding of how best to interact with other team members can add to stress for people in a virtual environment. The program or project manager must spend additional time with individuals who are struggling on a virtual team until they feel comfortable.

Inherent Sources of Stress in Program Management

While program managers experience some of the same types of stress as do project managers, program managers have even more responsibilities. These managers are not responsible for only one project, but for a multitude of projects with interdependencies among them, along with some nonproject work, and they must interact with an even greater number of stakeholders, many of whom are external to the performing organization. The longer life and complexity of a program may be especially stressful to the program manager. He or she may have trouble envisioning how the program will achieve all its planned benefits and come to a close. Even if the program finally comes to a close, the program manager is responsible for transitioning the benefits to the organization in a sustainable way. There may also be additional pressure on the program manager to be a leader and an effective communicator. Table 7-2 summarizes the stressors the program manager faces.

Managing Several Projects Plus Ongoing Work

The program manager will have a number of different projects in his or her program, in addition to other ongoing work or nonproject work. Some of these projects may have started before the program, and these projects with their interdependencies may be the reason the program was initiated. Other times, programs begin, and projects are initiated later. Regardless, projects can be initiated at any time during a program's life cycle except during the closing

Table 7-2   Inherent Stress in Program Management

Source of Stress	Type of Stress Placed on Program Manager	Optimal Stress-Management Approach for Program Manager
Managing several projects plus ongoing work	Pressure to make sure all the interdependencies between the projects are identified	Enlist the support of the project managers to prepare work breakdown structures (WBS) for their projects to lead so that a program WBS can be developed.
	Challenge of allocating resources across the projects and the nonproject work	Set up a resource profile of the knowledge, skills, and competencies of the people assigned to the program.
	Identification of a risk or an issue on one project that may also affect other projects in the program, positively or negatively	Work with the project managers to encourage them to escalate risks and issues to the program manager for review.
Working with numerous internal and external stakeholders	Demands to be available to meet with stakeholders continually throughout the program	Work with the project managers and core team to develop an approach to ensure stakeholder needs are met.
	Continual stakeholder-identification and management strategy development	Recognize that each time a new project is added to the program, the

		program manager will need to update the management strategy for the new stakeholders.
		Develop an approach for continual stakeholder identification throughout the life cycle.
Striving under pressure to be a good leader and an excellent communicator	Creating a sense of importance of the program for team members	Work with the project managers and each project team to develop project and team charters.
		Recognize one's own leadership and communication styles.
		Recognize that communication is the most essential interpersonal skill, and work to continually develop it.
Transitioning program benefits	Pressure to ensure that the benefits in the business case and in the benefits realization plan are met	Prepare a benefit transition plan.
		Enlist as stakeholders those who will be responsible for benefit sustainment.

process, and the program manager is responsible for ensuring that *all* of the interdependencies are identified and determining how best to manage them. According to PMI (2008b), managing these interdependencies involves:

- Coordinating the supply of components, work, or phases
- Resolving resource constraints and other conflicts
- Integrating activities across components
- Mitigating risk actions across components
- Ensuring that the program remains in alignment with the organization's strategic goals
- Resolving issues by escalating them to a governance board that may address scope, time, cost, and quality.
- Tailoring procedures as needed and managing interfaces.

Because programs are complex and important to the organization and typically take longer to complete than an individual project, any of the activities listed above can be a source of stress. One way to approach these challenges is to prepare a program work breakdown structure (WBS) by working with the project managers. Involving the project managers in the program WBS has two advantages:

- The project managers believe they are integral to the overall success of the program in the early stages.
- The project managers can ensure that the control accounts and work packages for their project are considered and recognized by the program manager and other project managers.

The program manager should have a group meeting (if working in a virtual team, a teleconference or computer-aided meeting) so that all of the project managers can work together to prepare the program WBS. Then, when a new project is added to the program, the project manager should prepare a WBS for his or her project, and the program manager should hold another meeting of the project managers to update the program WBS and to show everyone how the new project interfaces with the existing projects.

Another key source of stress at the program level involves resource allocation. While certain resources are critical to each project, familiarity with the knowledge, skills, and competencies of all of the human resources on the program can help the program manager allocate and reallocate resources. It may be that a key subject matter expert is required for one project in the program. However, another project may also benefit from this individual's contribution to certain deliverables. The program manager can set up a profile outlining each individual's capabilities and use the profiles to determine how to best use the available resources.

To complement the program WBS, a resource breakdown structure (RBS) and a RACI (responsible, accountable, consulted, informed) chart should be prepared at the project level and then rolled up to the program level. The program manager can use these documents to see when certain key resources are required on various projects. Then he or she can work with the respective project managers to determine how to best use the talent available. Such an approach also can help the program manager obtain resources who are not assigned to the program. If it is evident that the program requires a resource who is not assigned to the program, the program manager can work with the governance board and the human resource management group to find someone with the needed skills.

When working with project managers, the program manager should:

- Establish a climate of open communication so that moving a resource from one project to another does not add to the project manager's stress.

- Talk one-on-one with the project manager before reallocating a resource to determine the impact on the project.

- If reallocation presents a major challenge to the project manager, see if a compromise can be reached with the other project manager, and set up a mutually agreeable timetable for switching the resource.

- Publically acknowledge the willingness of the two project managers to work together to resolve this issue so that everyone else can see the benefits of teamwork and compromise.

Risks to the program are another area of stress. While it is impossible to identify all risks that may affect a program, because there will always be some unknown unknowns, the program manager must work collectively with the project managers. A risk identified on one project may also affect an interdependent project. Each project manager should prepare a risk management plan and share it with the other project managers. These plans will be used to help develop the program risk management plan.

When a risk actually happens, whether or not the proposed response is effective, the project manager should notify the program manager so he or she can inform others as required. The project manager should follow established escalation practices without fear of repercussions; similarly, the program manager should escalate risks as required to the sponsor or to the governance board. It may even be necessary to involve the portfolio review board if the risk is so significant (as an opportunity or as a threat) that it could affect a program or project under way in another part of the organization. An atmosphere of open communication is critical to help reduce the stress associated with risks in the program management environment.

Working with Numerous Internal and External Stakeholders

At the program level, there are far more stakeholders, both internal and external, than at the project level. Identifying and working with the various stakeholders at different levels is a complex process and a significant source of stress for program managers.

- Each stakeholder group will require different types of information and will probably be actively involved in some phases of the program and have less influence and impact in others.

- It is possible to overlook a key stakeholder even if the entire team works to make sure that this does not happen.

- Each time a new project is added to the program, new stakeholders will be involved, which means the stakeholder management plan and stakeholder management strategy must be updated.

To help reduce this stress, program managers should:

- Work with the project managers and the team to ensure stakeholder planning, identification, and management are ongoing throughout the program.

- Hold special meetings with the project managers and team members as needed that focus specifically on stakeholders: Are stakeholders receiving the information they need, or do they require additional reports and meetings?

- Meet regularly with the sponsor and the governance board, not just at key phase or stage gate reviews, but at other times to discuss the overall health of the program with a focus on stakeholder management. Sponsors and board members may have their own concerns and also may have come across a key stakeholder who is not included in the program's stakeholder management plan and strategy.

- Track activities underway to make sure someone from the team is working with the associated stakeholders.

- Periodically conduct surveys of stakeholders, using open-ended questions, to gauge their reaction to the program thus far and to ask how the program could better meet their individual needs.

Being a Program Leader

The stressors that affect project managers also affect program managers, but they are magnified at the program level. The program manager must constantly reinforce the purpose of the program to team members and stakeholders. He or she also must bring the team together even if its members are scattered across the globe and may never meet face to face as a group. Further, he or she must apply personal energy to building and maintaining the team, and this energy must continue throughout the long life of the program.

The program manager must make an effort to be viewed as a person who is fair and objective and who treats people at all levels with respect. He or she must have an open door policy with a co-located team. On a virtual team, the program manager should inform the team of his or her availability to speak on the phone and how quickly he or she will typically respond to emails.

If the program manager believes or learns that others think his or her leadership and communication skills need improvement, the best approach is to practice active listening and ask people for candid feedback. It may be difficult to not take a defensive posture, but feedback is important for anyone who strives to continually improve. Based on this feedback, it may be appropriate to call a team meeting to discuss what you, as the program manager, plan to do to improve your leadership and communication skills and your own operating style in the program. Later, you might ask the enterprise project management office to conduct an anonymous survey of your team to determine whether its members think you have made positive changes—and, more important, to find out what else you might do to improve.

Transitioning Program Benefits

Managing projects with interdependencies as programs reaps benefits that would not be realized if the projects were managed in a standalone way. In addition, most programs contain some elements of ongoing or nonproject work. The expectation of greater benefits means the program manager is under greater stress from the beginning than a project manager.

- Not only must additional benefits be realized from the program structure, but there are also more deliverables associated with the program.

- The benefits are listed initially in the business case but expand over time, so by the time the program manager is assigned to manage the program, he or she may have even more benefits to manage.

- Projects will be canceled or completed and closed at different times. When projects are closed, their associated benefits must be transitioned to customers, end users, or a product or customer support organization. This means the program manager is responsible for benefit realization from each individual project, plus benefits from the program as a whole. In addition to this, he or she must consolidate the benefits, transition them, and manage the transition effectively so that the benefits are sustained.

For many team members, the concept of a benefit may be new. PMI (2008**c**) defines a benefit as "an opportunity that provides an advantage to an organization" (p. 309). The program manager must define the benefits the program is to provide in a way that allows each member of the team to see his or her role in their delivery. The program manager also must make clear to everyone on the team the importance of benefit identification, planning, execution, monitoring, and control, as well as completing deliverables on time, within budget, and according to specifications, and meeting customer expectations.

To illustrate each person's contribution to overall benefits management and to reduce each person's possible anxieties about the importance of benefit management, the program manager can:

- Hold brainstorming sessions or use other group dynamic approaches to involve the team in the benefit identification process.

- Have the team prepare a benefits realization plan at the project level, which then is rolled up to the program level and maps to the program management plan so that each person can see how he or she is to contribute.

- Work with the team to develop metrics that will show how and when benefits are realized and that indicate whether any benefits cannot be realized as planned.

- Meet individually as needed with team members if the team is co-located, or through phone calls if in a virtual environment, to stress the importance of benefit management to team members who may not have experience with this requirement.

Many organizations have product or service departments that are responsible for sustaining program benefits. A consultant was hired to assist one such department that was having several problems communicating with the organization's program group. For example, the service department received no notice when it was to assume operational responsibility for a completed program, and it was unable to perform capacity planning and had to be on standby or use an informal network to learn of upcoming work. The consultant worked to help this department set up a project management office (PMO) and, more important, a process to align communications with the program group. The consultant suggested that the service PMO director set up formal weekly meetings with the program group and ask to be included as an observer in program-group reviews to learn about upcoming work. The service PMO director explained to the program group that his department had to be ready to support the program group's important work and that the use of proactive, horizontal communications could greatly assist him in doing so.

Often the recipient of the program benefit is not involved until the individual project or overall program is complete. He or she may know the program is underway, and if this person, for example, represents a product support or customer support group, may know that ultimately it will be his or her responsibility to sustain these benefits. At times, however, this key stakeholder is overlooked or is an afterthought; if the stakeholder finds out about this upcoming responsibility without time to plan for it, additional stress may be placed on the program manager. The program manager may need to ask the governance board for resources to continue the program even when it should be closed until this support group is able to assume responsibility.

To avoid the need to continue to support the program after it is complete, the program manager must ensure the ultimate group responsible for benefit sustainment is aware of the program and when specific benefits from each project and the program as a whole are expected to be delivered. The program manager should:

- Meet with the group responsible for sustainment early in the program and ask them how they wish to be involved. For example, do they wish to receive regular updates on progress and benefit realization reports, attend team meetings from time to time, or have regular involvement even as a member of the governance board or steering committee?

- Provide as much information as possible, perhaps through the joint development of a benefit transition plan to the receiving organization so they are prepared and can assume ownership once the program is closed.

- Ensure the receiving organization has access to the program's knowledge repository.

- Be available after closure in case the receiving organizational head has any questions, and be able to put members of the receiving organization in direct contact with program team members as required.

Inherent Sources of Stress in Portfolio Management

Stress levels differ at the portfolio level, although the portfolio manager is still responsible for being a leader, an outstanding communicator, and an effective manager of stakeholders. Project-based organizations' portfolios contain both internal and external programs and projects. In such a portfolio, people can work on different projects at different times, often in different roles. This means there can be role conflict, which, combined with the demands from program and project managers, add to stress. It is more difficult to achieve a work-life balance because the workload on the different programs or projects peaks at different times—or even at the same time, which maximizes stress on the individual and can ultimately lead to burnout.

The portfolio manager also faces pressure to guide the selection process, to continually work to optimize the portfolio, to measure and monitor the value of portfolio management to the organization, to work with multiple funding streams, and to continually assess the environment for changes that may affect the portfolio (Table 7-3).

Table 7-3   Inherent Stress in Portfolio Management

Source of Stress	Type of Stress Placed on Portfolio Manager	Optimal Stress-Management Approach for the Portfolio Manager
The pressure to guide the selection process	Creating a process that is considered objective and not overly bureaucratic	Work with sponsors who are preparing justifications for the inclusion of new programs and projects in the portfolio.
The need to continually optimize the portfolio	Ensuring the portfolio is reprioritized as necessary	Set up an optimization process by working with various stakeholders to monitor the overall status of the portfolio.
The requirement to monitor and measure the value of portfolio management to the organization	The challenge of determining the value proposition that portfolio management brings to the organization	Work with stakeholders to determine why the organization needs portfolio management and how it will help the organization achieve its goals. Communicate this value statement throughout the organization.
The need to work with multiple funding streams	Recognizing when funds can and cannot be moved to better optimize portfolio investments	Set up a process to rank portfolio components based on their funding streams and focus on resource allocation.
The importance of continual assessment of the environment to determine if changes should be made to the portfolio	Responding to changes that may result in a requirement to change the portfolio	Set up a process to track strategic changes to enable the organization to capitalize on new business conditions.

Guiding the Selection Process

Portfolio management represents a culture change for organizations. No longer can people work on programs and projects they feel will be of benefit to the organization; instead, they must follow a detailed selection process that will be used to evaluate whether to fund and allocate resources to a program or project. The portfolio manager may experience stress because he or she must:

• Describe why this process is being followed

• Provide guidance to people about what must be done to make the business case for a program or project and how to structure it so it is carefully considered by the portfolio review board

• Communicate to the proposer the decision of the portfolio review board, which, of course, is extremely difficult if the decision is not to fund the proposal.

The portfolio manager also may be tasked with developing the selection process, which requires analytical skills, as well as communication skills—the portfolio manager must explain the process to people at all levels and get their buy-in to the new process. Additional responsibilities that may cause stress include coordinating the development of the selection process with others in the organization and evaluating the selection process periodically to make sure it is serving its purpose and is not considered cumbersome and too bureaucratic to follow.

Once the selection process has been set up, the portfolio manager should work with program and project sponsors as they prepare their business cases to make sure they understand items to include. If a sponsor's business case is not accepted by the review board, the portfolio manager must inform the sponsor about why it was not accepted—which could bring on even more stress. (When the portfolio manager delivers bad news, he or she should focus on pointing out why other programs and projects were selected over this one and on ways to better justify the proposal before the next meeting of the board.)

Optimizing the Portfolio

Because a portfolio is not static, the portfolio manager must work with the portfolio review board to continually optimize it. Rebalancing is an ongoing occurrence as new programs or projects are added to the portfolio, others are terminated after board meetings, and others are completed as planned. These frequent changes are typically stressful for the portfolio manager.

With each change, the portfolio manager must communicate decisions to the various stakeholders and also must work to reallocate resources to newer, higher-priority work. The portfolio manager must have negotiating skills to work with the various program and project managers involved. In determining the most optimal mix of resources, the portfolio manager can enlist the support of existing program and project managers for changes.

Ultimately, however, the portfolio manager usually makes decisions about the portfolio mix with support from the review board. It is common for these decisions to engender resentment in people who are moved from their existing work to a new program or project as well as in their managers. The portfolio manager must explain why the changes are occurring and individuals' roles in the process. He or she may be able to negotiate with displaced employees' new program or project managers so they can at least be available for consultation or can return to their previous assignments once they have completed their new assignments.

The portfolio manager can simplify the portfolio rebalancing process and minimize the associated stress by:

- Continually performing capacity planning so that he or she can inform the portfolio review board of the impact of portfolio changes

- Communicating as often as possible with program and project managers whose work is considered to be high or medium priority about changes that may affect the portfolio so that any change is not viewed as a complete surprise

- Consistently providing information to everyone in the organization about the value of the portfolio management process and any changes so that the process is as transparent as possible.

Monitoring and Measuring the Value of Portfolio Management

While every organization has some kind of portfolio, not everyone in an organization may be aware of the actual portfolio of programs, projects, and other work. If an organization has a defined portfolio-management process, involving a portfolio manager and a portfolio review board or comparable group, the portfolio manager may be under pressure to show the rest of the organization—at the executive level and at lower levels—why this process is valuable. If others in the organization do not understand the value of the process, the portfolio manager will struggle to get buy-in; people will feel their time is better spent elsewhere.

Senior executives on the portfolio review board may not appreciate a process that prevents them from pursuing pet projects they believe are essential to the organization, and they may not wish to be part of the formal portfolio selection process, may not take the process seriously, and may delegate attendance at board meetings to others rather than actively participating in them.

The portfolio manager can prepare a thought paper or white paper that concisely describes why the organization is following a structured portfolio management process. People need information about:

- Why portfolio management is important
- The tools and techniques being used
- Specific roles and responsibilities
- The overall value a defined process brings to an organization.

To prepare this thought paper, the portfolio manager should:

- Draft a value proposition for portfolio management that states its goals, objectives, and benefits and how they will be monitored and measured.
- Work with stakeholders in a cross-functional group to review and revise the thought paper. List factors for the success of portfolio management in the organization.
- Submit the thought paper to the members of the portfolio review board for their buy-in and comments.
- Circulate the thought paper throughout the organization.

Working with Multiple Funding Streams

Many organizations have multiple funding streams. This is typical in consulting firms, a joint venture, or a joint services organization such as in the Department of Defense or other governmental agency. In this kind of environment, the portfolio manager cannot move funds from one funding stream to pursue a project or program that is considered to be of higher priority and importance but is not covered by the funding agent. He or she must have an in-depth understanding about what can legally be done and what cannot be done and must be able to explain the process to stakeholders at various levels. The portfolio manager may be put in a difficult position if executives want to execute a program or project but lack the needed funds to do so. A portfolio manager who is frequently in this situation must have skills in resource allocation techniques, trade-off analyses, negotiation, and decision-making to help manage the stress associated with the position.

Assessing the Environment for Changes to the Portfolio

With the increase in downsizing, joint ventures, outsourcing, and off-shoring, as well as the need to keep up with and outpace the competition, the portfolio process is characterized by constant change. To help mitigate the stress these changes may bring, the portfolio manager should strive to:

- Build relationships with people in the organization who work in strategic planning, marketing, sales, and business development

- Cultivate relationships with people who specialize in organizational change to help prepare people at various levels for these changes

- Recognize that the portfolio management process is not a static one. Even if there are no changes, it is helpful to review the criteria from time to time to see if they are still applicable and to practice a policy of being receptive to and embracing change.

Stress Caused by Dysfunctional Organizations

Organizations operating in dysfunctional ways create stress for managers. A dysfunctional organization is one in which formal or informal processes and culture operate in ways that are not healthy or conducive to a positive work atmosphere. Too frequently, portfolio, program, and project managers working in a dysfunctional system become lightning rods for all that is wrong with the organization simply because they are prominent people at the center of the action.

One way to combat dysfunction is for organizations and leaders to demonstrate congruence between spoken or written words and actions. This is "walking the talk." When people or organizations say one thing but do another thing, this lack of congruence heightens the stress level for stakeholders. A lack of organizational congruence is more than simply a nuisance for team members and portfolio, program, and project leaders. People who are repeatedly exposed to situations in which a lack of congruence exists frequently display a variety of troublesome symptoms and reactions. For example, when people notice that organizational words and actions do not match, they are often puzzled, saying, in effect, "Am I wrong in my perceptions or is the company wrong?" This creates self-doubt, and this self-doubt can begin a spiraling process in which the person loses motivation and becomes chronically distrustful or cynical.

A situation involving a lack of organizational congruence is a no-win situation for the portfolio, program, or project manager, given that a single manager is unable to change the culture of an organization. Many managers experience high levels of stress when faced with a no-win prospect. The best way to avoid too much personal stress in these situations is to seek a middle ground—acknowledging the team members' perceptions about the organization's lack of congruence without getting stuck in too much negativity. The manager might say something like:

> Like you, I also believe the company may not be walking the talk on this issue. However, I do not want to spend too much time trying to understand where senior management stands on this issue. Instead, I suggest we focus on what we can do on our level to resolve the contradictions in a way that allows us to go forward and feel as positive and productive as we can about the project.

The tone of this message validates the perceptions of the team in a forthright manner but does not slip into company bashing.

To manage personal stress in situations involving an organizational lack of congruence, the portfolio, program, or project manager should be realistic about what can and cannot be done to correct the situation.

- Project managers should intently focus the team on what can be done at the team level to resolve the discrepancies and keep the project moving forward in a positive manner.

- If working on a program, keep the team focused on the program's vision and mission and its importance to the organization.

- If you are the portfolio manager, try to focus on why changes are occurring and communicate them as quickly as possible to everyone involved.

Portfolio, program, and project managers can get mired in attempting to right the wrongs of the organization. These managers experience excessive stress if they assume too much personal responsibility for correcting dysfunctional organizational behavior that is beyond their control. Do what you can, but take care that you do not ask too much of yourself.

Stress Caused by the Manager's Personal Traits and Habits

A person's personality can directly contribute to the level of stress he or she experiences (Table 7-4).

Table 7-4   Personality Traits That Can Increase Personal Stress

Source of Stress	Resulting Stress on Manager	Adaptive Approach for Manager to Use in Reducing Stress
Using maladaptive coping approaches such as giving up, indulging, denial	Negative habits are reinforced, and stress is never directly addressed or resolved	Stay vigilant for these tendencies, and develop new approaches as needed.
Perfectionistic attitude	Self-imposed pressure (experienced as anxiety, anger, or guilt) to do everything at unrealistic levels of achievement.	Realistically consider what is crucial, and lower expectations of oneself or others for tasks not requiring perfect performance.
Tendency to overcontrol people and tasks	Anxiety, fear that tasks will fail unless one is intimately involved in all the details	Look for competency in others, and remember that some things will go wrong but probably can be corrected.
Unregulated sense of time urgency and immediacy	Intensity, anger, and anxiety coming from the belief that everything must be done now	Pause and ask if this action must be taken now or if it could be done at a later time.
Runaway personal myths (such as the need to play the role of the hero)	Unrealistic expectations leading to high levels of self-created pressure to pursue actions that may not be realistic.	Think through what is motivating your actions, and see if a personal myth is propelling you toward unrealistic or self-defeating actions.

Four personality traits that particularly contribute to managers' stress include perfectionism and time urgency, an overcontrolling approach to work, an unconscious adherence to certain personal myths or beliefs, and excessive multitasking.

Perfectionism and Time Urgency

The portfolio, program, or project manager with perfectionistic tendencies understands on an intellectual level that perfection is not achievable, but this awareness often is not reflected in his or her behavior. A person with a perfectionistic style combined with a sense of time urgency often has the makings of a Type A personality (Friedman 1996).

A portfolio, program, or project manager with perfectionistic qualities and a sense of time urgency may believe that:

- There is only one acceptable level of performance.

- Anything short of that level of performance will be viewed as a failure.

- Work needs to be done as soon as possible, with little consideration of whether it really matters.

The perfectionist manager needs to keep these qualities under control so that they do not cause personal turmoil. Before a task begins, he or she should spend some time listing all expectations—realistic and unrealistic—for his or her own performance and for the result and timing of the project. Keep this list on hand throughout the project and refer to it regularly. Determine whether you are allowing yourself to drift into activities that have little impact on project success.

Overcontrol

An ongoing challenge for a manager is to define the often nebulous point at which exercising appropriate control over a program or project becomes a matter of overcontrol. When not held in check by personal awareness, a tendency toward overcontrol creates stress for the portfolio, program, and project manager. He or she is unable to relax, believing that he or she must remain vigilant to control unseen forces or to avoid problems that have yet to occur.

If you believe that overcontrol may be a personal issue for you as a manager, you can explore that possibility by noting any thoughts that suggest you are trying to take too much responsibility for or control over a situation—for example, "If I do not personally review all of the technical drawings, something big will be missed and we will fail." After compiling a list of these types of thoughts, ask yourself the following questions:

- What would be the worst consequence if this event occurred?

- What is the risk of that consequence to the overall portfolio, program, or project?

- How bad is that consequence?

- How could I manage that consequence?

- Could the portfolio, program, or project and I survive if that consequence actually happened?

The process of delineating fears and worst-case scenarios can have a calming effect. Once the manager has explored the negative consequences, he or she can create a survival plan. This process allows the manager to let go of some of the emotionally charged aspects of the situation.

Runaway Personal Myths and Beliefs

All of us have reasons for doing the things we do. Some of these reasons are known to us on a conscious level; other reasons operate on less conscious levels. Many of the reasons we do any task are based on deep, substantive personal myths that we bring with us to the work world.

Personal myths are beliefs that we use to describe ourselves and our motivations in life. Myths are developed in early years and at formative turning points in our lives. For example, a personal myth developed early in life might be: "I am the smartest kid in my class, and I need to show others that I can solve any problem." Such a personal belief may be grounded initially in fact and then reinforced by teachers, parents, other students, and the world at large.

Personal myths are important because they help motivate us to take action by providing a generalization that we can apply in the workplace. The generalization provides an identity for us—something that tells others, as well as ourselves, who we are. Examples of these identities or personal myths include:

- Hero

- Innovative problem solver

- Brightest person in the group.

Myths serve a positive purpose when they give us a role or purpose on a team. However, if a myth is operating within us on an unconscious level, we may eventually notice that it has taken control of our behavior and has placed us in stressful situations. Personal myths need to be made conscious. Gaining awareness of our personal myths helps us avoid being managed by them. If we do not have an awareness of what is driving us, we may experience excessive distress, personal pain, and professional problems. How does one become more aware of personal myths? Here is a suggestion.

Imagine you are working on a virtual team. No one else on your team is in your location. You have been promoted in your organization many times in a short period of time and have also obtained your PMP and an advanced degree in project management. You believe, therefore, that you have more knowledge than anyone else on your virtual team. You find that you are constantly asking team members how you can help them, seeking new assignments, asking the project manager how you can work more with various stakeholders, asking to lead team meetings, and taking on the most challenging work packages on the project. But by taking on so many assignments, in addition to your own work, you are creating undue stress for yourself.

Excessive Multitasking

Many people thrive in a multitasking environment. They consider it a success to be able to do two or three things at once, such as using a smartphone or netbook to answer emails during a meeting. This multitasking work style has become so common that some people think it is necessary. Jones, for example, writes, "Project managers obviously can't do it alone. They're going to need a team of multitasking experts as well" (2009, p. 54).

Although we often do not have the luxury of working on a single assignment, we must approach multitasking carefully because it can become a source of stress as well as a drain on productivity. Shellenbarger (2003) points out that "multitasking creates the illusion of progress by creating busyness while robbing people of time and mental cycles. Humans are not particularly good at switching contexts." Each time we switch to another task, we lose time because we must then revisit where we were when we last worked on that task, gather required information, and then review it before we can proceed. Therefore, portfolio, program, and project managers can best guide their teams by prioritizing what must be done today or this week and what can wait until later. Of course, they may not be able to work on only the highest-priority task, but at least they can set the majority of their time aside to do so and can increase overall productivity while reducing stress.

Stress-Management Tips for the Portfolio, Program, or Project Manager

- Prepare a charter to define your authority and responsibility, and ask your team to prepare a charter for use by the team to empower itself.

- For resource assignment and reallocation, use a knowledge, skills, and competency database if available, or ask that one be set up.

- Perform detailed planning, beginning with a WBS, and then link each work package (or program package at the program level) to a specific individual or organization.

- Focus on the assigned work and limit multitasking. Set up a specific time to answer emails, return phone calls, or talk informally with others.

- Keep emphasizing the vision of your program or project to your team and its importance to the organization's strategic goals.

- Use your organization's knowledge management system, if available, for assistance in solving difficult problems, for collaboration with others, and for locating key experts.

- Set up discussion forums or blogs for your team.

- Ensure that everyone on the team has access to the same type of software for ease of communication.

- Continually focus on stakeholder identification and a stakeholder management strategy.

- Recognize that risks can be both opportunities and threats and will affect your program or project. Identifying them and developing responses, as well as monitoring and control, should be ongoing throughout the life cycle.

- Realize changes are inevitable, establish a process to effectively manage them when they do occur, and communicate the impact of each change and decisions made as a result of each change to your stakeholders.

- When problems arise, do not jump to an immediate decision. Take time to consider what has happened and why, as well as how you feel about what has occurred.

- Establish a "no surprises" policy for your team and with your sponsor or governance board.

- Focus on open communication, and make a sincere effort to involve people as much as possible in the decision-making and conflict-resolution processes.

Summary

Personal demands on portfolio, program, and project managers are numerous and complicated in today's fast-paced environment. Stressors have many sources, including organizational issues, the complexities of program and project management, and the manager's personal traits.

Managers should work to develop a solid understanding of what their own sources of stress are and must also recognize that what might be stressful for one manager may not be stressful for another.

When creating a personal stress-management action plan, portfolio, program, and project managers must be creative and willing to experiment with different approaches. Develop a personalized approach to stress management that fits your style. Following and continually improving upon a personalized stress-management approach will help you remain vital, excited, and content, even in the face of complex demands and challenges.

Discussion Questions

A project manager operating within a matrix organization encountered significant frustration even before the project got started. This manager discovered that three functional managers were balking at releasing skilled employees to work on the new project. All three functional managers told the project manager that they were understaffed and could not afford to give up good people.

For three weeks, the project leader held meeting after meeting with these functional managers, trying to convince and cajole them into releasing the needed employees. The functional managers' arguments seemed shallow and incomplete to the project manager. He viewed their actions as obstructionist, not professional, and they all appeared to resist any attempt he made to reason with them.

After four weeks, the project manager realized that his anger was increasing, so much so that he was hoping to avoid seeing these functional managers in the hallways. His sleep was interrupted by recurring worries about what he was going to do if he could not get these three people for his team.

After days of inadequate sleep, he finally appealed to his project sponsor for support—and the three people were assigned to his team. By that time, however, he felt discouraged, fatigued, and unmotivated. And the real work of the project had yet to begin.

1. What should the project manager have done to address these personal feelings before starting work on the project?

2. What would you do if you were in such a situation?

3. In general, what can project managers do to minimize stress while working in a matrix environment?

You just obtained your PgMP and have been a successful program manager in your organization. You were recently assigned to manage a program in a different business unit in your company. You will be leading a virtual team with members located on two continents and in seven different locations. So far, there are four projects in your program.

One project has a major milestone due to its customer in three weeks. Today, the project manager told you that he is concerned that he cannot meet the deadline. This is particularly problematic because this project has dependencies with two other projects. The project manager told you that a critical subject matter expert (SME) recently quit the company abruptly without giving any notice; another key SME is ill and is not expected to be able to return to work for another month; and a vendor, who is responsible for a major part of the deliverable, is waiting for new technology to be installed.

You know that no one on your team has the same skills as the two SMEs who are no longer available, but you think that another part of the business unit may have resources you could use. You are new to this organization, though, and you are not certain. You also think that you might be able to find another vendor if you could get a meeting set up with your contracts department and review the qualified seller list.

1. As the program manager, what would you do if you were in this situation?
2. What should you have done when the program was established to avoid such a situation from occurring in the first place?
3. What stress-management approaches might you use to reduce this stress that would work for you?

Resolving Conflict and Managing Agreement

Conflict is inevitable in portfolio management, program management, and project management because of the complexities involved, the myriad different stakeholders, the requirements to show the value and benefits of the work that is to be done and then to realize these benefits, and the need to complete programs and projects on time, within budget, according to specifications, and with customer satisfaction. PMI (2008a) notes that conflicts arise because:

- Necessary resources are lacking
- The schedule has been imposed on the team rather than developed by the team
- There are differences in the personal work styles of each team member and the project manager.

By using a team charter (or, as PMI recommends, establishing ground rules), planning communications, and defining roles and responsibilities, teams may be able to reduce conflict. They will be more productive and build a more positive, collaborative relationship.

Keep in mind that conflict does not have to be negative. Conflict can actually be a way to boost a team's creativity—it can become the energy that loosens the attachment to old ideas. And, if the team takes advantage of its diversity by devising a solution that brings together different points of view, it also can improve the quality of the team's decisions.

If the team cannot resolve a conflict on its own, it is the project manager's responsibility to do so. (Meredith and Mantel write that the project manager "who cannot manage conflict is doomed to failure" [2009, p. 219].) PMI (2008a) suggests the project manager use a direct, collaborative approach, working privately with the people involved in the conflict as much as possible. PMI discusses several different approaches to resolving conflict, which this chapter discusses further. Briefly, the following factors should be taken into account when trying to determine how to manage a conflict:

- The importance and intensity of the conflict

- How much time is available to resolve it

- The emotional attachment each involved person has to his or her point of view in the conflict

- Whether it is best to devise a long-term or short-term solution.

Remember that it is important to focus on positions, not on the personalities involved; to emphasize the present; and not to resurface old grievances or concerns in the process.

The project management literature has for years addressed conflict resolution skills and the effective management of the conflict resolution process as a key role for project managers. A PMI monograph (Kirchof and Adams 1982) is devoted to this topic. Kirchof and Adams assert that "conflicts *will* exist in all project environments" (p. i) and explain that matrix management intensifies conflicts because the working relationship between the project manager and the functional manager involves balancing authority, accountability, and responsibility. If a project manager fails to recognize and carefully manage conflicts, the project team could totally collapse.

But conflict management is not just the project manager's domain. It is also part of program and portfolio management. PMI (2008c) says that the program manager's approach to resolving conflict defines how conflicts among stakeholders will be managed and creates escalation paths. The ability to resolve conflict is a key skill for portfolio managers, too (PMI 2008b), especially because the portfolio manager interacts with a wide range of internal and external stakeholders at varying levels.

This chapter describes the positive and negative aspects of conflict in portfolio, program, and project management; describes the types of conflict that can happen in various phases of the life cycle; describes a variety of conflict resolution approaches and explains when each one is helpful; provides a checklist that can guide managers in assessing and managing conflict; notes the consequences if conflict is not addressed; and also discusses the importance of managing agreement.

Types of Conflict

Rapport (1960) says that there are two basic types of conflict: competitive and disruptive. In *competitive* conflicts, the people involved have goals that are mutually incompatible, and each is striving to win. The conflict is resolved when the result is one that everyone involved can accept and is obvious. A *disruptive* conflict is one in which people are not following a mutually agreed-upon set of rules (for example, a team charter) and want to weaken, defeat, harm, or drive away the other party. The atmosphere is very stressful, requiring immediate action to diffuse it. Typically, conflicts are on a continuum between competitive and disruptive.

Thompson and Border (2007), building on work by Robbins (2003), write that conflicts can be functional or relational. *Functional* conflicts are positive conflicts. They are basically disagreements about how to best proceed on the work of a program or project and the specific processes that should be used to do so. *Relational* conflicts are caused by emotional differences. They do not involve processes, procedures, or functions, but rather personal styles, choices, and work habits. They also may be rooted in relevant social or political issues outside the work environment.

Thompson and Border say that project managers must monitor relational conflicts to prevent the development of damaging differences of opinion, even if these conflicts are subtle (which is especially likely on virtual teams). If relational conflicts are not resolved, they can lead to larger conflicts that are time-consuming and costly to the program or project. The authors say that relational conflict leads to team decomposition in three stages:

1. ***Communicative detachment.*** People are unwilling to constructively communicate with their teammates, and often they will take hard stands on an issue that may not be important.
2. ***Selective detachment.*** Like-minded team members form alliances—sub-teams—with others to prepare strategies to deal with the conflict.

3. ***Factionism.*** Now there are multiple teams, rather than a single team that is united toward common goals and objectives—leading to duplicated effort, confusion over roles and responsibilities, and in the long term, increased cost.

When relational conflicts are disruptive to the team, the manager must refocus team members around the program's or project's goals and objectives.

Individual Sources of Conflict

There are many possible individual sources of conflict on program or project teams, including:

- Two team members who constantly irritate one another

- A team member's poor communication skills

- A team member whose acute personal programs (e.g., family problems) affect his or her work performance

- The different perspectives held by team members who were originally trained in different disciplines

- A team member's lack of interest in being assigned to work on the program or project

- Unclear roles and responsibilities

- The need for one team member to rely on someone he or she does not trust or respect

- A team member's lack of respect for the technical capabilities of fellow team members, based on prior experiences with them or knowledge of them from other sources

- Team members having incongruent goals and objectives (Kirchof and Adams 1982).

Conflict on Program and Project Teams

The reasons for conflict on program and project teams are varied; they can be related to the personal characteristics of team members, the systemic challenges

Table 8-1   Positive and Negative Aspects of Conflict on Programs and Projects

Positive Aspects of Conflict	Negative Aspects of Conflict
Productively challenges existing beliefs or paradigms	When not addressed in a productive manner, can demotivate team behavior and increase interpersonal withdrawal
Reduces the risk of intellectual compliance within the team (groupthink)	Decreases interpersonal communication, increases cynicism
May create the opportunity to forge more effective team and stakeholder relationships and revitalize team energy and boldness	Adversely affects initiative and the willingness to take risks

of completing tasks within complex and challenging environments, some combination of these factors, or relevant external events. Every organization and industry has conflicts. They are simply part of doing business, and the program and project manager should consider both the positive and negative aspects of conflict (Table 8-1).

There are many sources of conflicts on programs and projects. Systemic sources include conflicting loyalties and alliances or ambiguous jurisdiction (Filey 1975)—for example, when a project team member works for both the project manager and the functional manager, or when a project team member works on multiple projects, sometimes working for a manager on-site and other times working for a manager in a different location, where there will be no face-to-face interaction during the project.

Conflicts also arise with downsizing and reductions in force. While the people who are no longer employed may harbor resentment toward those who remain, the surviving employees also struggle. They are forced to do more with less and may have trouble getting the resources needed to complete the work; they may feel guilty about being retained while some of their peers were not. They also may worry that they will be the next to be released if they believe other reductions in force lie ahead; their focus might shift from enthusiastically completing their assignments to locating another job.

A government agency preparing for an announced reduction in force evaluated its workforce and decided the most expedient action was to outsource the IT department. If the IT staff were let go but the positions were not outsourced, other staff members in the organization would take over the IT employees' duties but would lack the knowledge and skills required to perform the work.

The program manager worked hard to help the staff find positions in other organizations, and she was temporarily retained to assist with the transition. Then she was told that once the outsourced team was fully engaged, she too would lose her job. When she realized she had to make sure she had another position, her enthusiasm for helping the outsourced team obviously diminished. She did not provide the outsourced team with the key information they needed, delaying the completion of many key projects for the agency.

Other conflicts arise when a program or project ends, especially in projectized organizations, in which team members lack a functional home in the organization and must look for new positions each time a project ends. They tend to delay the closing tasks as long as possible. Though they realize it is important to finish the work, they are more interested in their own safety and security and in locating another position.

Conflicts will invariably arise on virtual teams, though they may not be apparent, especially if only two or three team members are involved. On a virtual team, it is easy for a team member to have an "out of sight, out of mind" attitude, especially if he or she is not enthusiastic about being on the team. Virtual team members, particularly those who have this attitude, may not involve the project manager in resolving conflicts and may not follow the team charter (if one exists).

Conflict in Portfolio Management

The portfolio manager interacts with such a large number of stakeholders that a variety of conflicts can arise. Most of these conflicts involve the organization's portfolio management process. People will resist using this process if they do not believe it is equitable and fair. They may believe that the process will restrict their freedom to do a project that they believe is necessary for the organization because it will not meet the selection criteria. See Table 8-2 for some examples of the positive and negative aspects of following a portfolio process.

Table 8-2 Positive and Negative Aspects of Following a Portfolio Process

Positive Aspects	Negative Aspects
Promotes an unbiased method to allocate resources	Increasing resistance by stakeholders if they feel the structured approach is not in their favor
Provides a sense of importance to people because they know the priority of their work to the organization	Decreasing interest in working on a program or project if it has a low ranking in the organization
May help unify the executive team as portfolio management is embraced as the way to ensure successful programs and projects are undertaken	Increasing frustration from some executives if they wish to propose a program or project that does not meet the defined criteria

The portfolio manager must continually communicate with stakeholders at all levels about the value of portfolio management and why it is important to use it in a structured way in the organization. He or she also must have a positive outlook on changes. When a change does occur or is about to occur, he or she must be able to assess its impact on the organization so it can be managed effectively and turned into an opportunity that will enable the organization to obtain new customers, enter new markets, and pursue programs and projects that it might not have considered previously.

Conflict throughout the Project Life Cycle

Thamhain and Wilemon (1975) identified seven types of conflict that tend to occur in project environments and then related these types of conflicts to specific phases in the life cycle in priority order. (See Table 8-3.)

Conflicts over personnel concern the human resources who are proposed for the project team, while those about personalities involve disagreements on interpersonal issues. Thamhain and Wilemon found that the greatest number of conflicts involved personnel resources, even if the people remained in their functional departments and worked in a weak matrix-type environment. They also noted that personality conflicts were the most difficult for managers to deal with in an effective way. All the sources of conflict were significant in Thamhain and Wilemon's study, however, and varied in intensity from team to team.

Table 8-3   Types of Conflict by Project Life Cycle Phase

Initiating	Planning	Executing	Closing
Project priorities	Project priorities	Project priorities	Project priorities
Administrative procedures	Schedules	Schedules	Schedules
Schedules	Administrative procedures	Administrative procedures	Personnel resources
Personnel resources	Technical opinions	Technical opinions	Personalities
Cost	Personnel resources	Personnel resources	Cost
Technical opinions	Cost	Cost	Technical opinions
Personalities	Personalities	Personalities	Administrative procedures

In reviewing Thamhain and Wilemon's work, it is interesting to note that personnel resources were among the top three sources of conflict in the executing and closing phases. The majority of the work of the project or program is performed during the executing and monitoring and controlling phases (PMI 2008a) or the delivery of the program benefits phase (PMI 2008c), which is why the resource issue is so critical. Good personnel planning may help avert conflict. PMI recommends preparing a program resource plan (2008c) or, for projects, a human resources plan that includes a specific staffing management plan describing how and when the staffing resources would be met on the project (2008a). This plan describes how resources will be acquired, where people will work, when they will be needed, how people will be released, training requirements, and rewards and recognition.

It is not surprising that personality conflicts are ranked high during the closing phase, especially if people are unsure about their next assignment or whether they even will have a job once the program or project ends. Personnel resources are another significant source of conflict during closing because there may not be enough people available to complete the activities in this phase; people have moved on to other opportunities. If personality conflicts arise or competition for resources develops during closure, program and project managers should:

- Meet individually with team members to discuss their future and their contribution to the program or project.

- Recognize and reward team members for their work.

- Work actively with people who do not have a new assignment to help them locate one, using the services of the human resources department as appropriate.

- Recognize, however, that resources are needed to close the program and project. If a team member's new assignment can be deferred, ask him or her to remain with the program or project as long as possible to help complete the closing tasks.

If it is impossible to obtain sufficient resources for the closing phase, the manager should work with the program sponsor to see if someone can be brought in to work with the program or project manager to handle the closing tasks. Other considerations for ways to best manage conflicts in the various phases of the life cycle follow.

Initiating Phase

During the initiating phase on a program or project, the first step is to prepare a charter to describe the key roles, responsibilities, accountabilities, and authority of the program and project manager. The sponsor should prepare this charter, but in many situations, the program or project manager must do it and then have it approved by the sponsor, members of the governance board or steering committee, if applicable, functional managers, and other key stakeholders. The program or project manager can use this charter to obtain needed resources from functional managers throughout the organization.

The program or project manager attends to all activities that are required to begin a major piece of work that is linked to the organization's strategic goals and objectives, including identifying key resources or required personnel, determining specific success criteria and how success will be measured, specifying required technology and other resources, and clarifying roles and responsibilities and policies and procedures. If the organization is at a high level of maturity in program and project management, it probably has a detailed methodology to follow. Some aspects of this methodology, however, may not be required for a given program or project. If this is the case, to avoid future conflicts later, especially if there is an audit, the program or project manager should consult with the enterprise program or project management office (EPMO) staff and get a waiver from key requirements in the methodology that are not applicable.

Meredith and Mantel (2009) note the need during the initiating phase to focus on setting the stage for open discussion of conflicts. Team members take their cues from the leader at this formative stage. If the program or project manager is sending the message that conflict should be avoided, then team members will respond accordingly. This situation is particularly true if the team members are new to the organization or are more junior and have a diminished sense of their own competencies. At the beginning of a project, at the kickoff meeting, encourage the entire team to look at conflict in a positive light rather than viewing it as something to be avoided and to frame issues as problems team members can solve collectively.

Parker (1994) points out the importance of setting clear goals at the beginning of a program or project, especially when working with a cross-functional team, as a way to ward off future conflicts. He explains the importance of having a common goal that all members of the team support. A team charter also is critical at this stage; it promotes team buy-in and commitment by taking the overarching goals from the program or project goals and making them more specific to the work to be done by the team.

During the initiation phase, the program or project manager can establish a good precedent for handling conflict by serving as an example, role-modeling conflict resolution behavior early and often, and reinforcing that behavior in team members.

Planning Phase

One of the main challenges for the leader during the project planning phase is developing relationships with key stakeholders such as the supporting functional managers. As program and project managers can attest, relationships with functional managers can be fraught with complexities as the program or project manager attempts to gain the needed funds, materials, and personnel.

Working with a functional manager presents many opportunities for conflict. The program or project manager must clearly think through the needs, priorities, and motivations of the functional manager—which may be different from those of the program or project manager—as fully and as carefully as possible.

While the program or project manager and functional manager are building a relationship, the functional manager may attempt to resolve a conflict by claiming to be the "technical" expert, while indirectly casting the program or project manager in the less technically sophisticated role of a "generalist." It is best for the program or project manager not to confront the functional manager directly if he or she takes this approach because the functional manager will likely react defensively. The best approach is for the program or project manager to let those comments pass and to stay persistently focused on specific requirements. The program or project manager is well advised to simply acknowledge the functional manager's competency in the technical area and keep the discussion moving forward.

Executing Phase

This phase is the longest in both the program and project management life cycles. Typical conflicts revolve around technical issues the team encounters. By this time team members are familiar with one another, and each person understands what he or she is to contribute. Everyone on the team should understand how other team members can help if needed. For virtual teams, it is critical that the program or project manager set up a method everyone on the team can use to communicate regularly.

Key issues during this stage involve the resolution of risks and issues. The team should be able to resolve most of them on their own. If project work is being done within a program structure, team members should tell the project manager about any risks or issues and how they have been resolved so that he or she can inform the program manager in case the issue or risk involves other components of the program. No one should be afraid to escalate an issue or risk to a higher-level person. This includes the program manager, who should consult the governance board or steering committee when necessary. The portfolio manager should be consulted or informed about risks or issues that could affect another program or project underway elsewhere in the organization.

The project manager leading a project involving railroad safety retired, and a new project manager was hired to fill this position. This new manager took a command-and-control approach unlike the collaborative, participative approach of his predecessor. The project sponsor thought the team was working well together because the project manager called her daily to tell her about the work underway, though he also tended to talk about things not related to the project. She was unaware that the team, previously a high-performing group, had regressed into a storming team because of the personality of the project manager.

As the deadline for the project's deliverable approached, she learned that the team had made little progress; the project manager was focusing on other work because this was not his only assignment. The team members had been afraid to tell the sponsor about their conflicts with the project manager because of the project manager's command-and-control approach. It took heroic efforts on the part of the sponsor and the team members, plus the previous project manager's help, at the sponsor's request, to complete the project on time.

Other conflicts during this phase involve personalities. Team members are under stress to complete the program and deliver its promised benefits or to complete project deliverables on time and ensure customer satisfaction. Burnout is common during this stage, and program and project managers should be alert to signs of significant stress in team members so they can intervene and help as needed.

Program or project managers also may have to counsel dissatisfied team members. If a team member is disgruntled because he or she is not achieving a personal goal on the project, the program or project manager can respond by:

- Talking with the team member and acknowledging that his or her personal goals may not be addressed during this project.

- Encouraging him or her to establish new personal goals for the remainder of the program or project that might increase his or her motivation.

Closing Phase

One might think the closing phase is rather easy because the work of the program or project has been completed, but in reality, it presents new challenges for the leader. Team members are often emotionally and intellectually fatigued. The pressure to complete tasks against time and resource limits has diminished personal resiliency. Team members may be uncertain about their next assignments, which can distract them from their closing responsibilities. Some team members may experience a sense of loss when they must emotionally disengage from the team and the program or project, which also can hamper productivity.

The program or project manager should be sensitive to these potential sources of conflict when driving the group toward project completion and closure. During the closeout period, the program or project manager can be helpful by:

- Assuming that each team member may be a little burned out and not at full emotional or intellectual strength

- Paying individual attention to each team member, noting the best ways to help each one flourish during this trying period.

The Thomas-Kilmann Model of Conflict Resolution

The Thomas-Kilmann Conflict Mode Instrument (TKI) is a self-assessment tool based on work in conflict resolution by Thomas and Kilmann (1974). This instrument helps the user define his or her primary and secondary conflict resolution styles, which include "competitor," "accommodator," "avoider," "compromiser," and "collaborator." Many portfolio, program, and project managers and team members have found this instrument a helpful way to get a quick assessment of their preferred conflict resolution approach. By knowing one's primary and secondary conflict resolution method through the TKI, one can then be aware if he or she is over-using a preferred style when another approach might be more beneficial given the situation.

The TKI is based on work done by Blake and Mouton (1964), who identified five methods of conflict resolution. The methods differ primarily in the degree of assertiveness and cooperation shown by the person who employs them. Their work led to the current concept of five conflict resolution modes (PMI 2008a):

1. Smoothing

2. Forcing

3. Withdrawal

4. Compromising

5. Problem solving.

Combining the Blake and Mouton work with that of the TKI, there are five main approaches to conflict resolution:

1. Smoothing or accommodating

2. Forcing or competing

3. Withdrawing or avoiding

4. Compromising

5. Problem-solving or confronting.

A sixth mode is collaborating, which is similar to problem-solving or confronting.

The following sections describe these approaches and how they are used in portfolio, program, and project management. Each style is appropriate in certain situations, and each person uses all five styles from time to time. The TKI instrument identifies one's primary and secondary conflict resolution style, but everyone uses all five styles from time to time. Kirchof and Adams (1982) note that in project management, the most effective one is problem-solving or confronting, but they add, "No single 'best' method of dealing with conflict exists. Depending on the situation, the project manager needs to have the ability to use all of the conflict management methods as necessary" (p. 29).

Smoothing or Accommodating

This approach involves retreating from an actual or perceived conflict situation (PMI 2008a). The accommodating individual displays a high degree of cooperation but is low on assertiveness. Often, the accommodating person focuses on meeting the needs of the other person, occasionally at the expense of his or her own agenda. Examples of accommodating or smoothing statements include:

- "That's fine... we can do it whenever you want."

- "Let's try to get some more information and then revisit the problem."

- "Maybe we can find someone else who might help us. Let's not take any drastic action now."

Using the smoothing or accommodating approach to conflict management can help a person demonstrate open-mindedness, particularly during the early, formative stages of the team. Other reasons for using this approach include preserving harmony and avoiding pointless debate over insignificant matters.

But overuse of smoothing or accommodating can severely undercut a portfolio, program, or project manager's standing in the eyes of team members and other important stakeholders. The manager who overuses it may be viewed as weak and ineffectual, and team members who believe that their positions and needs are not being pursued forcefully may become angry. When considering taking an accommodating approach, the portfolio, program, or project manager should first answer the following questions:

- Is accommodation too much a part of my character, something that I use too often?

- Will my team react negatively to the use of accommodation?

- What are the long-term implications for my reputation in the organization if I accommodate the other party?

Forcing or Competing

The forcing or competing approach is one in which one person pushes his or her point of view at the expense of others, creating a win-lose situation (PMI 2008a). Kirchof and Adams (1982) say that the forcing or competing approach is valid when time is of the essence, stakes are high, and no other alternatives exist.

This approach is grounded in a combination of assertiveness and uncooperativeness. It is often driven by a need for power, with individual concerns and goals pursued at the expense of other parties' goals. It can be useful in specific situations in which unpopular actions must be taken, in a fast-paced environment, and when an individual is certain that his or her position is correct.

For example, assume you are managing a construction project. Two of your team members are engaged in a heated discussion. You believe you must intervene; there is no time for arguments. You decide that you need to tell them what to do so the project is not delayed. As another example, a portfolio manager might need to resort to forcing or competing if he or she learns that someone in the organization is pursuing a project that has not been formally approved through the portfolio management process.

Here are examples of forcing or competing statements a manager can use when the situation warrants:

- "Bill, I understand that you want to do it your way, but I cannot approve that change. We have to follow the existing document."

- "We have to get this deliverable to the client tomorrow; while other options may be more desirable, we lack the time to explore them now, so save your opinions for later, and we will discuss them."

- "I know you do not like the EPMO's policies, but we have to follow them because we have a quality audit scheduled in one week. After the audit, we can meet with the EPMO staff to discuss your concerns."

While forcing or competing may be effective in certain situations, it must be used judiciously, not as a primary tool. When it is applied in the wrong setting or at the wrong time, it can stalemate the conflict, alienate stakeholders, prevent the other party from being heard, and cause team members to lose sight of the overall goals and objectives of the program or project. Before using the forcing or competing approach to conflict resolution, a manager should:

- Attempt to use other, less confrontational approaches

- Consider the long-term effects of the approach on ongoing working relationships with all stakeholders.

Withdrawing or Avoiding

The withdrawal or avoiding approach is one in which the individual retreats from what he or she perceives to be either an actual or a potential conflict situation (PMI 2008a). This approach, of course, fails to resolve the issue, so as Kirchof and Adams (1982) point out, it is not one to follow if you desire long-term resolution.

Examples of withdrawal or avoiding statements include:

- "I realize that's an issue… let's leave it for now and get back to it next week."

- "Let's bring in a facilitator to help us with this issue and resolve it then."

- "We can wait on this one a while because we have more pressing problems to solve, so we will bring it up during the quarterly meeting of the steering committee, when it reviews the existing portfolio."

Withdrawal or avoiding is acceptable when the issue at hand is trivial, if there is little chance of winning an argument, if more information or data are needed, or when interactions are emotionally heated and a cooling-off period is warranted. This approach can be harmful, however, when it results in unnecessary delays for the program or project or when it hinders communication. Moreover, someone who regularly responds to conflict by withdrawing runs the risk of being perceived by others as too passive. Before applying the avoiding approach to conflict, the program or project manager should:

- Determine whether the issue is crucial or trivial
- Assess the risk of possible delay in completing the deliverables
- Consider the effect on personal reputation and the perception of others.

Compromising

Compromise is used to find solutions that bring a degree of satisfaction to all parties (PMI 2008a). Kirchof and Adams (1982) note that it is especially useful in contract negotiations and in informal negotiations, especially if the project manager can afford to give up something in return for agreement.

In this approach to conflict resolution, both individuals give a little and try to find middle ground. An example of a compromising statement is "OK, I can change the completion date, but I need you to alter the amount of funding I will receive." Compromise seems similar to the confronting or problem-solving approach, but it is a more short-term solution; it works well in situations in which temporary agreements need to be reached quickly.

Filey (1975) points out that because team members and managers are basically interdependent, they may choose to use the compromising approach because they want to resolve conflicts quickly, believing that continued disagreement is more costly than compromising.

Program or project managers should consider using compromise when:

- A short-term action needs to be taken quickly, and the compromise may not be of great significance

- A need to demonstrate openness and flexibility exists

- It can easily lead to a contract that is critical to the program or project and that both parties can support

- The manager must obtain a key resource from a functional manager; the program or project manager can offer support for the functional manager's team on a technical issue in exchange.

Compromise directs the energies of the people involved toward one another, and they approach issues as solutions rather than problems. The people involved want to sacrifice, but they are not necessarily focused on devising a solution that is beneficial to all parties. The conflict ends when all involved accept the proposed compromise.

As with the confronting/problem-solving and accommodation/smoothing approaches, the manager who uses compromise runs the risk of being perceived as too willing to give in to the other side or to give up on his or her original position.

Problem-Solving or Confronting

The manager or team member who emphasizes both assertiveness and cooperation and is willing to consider the merits of the other person's perspective takes a problem-solving/confronting approach to conflict. This manager has a give-and-take attitude, and he or she works to combine the best of both parties' positions. This approach is ideal for use in culturally diverse teams because it brings divergent points of view together for a common solution.

A project manager leading an effort to reorganize a government agency noted that the agency lacked an IT group and was using a variety of contractors with varying results and without a single point of contact. No one in the organization had the needed competencies to oversee the contractors and ensure that the requirements were met. The project manager recommended that as part of this reorganization the agency set up an IT department. While the administrator supported this recommendation, none of the senior staff wanted to assume the responsibility of supervising IT staff and contractors. The administrator did not want to force someone to take on this new group and instead hoped someone would volunteer to do so. He met with the senior staff again to see if someone would volunteer. When no one did, rather than simply appoint someone to do it, he said, "Let's sleep on this matter for a while, and we will meet again and try to resolve this conflict." This was essentially a withdrawing/avoiding approach to the conflict.

In the meantime, chaos continued, and the agency ended up not getting the results it needed from the contractor staff. Finally, an audit by the inspector general of the department made the same recommendation: This agency needed an IT department. The administrator could no longer "sleep" on the matter and instead got the senior staff together. This time, he used a problem-solving/confronting approach as he told the staff members it was essential that they reach an agreement on how to handle the IT problems. He asked the group to meet for a day to come up with a solution everyone would support. During the meeting, one of the leaders accepted responsibility. The other leaders indicated they would support him by setting up a steering committee to oversee the operations of this group and make sure it followed project management practices. The steering committee decided to conduct group interviews of candidates for the IT director position to ensure the person selected had the necessary skills and competencies in IT and in project management.

PMI (2008a) recommends the problem-solving or confronting approach. It is the preferred conflict resolution method in project management, especially if time is not a major issue and the parties involved trust one another. This means it is especially helpful in a program or project team that is in the performing stage and in which mutual respect and trust exists among team members.

Some examples of confronting/problem-solving statements are:

- "This is a good idea. I had not thought of it before. Let me tell you about my idea, and then maybe we can somehow combine them."

- "I like your approach, but before we adopt it, I would like to provide some information about another way we might solve this issue that builds on your suggestion."

- "Your suggestion is a good one for us to consider, but before we adopt it, I would like to involve some other people from our team with expertise in this area. I will plan a brainstorming session to see if we are definitely on track with this solution."

The emphasis in this approach is on developing a long-lasting solution. Other programs and projects underway in the organization may benefit from the solution, so it may be helpful to involve the EPMO staff as well to document lessons learned and for knowledge management purposes.

On virtual teams, using the problem-solving or confronting approach may require more planning to ensure that the key people are available to help solve the problem. It also may be beneficial to use a facilitator (this could be a suitable role for an affiliation-type person who is not directly involved in the conflict) to assist in alternatives analysis to explore and document all possible solutions before determining which solution to pursue. (A facilitator may also be appropriate on co-located teams to help to make sure everyone on the team contributes and interacts with one another.)

Problem-solving/confronting is ideal for use in situations in which both positions are considered important and viable; insights from both perspectives are valid. The emphasis is on clarifying areas about which there is agreement and disagreement. The parties involved discuss facts and feelings and offer feedback without fear of reprisal (Filey 1975). It is important, for example, to use this approach when developing a portfolio management process so that all units of the organization will support it.

But even this approach has some negative aspects. It is generally inappropriate in situations in which a quick response is necessary, as in an emergency, because the approach does not allow for immediate action. It also may result in a faulty product if some of the integrated points were incorrect and were not explored in detail before the solution was determined. Including a subject matter expert or a customer representative in resolving the conflict can help ensure the end result is acceptable.

The portfolio, program, or project manager should address these questions when considering taking a problem-solving/confronting approach:

- Are both positions really important and accurate, warranting a collaborative approach?

- Will the resulting product warrant the extra time that a collaborative approach requires?

Collaborating

PMI (2008a) adds collaborating to the five classic conflict resolution approaches discussed thus far, noting that it serves to incorporate multiple points of view from different perspectives and then merges them, leading to consensus and commitment. It is similar to the problem-solving/confronting approach.

Building a Culture of Conflict Resolution

To facilitate a team culture in which conflicts are resolved effectively, the program or project manager should:

- Emphasize early in the program or project that conflicts will occur, and let the team know how to escalate them as necessary.

- Encourage the team to refer to the team charter when attempting to resolve a conflict, and revisit the charter periodically in team meetings to ensure that it is effective.

- Continually communicate the vision for the program or project and its importance to the organization to make sure everyone knows their specific roles and responsibilities and their importance to team success.

- Point out that conflicts, if managed effectively, can be used to generate new ideas and creative solutions to problems the team may be facing.

- Review conflicts that have occurred to determine if changing any processes or procedures the team may be using to do its work is warranted. Involve the team in the change process as necessary.

- Show genuine interest in the work each team member is doing at group meetings and in one-on-one meetings, phone calls, emails, or instant messages.

- Remove any barriers to communication, such as a lack of common software, to facilitate more effective communications so that when conflicts do surface, team members are less likely to avoid dealing with them.

- Ask probing, open-ended questions to determine whether there are conflicts that team members are not talking about openly with others.

- Actively listen to all stakeholders, even those who may not have a direct interest in a specific phase of the program or project, to broaden your perspective and potentially avert conflicts.

When the program or project manager embraces and processes conflict in a constructive manner:

- An intellectually stimulating environment is built as team members challenge paradigms and constructs, pushing their performance to higher levels.

- Teams avoid groupthink; members challenge status quo approaches to solving problems.

- Opportunities emerge to forge improved working relationships and to revitalize team energy.

Conflict Resolution Checklist

The following questions and answers can help you resolve a conflict in a productive, efficient way.

1. *What phase is the program or project in?* Each phase has unique sources of conflict.

- *Initiating phase.* Conflicting priorities, administrative procedures, and schedules are common in this stage.

- *Planning phase.* Conflicting priorities, procedures, and schedules can affect the program or project in this phase, too. Issues with functional managers and general personality disputes also may give rise to conflicts.

- *Executing phase.* Schedules, technical challenges, and staffing issues are often sources of conflict.

- *Closing phase.* In addition to schedules, clashing personality styles (possibly due to job stress and fatigue) and staffing uncertainties (with regard to team members' next assignments) can be primary sources of conflict (Thamhain and Wilemon 1975).

Managers who are aware of the kinds of conflict common in each phase can maintain the perspective needed to respond appropriately.

2. *Is the conflict the result of a lack of information or knowledge?*

A lack of information often results from inadequate communication among stakeholders. Make sure all important information (both factual and personal or feeling-based) is communicated to stakeholders. Such efforts to keep communication flowing are especially crucial when working with virtual teams.

3. *Is the source of the conflict functionally based?*

Functionally based conflicts arise between program and project managers and functional managers or between portfolio managers and their stakeholders. The project team or an external interested party (such as the customer, a subcontractor, or the public) may also cause a functionally based conflict—i.e., a conflict in which one's authority and accountability are unclear.

When working with functional managers, program and project managers can minimize the risk of these conflicts by striving to understand the functional manager's needs and concerns. Problem-solving/confronting approaches are appropriate when working with functional managers. For example, if an organization is undergoing downsizing, and if functional managers are rewarded when their staff members are fully employed, a program or project manager can point out to the functional manager that the upcoming program or project work will ensure that certain people on the functional manager's staff are fully employed. Program or project managers can then work with the functional manager to prepare a resource management plan to show specifically when and for how long a functional team member will be needed, whether the work is full- or part-time, and when the team member can expect to be released from the program or project. Both functional and program or project members also can determine how they will recognize the team member's work on the program or project in addition to the usual work he or she does for the functional organization.

Similarly, portfolio managers should strive to use problem-solving/confronting approaches when trying to obtain sponsors' and other managers' commitment to the portfolio management system and buy-in to its value. They also should solicit ideas for improvement from these stakeholders, demonstrating that they are receptive to change and continuous improvement.

4. *Is the conflict personality-based?*

Personality-based conflicts include clashes of personal styles; for example, conflict might develop when two people with competitive styles deal with each other. Understanding the psychological preferences defined by the Myers-Briggs Type Indicator (MBTI) can be helpful in resolving personality-based conflicts.

Managing Agreement

Conflict can be resolved through various forms of agreement, such as accommodation, collaboration, and compromise. One potentially negative aspect of these agreement-based strategies, however, is the risk that necessary team conflict may be overlooked, resulting in less optimal solutions coming to the forefront. The portfolio, program, or project manager may be viewed as an inadequate manager of agreement if stakeholders and team members never bring appropriate conflict to the surface.

Harvey (1974) devised the Abilene paradox to elucidate the consequences of excessive agreement, the result of efforts to avoid conflict and offending others. Through an example of a group of people deciding to go to Abilene, Texas, though no one actually wanted to go at all, Harvey illustrated the truth that people in groups often do things that they really do not want to do just to avoid a conflict. Their agreement is really a mask, and serious problems may lie ahead for both the organization and the people involved.

Team members and portfolio, program, and project managers can easily fall into the trap of excessive agreement. People within groups can slip into groupthink, the creation of unwritten group norms regarding how tasks should be accomplished. These unwritten rules of behavior—in this case, the need to agree with the manager or with other team members as a means of demonstrating support—become established and codified as a result of team members taking performance cues from the behavior of the team leader.

Under the influence of groupthink, team members may withhold disparate points of view because they are concerned about not being viewed as team players. As team members continue to withhold contrary views, they become disengaged, motivation wanes, and innovation suffers. "Agreement" keeps the program or project moving forward, but often at the expense of the quality and sophistication of the work.

How can you as a manager manage the risk of having too much agreement on your team? The following are some ideas to consider:

- Observe and understand closely your own approach to conflict resolution. Are you an accommodator? A confronter?

- Consider whether you reward or show some type of favoritism toward team members who follow your unspoken requests for "agreement."

- Share the Abilene paradox with your team during its kickoff meeting and encourage team members to guard against similar situations. Create an environment that encourages active discussions of issues involving the team and the program or project work. This process should be combined with the development of a team charter laying out ground rules for the team, including guidelines for open and honest communication on matters of conflict.

Consequences are significant at the program level if there is too much agreement. For example, if everyone on a project team agrees with an approach to resolve a risk without adequately discussing all alternatives and later the response proves unsuccessful, not only is the specific project affected, but other projects in the program also may suffer if the response involved other work underway. If the entire team is in agreement on an issue because they have not really discussed alternatives and the program or project manager does not inform the governance board about the issue, other programs or projects may be affected. At the portfolio level, if everyone unquestioningly follows an outdated portfolio management process, and no one attempts to review and revise it, the organization may stagnate. For example, people may be discouraged from submitting new ideas by a process that does not make sense.

Summary

Conflict is a natural part of any program or project and also is natural at the portfolio level. Ideally, the conflicts that surface create an intellectually challenging and stimulating setting.

Addressing conflict in an active fashion is key for the successful portfolio, program, or project manager. Left unaddressed, conflict impedes the development of effective interpersonal relationships among team members and other stakeholders.

Conflict can be resolved through a number of approaches, including smoothing/ accommodating, forcing/competing, withdrawing/avoiding, compromising, confronting/problem-solving, and collaboration. Each of these approaches can be effective, depending on how it is applied and the situation at hand.

To successfully resolve conflicts, the portfolio, program, or project manager must first be aware of his or her own preferred approach to resolving conflict. This self-awareness serves as the foundation from which the manager can make necessary adjustments when working with team members who have different personality styles and respond to conflict differently.

Managing agreement is another challenge for portfolio, program, and project managers; too much agreement in a team often masks conflict and hinders the free exchange of disparate ideas, which can lead to creative and innovative solutions for programs and projects, as well as breakthroughs and transformation at the organizational level.

Discussion Questions

A project manager in an aerospace company was leading a multidepartmental team assigned to work with another company to develop a new product. Each company had recently undergone significant layoffs, and the mutual goal was to use this new joint project to boost the viability of both organizations.

The project manager, aware that team members from both companies were still stunned by the recent layoffs, tried to adopt a posture that would help the team members remain positive and stay motivated. But the manager's approach was misguided.

During the first several project team meetings, the manager minimized conflicts between team members from both companies. The teams never addressed disagreements over the technological requirements, and the project manager did not try to resolve disputes among team members regarding roles, responsibilities, and reporting relationships. The project manager believed that these issues would clear themselves up over time.

During the project planning phase, the team members and the sponsors noticed that core priorities had not been established and that no one had obtained key commitments from senior managers. On top of this, teamwork was minimal because the teams had not addressed their personal clashes over roles, style, and status. Conflicts became the norm among the team.

1. What should the project manager have done in this situation to avoid these problems in the first place?
2. Now that team conflicts are the norm, what type of conflict resolution approach would be the most appropriate for the manager to use?
3. Why do you think this manager avoided active conflict resolution?
4. If you are working for a manager who tends to avoid conflict, but you realize that conflicts are arising that are detrimental to your team's work, what can you as a project team member do? What strategies would you use?

Critical Incidents: Coping with Traumatic Events 9

A critical incident is a painful or traumatic event that is outside the range of normal day-to-day events and involves some component of loss or harm. The event elicits a variety of emotions in the individuals involved, including grief, shock, fear, confusion, or numbness. Examples of critical incidents include the death or sudden illness of a team member, violence in the workplace, the experience of surviving a natural disaster, or being the victim of domestic violence (Herman 1992). Less obvious events, such as the firing of a valued team member, extensive company layoffs, client or supplier delays, negotiation issues, taxation problems, or regulatory compliance dilemmas also can be critical incidents. Research by Mallak and Kurstedt (1997) shows that crises are inevitable in projects, and as a result, project-based organizations must learn how to deal with them on a regular basis.

Critical incidents affect not only the individual team member (the victim) but the team as well. The portfolio, program, or project manager can take actions that will help the individual and the team return to normal levels of productivity. In situations in which a critical incident causes extensive disruption to a team, the manager may need to implement a recovery plan, or the EPMO may need to bring in a program or project recovery manager, to save the program or project.

Critical incidents such as a hurricane, a fire, a death on site, or a threat to the organization's security can affect the entire organization, whether it is small or large. Incidents of this scale focus negative attention on the organization and adversely affect its financial condition, stakeholders, stockholders, and customers as well as its reputation in the marketplace (Reid 2000).

They may also necessitate rebalancing and reoptimizing the portfolio. They may be abrupt or cumulative, but regardless, executives and other managers are not prepared for their occurrence. They are not considered during risk management planning or during the continual risk identification process, so responses to them are not planned or considered in advance.

Impact on the Victim

A team member who experiences a critical incident, such as a physical assault, may exhibit a number of reactions and behaviors that will affect his or her work performance. These may include:

- *Heightened fear and anxiety.* The traumatized individual is more vigilant and on guard and is easily agitated by noises, routine events, or any situation or stimulus that is reminiscent of the traumatic event.

- *Somatic problems.* Sleep disturbances, fatigue, changes in appetite, increased risk for illness, and weight gain or weight loss are examples of somatic problems. It is common for some trauma victims to have difficulty falling asleep or staying asleep. Other victims may sleep for 10 to 12 hours every day but still feel fatigued and listless.

- *Temporary cognitive effects.* Decreased concentration skills, a reduction in short-term memory capabilities, confusion, a loss of objectivity, and a diminished capacity to make decisions are examples of cognitive effects following trauma. During the weeks immediately following a traumatic event, some victims have difficulty learning new tasks that require significant cognitive focus and attention.

- *Presence of intrusive thoughts.* For many trauma victims, flashback memories of the traumatic event flood their consciousness with little or no warning. What makes these flashbacks so frightening and upsetting is that other sensory experiences accompany the visual memory of the event. Frequently, the victim will notice smells, textures, and other sensory cues that were a part of the original event.

- *Emotional problems.* Depression, emotional numbing, apathy, alienation, and feelings of helplessness and isolation are examples of emotional reactions to trauma. Each trauma victim responds to a situation with different feelings, based in part on his or her personality and history before the event.

- *Issues with substance abuse.* During the tumultuous, emotional periods following a traumatic event, it is not unusual for the victim to seek any form of available relief. Occasionally, this search for relief results in periods of substance abuse as the victim attempts to self-medicate the pain away through excessive use of alcohol or drugs.

Helping the Victim

While the victim needs to take the lead in adopting coping strategies, the program or project manager can be helpful by:

- *Encouraging the victim to talk with others,* such as family members and friends.

- *Encouraging the victim to continue regular activities,* such as spending casual time with friends and family, and to stay involved in activities that have been pleasurable in the past.

- *Encouraging the use of humor, when appropriate, to get through this period.* Even during periods of crisis, one may be able to find small aspects of the experience that are humorous. These rare moments should be enjoyed; they are subtle reminders that life may not always look as dark as it looks now.

- *Suggesting counseling resources if the problems persist.* It is not the role of the program or project manager to direct a team member to personal counseling, but such a resource can be helpful if the victim of the traumatic event feels that he or she is not making progress in recovering from the incident. Individual counseling or psychotherapy with a professional experienced in helping people deal with trauma can aid the natural recovery process and help the victim return to normal levels of productivity. The human resources department should be able to make such a referral should the team member desire professional assistance.

- *Considering whether it makes sense to temporarily reassign some of the person's tasks* to other team members.

In assisting a victim of trauma, the program or project manager should remember that the primary goal is to maintain a supportive and understanding but business-focused relationship with the affected team member. The manager should avoid the inclination or pressure to become a counselor. He or she should respond with empathy but should also feel comfortable setting some limits on discussion of the traumatic event. The trauma victim may ask what other team members know about the details of the traumatic event. He or she may not want to have to tell his or her story repeatedly to all the team members. As team leader, you can pass that request on to the other team members.

Frequently, trauma symptoms are worse after a week or more has passed following the event; performance may actually decrease over time. Continue to strive toward a posture that is supportive, attentive, and task-focused.

Impact on the Project Team

When a critical incident strikes a member of the project team, other team members will be affected in personal and professional ways. Consequently, the project itself may suffer. The reactions of team members will vary and will often be surprising. The most common reactions that team members have when a traumatic event happens to a fellow team member include:

- *Emotional reactions.* Team members will display a variety of emotions, including sadness, shock, anxiety, denial, and remorse. Some people will display these feelings immediately, while others will show the feelings after a day or two has passed. Others may display no overt emotions or feelings.

- *Responses that affect workplace duties.* Some team members will talk among themselves for a few hours, unable to focus on the work to be done. Others will ask questions and gather information. Some people may volunteer to pick up some of the extra workload.

- *Surfacing of old grievances.* Traumatic events often evoke old issues, angers, emotional injuries, and grievances held by the team members. For example, the death of a team member may prompt a surviving team member to say that he or she thinks the company has always worked people too hard. Often, the grievances that emerge have no direct connection to the current issue. When these feelings surface, the project manager should work to help the team maintain its focus on goals, objectives, and deliverables.

The project manager may react to a trauma with personal guilt, questioning whether he or she could have done anything to prevent the event. Frequently, the event is clearly out of the manager's control. However, events whose causative factors are less clear, such as an employee who has been working long hours of overtime experiencing a stroke, often cause the manager to examine his or her own behavior. Specifically, the project manager may wonder if he or she pushed the team member too hard.

If you, as the manager, feel personally guilty or responsible for the traumatic event, you can try a personal exercise to help put those feelings in perspective. Take a piece of paper and divide the page down the middle into two columns. In the left-hand column, list all aspects of the traumatic event over which you had no control. For example, if a team member suffered a heart attack when traveling on business, items in the left column could include:

1. The team member was at high risk for heart attacks and had discussed his medical condition with you.

2. He had poor dietary habits.

3. Weather conditions delayed his travel and increased deadline pressures.

In the right-hand column, list factors over which you do have control. For example:

1. I can continue to push for an increase in staff, therefore reducing the need for individual team members to travel.

2. I can push for flex time for the team member as he recovers from the heart attack.

3. I can distribute some of his tasks to coworkers.

This method is a good way for a manager to take a realistic look at what he or she is and is not accountable and responsible for. Without this clear focus, it is easy for the manager to assume undue responsibility for certain types of traumatic events.

Impact on the Program Team

Because program teams are larger than project teams, it is not uncommon for people to be unaware of a critical incident that has affected a member of another project team within the program. However, the program team itself (project managers, people responsible for nonproject work, members of the EPMO, and any other core staff members reporting directly to the program manager) faces challenges similar to those a project team faces when a member is the victim of a crisis.

Each project manager, when a critical incident affects only his or her team, should inform the program manager as soon as possible so that he or she can offer assistance. For example, the program manager can help recruit someone from another project in the program to help out for a short period of time until the project team member can return to work or help the project manager quickly hire a replacement or find a consultant. If the project manager seems to feel personally guilty about the crisis, the program manager should talk privately with the project manager to reassure him or her that it is not his or her fault.

If a critical incident strikes the project manager, the program manager may need to step in and fill this role temporarily. (At the program or single-project level, this role would fall to the sponsor.)

What if the project manager abruptly quits the team, leaves the organization, or is fired? These possibilities are often overlooked, especially on high-performing teams. If this happens, the program manager must:

- Meet with the project team members as quickly as possible to share the facts about the situation

- Let the team know that, if the project manager was fired, it was not their fault and was due to other causes

- Tell the team that he or she is available to talk with team members individually to discuss what has happened

- Fill the role of project manager until someone else can be hired.

As the program manager or the program or project sponsor, you may at times be aware that a project manager is dissatisfied with his or her work but has a positive relationship with his or her team and can contribute to the organization's goals. You value this individual greatly, and in a sense his or her departure could in effect be comparable to a critical incident. In these cases, consider the following approaches to help retain this person:

- Meet with the person to discuss his or her long-term career goals and how you might help him or her realize them through work on this program or project.

- Assign someone else to manage a phase of the project that the person dislikes—for example, if he or she dislikes closing projects, you could choose a closing manager to fill in for this person.

- Offer educational opportunities, such as attendance at conferences, participation in training programs, or reimbursement for courses.

- Work with the person to outline a possible career path to show that the organization values his or her contributions and wants him or her to eventually become part of the management team.

- Create opportunities for this person to interact with members of upper management in forums such as a meeting of the portfolio review board or during luncheons to get to know executives one-on-one.

If the project manager remains dissatisfied but you still believe he or she is an asset to the organization, offer to reassign him or her to a functional unit or another project as quickly as possible. You do not want this manager's dissatisfaction to affect the team's morale. Locate a replacement quickly, and ask the former project manager to work with the replacement as necessary. If the project manager plans to leave the organization, ask him or her to do so as soon as possible, again so that his or her dissatisfaction does not affect the project team further.

Critical Incident Stress Debriefing

Immediately after a critical incident occurs, program and project managers should consider holding a critical incident stress debriefing (CISD). This debriefing is a structured meeting, usually facilitated by a mental health professional skilled in working with people who have faced trauma, in which employees are presented with the facts of the critical incident and are given an opportunity to ask questions or share their reactions.

The human resources department of most companies can identify a facilitator to lead this type of meeting. The debriefing is not group therapy. It is intended to help people begin to adjust to the loss and to help prevent a significant decrease in team productivity.

Beginning the Debriefing Meeting

The program or project manager opens the debriefing meeting by telling the team that the debriefer is present to help the team members process their reactions to the traumatic event. The debriefer tells the group that the meeting is confidential and that verbal participation (in an in-person meeting) or, for virtual teams, active participation in the videoconference or teleconference, is voluntary. (Before beginning a virtual meeting, make sure that all team members are available and able to use the technology and that the technology is ready to go.)

The first step is to ask each person to tell the group how he or she learned about the critical incident. As team members listen to each other speak, information gaps are filled. On large teams, several debriefing sessions may need to be held so everyone has an opportunity to speak. Each group should be fairly small; three to ten people may be best.

The debriefer does not push people to speak or to bring up strong feelings and emotions. The debriefer asks structured questions (such as "How did you learn about the incident?") to facilitate the discussion. The debriefer takes cues from the members and does not push beyond what is appropriate.

Letting Team Members Tell Their Stories

As team members tell their stories, the debriefer periodically acknowledges what they are saying by commenting on the natural process of going through a trauma; for example, he or she might say, "As John is saying, shock and numbness are often big parts of these experiences."

The process continues, with team members occasionally and voluntarily offering favorite memories of the affected person or making suggestions about how they might help the victim's family. Many of these issues cannot be resolved immediately, so some of the CISD process is usually spent brainstorming how these personal needs can be addressed at a later time.

Usually, some team members remain silent. Other members may become overly involved in the process, talking too much and taking up too much time. The debriefer should be sensitive to their needs but should help establish some boundaries that reflect the purposes and limitations of the debriefing.

Concluding the Debriefing Meeting

Generally, a debriefing meeting lasts about 90 minutes. As the debriefing concludes, the debriefer summarizes the group's general thoughts and reactions. He or she may distribute written materials, often a two-page handout describing common reactions to trauma and the recovery steps the victim and others can take. If the organization has an employee assistance program, the debriefer provides the phone number and email, reminding team members that counseling services can be a helpful resource when going through a difficult time.

When the debriefing ends, the debriefer, the human resources representative, and the team leader meet separately to talk about how the meeting went and to discuss any follow-up steps. One of these steps may be for the counselor to be available on-site (if the team is co-located) or easily accessible by phone or email (if the team is virtual) for voluntary meetings and confidential discussions with employees.

In short, the goal of the debriefing is to support the affected team members by providing them with a safe setting to discuss initial reactions and to receive appropriate information on how to handle the normal processes of recovery and how to return to normal levels of productivity.

The Recovery Plan

Even in the best of situations, critical incidents can have such a negative effect on the status of the program or project that the manager must consider extraordinary measures to save the program or project from failure. When a crisis has a significant impact on project benefits, time, cost, technical performance, customer satisfaction, or overall value, the team should immediately begin a salvage process. This rescue attempt, although equally applicable to programs and to projects, is called project recovery here.

A project team that has had its efficiency, productivity, and focus disrupted by the turmoil resulting from traumatic events in the workplace is a team whose project is at risk. Four indicators in particular suggest that the project is in trouble and a project recovery plan should be considered:

- ***The project customer is giving signals of dissatisfaction with the product, service, or project status.*** These signals can be overt (such as an angry exchange during a project meeting or a critical letter or phone call) or subtle (such as not returning phone calls or barely participating during project reviews). Whether overt or subtle, these signals must be addressed immediately and actively. Waiting for the customer to come around and regain a positive attitude toward the project is risky and may result in permanent customer dissatisfaction over the life of the project and in the future.

- *An excessive amount of project rework is necessary because of poor project quality, team members' performance, or technical errors.* Technical errors have become routine, and ensuring quality is less often a priority on projects. Without giving adequate attention to quality assurance and quality control, project teams will continuously have to rework, which will affect their morale and lead to further customer and sponsor dissatisfaction later on in the project.

- *An unacceptable level of project variance in one or more key areas (project time, cost, technical performance, customer satisfaction, or benefit delivery) has become routine* for this team, possibly because the traumatic event forced everyone to fall behind in their work. Operating behind schedule often forces teams to rush their work, increasing the probability that the project's product, service, or result will have errors that require rework by the team. This process of rushing to catch up becomes a vicious cycle for the team. Trying harder and working longer hours do not necessarily mean reducing the key variances. In fact, trying harder often makes things worse and typically increases project costs because it requires overtime.

- *Standard project controls, such as earned value data, show that it will be basically impossible to get the project back on track.* This indicator is especially significant if the project has passed the 20 percent completion point and the cost and schedule variances are too major to overcome.

These four indicators of the need for project recovery are often obvious to the project manager. However, when the manager is dealing with the fallout from a traumatic event on the team, it is easy to miss these indicators. (Sometimes the project manager sees the symptoms of a problem but hopes that they correct themselves over time.) The goal is for the project manager to locate the root cause of the problem and to take action.

Taking Steps toward Project Recovery

There are four distinct steps to building a project recovery plan:

1. *Identify actions or alternatives* that will help eliminate the significant variances in project time, cost, and technical performance. The project manager should identify ways to minimize damage to the off-course project, such as adding or subtracting team members, obtaining additional funds or resources if needed, and revising the schedule to expedite delivery

of the product to the customer, even if this means deviating significantly from the plan or from the project management policies and procedures.

2. ***Take actions*** that may help reduce the project variances. The project manager might conduct team-customer meetings to establish a turnaround strategy, discuss possible recovery options, and conduct a concrete review of the project scope.

   This process may result in the preparation of a project recovery plan, with a schedule of activities to be performed during the recovery efforts and a budget for the recovery initiative. Activities might include adding or subtracting team members, acquiring additional funds or resources (through outsourcing or using resources elsewhere in the organization), revising the schedule through fast tracking or delaying certain tasks in the schedule not on the critical path, or taking other actions to expedite a reasonable delivery of the product, service, or result to the customer.

3. ***Closely monitor the project recovery plan against the executed actions.*** The project manager must review the revised scope of the project frequently, consult with subject matter experts regarding documentation, hold regular—as often as daily—status reviews with team members, and regularly schedule customer meetings, technical reviews, and audits.

4. ***Control specifications and alternatives*** designed to reduce the unacceptable variances. It is necessary to take actions to minimize the risk of project disaster and ensure that similar project variances do not occur again. Lessons learned from the problems encountered in the current project can be documented in a lessons-learned database or repository and applied proactively to establish risk-management responses for future work on the current project and for future projects in the organization.

Assessing Team Effectiveness and Performance

As the project manager begins to craft the four-step recovery strategy following a critical incident, he or she should assess the effectiveness of the project team as a whole as well as that of the individual team members. The project manager should review performance reports to determine the level of team performance and should investigate whether members are using the resources they are given to meet deadlines and milestones. Alternatively, the project manager can request feedback from all team members to evaluate how the team is functioning as a unit and how individual team members function when working alone.

The success of the recovery effort is not solely the responsibility of the project manager. Indeed, there are specific actions that team members must take to assist in the recovery process. Team member responsibilities include:

- Informing the project manager immediately as new project problems and risks are uncovered

- Actively supporting the project manager in developing and implementing project recovery strategies

- Regularly updating the project manager on the effectiveness of the recovery strategies, providing frequent status updates regarding project schedule, cost, and deliverables.

The Project Recovery Manager

Even the best project recovery plan is not always successful. In certain situations, the existing project structure (i.e., the project manager and the project team) may be unable to execute the recovery plan. The EPMO or project sponsor may need to identify and appoint a new person to serve as the project recovery manager and reassign the project manager to another initiative.

The primary mission of the project recovery manager is to ensure that project recovery risks are accurately defined, identified, and assessed so that concrete action can be taken. He or she may wish to establish a task force to focus on the recovery process. A recovery manager should have previous experience with similar projects and the skills needed to motivate the team members, work with the stakeholders, make decisions, and hold the team accountable for achieving the project's goals (Rad and Levin 2003).

The new manager must develop a clear project recovery plan that is approved and supported by internal management. Without management's true, meaningful support, the plan's chances of success are minimal. A key element of the recovery plan is the project recovery manager's review of the results of any project assessments conducted thus far by the original project manager and his or her team.

Once the recovery plan has been created and implemented, the recovery manager must focus on reviewing progress and assessing future risks. He or she can hold frequent reviews with the project team members and discuss risks at each project team meeting. After each review, the recovery manager must update the recovery plan as necessary. Also, the recovery manager must keep detailed records and track the financial implications of the action items in the recovery plan.

Another key focus for the recovery manager is making certain that communication with senior managers, functional managers, customers, suppliers, and other stakeholders is open, regular, and effective. The recovery manager should be aware of the type of communication stakeholders need and how often it should happen. He or she should consider preparing an analysis of stakeholder information requirements to be certain that important information is provided to project stakeholders in a timely manner. Stakeholders should also have access to information between scheduled communications.

The recovery manager should update the project's communications management plan, review its effectiveness frequently, and often ask, "Who else should we be talking with about the needs and status of the recovery effort?" During a stressful recovery effort, it is easy to overlook a key stakeholder because the team is focused on day-to-day activities.

Leading a project recovery effort can be a thankless job, given all the problems that must be corrected and the strong risk of high-visibility failure. This role is not for every project professional.

Leadership Skills

It is crucial that the recovery manager demonstrate leadership skills under trying circumstances. He or she must be able to:

- Motivate team members (see Chapter 3) and make difficult decisions
- Hold the work group accountable for achieving goals in a timely manner.

Interpersonal Skills

The recovery manager should be proficient in applying a wide variety of sophisticated interpersonal skills, including the ability to:

- Resolve conflicts (see Chapter 8)
- Build (or rebuild) a sense of team without critical fault-finding or finger-pointing (see Chapter 2)
- Make decisions (see Chapter 6).

Customer Relations Skills

The project recovery manager should also have excellent skills in customer relationship management. He or she must address customer issues and needs forthrightly without attempting to defend the previous work of the team. Trying to defend the team at this point leads to a "yes, but" interaction between the customer and the team that becomes circular and does not help get the project back on track.

Some project recovery managers enjoy the challenge of the recovery process but do not spend sufficient time on customer relationship management issues, choosing instead to immerse themselves in the technical content of the project and team details. It is often easier to avoid situations that may be confrontational. This is a natural response, but it can become a serious problem if the manager pays insufficient attention to customer satisfaction. Ideally, the recovery manager will balance time spent working on the technical details of the project with time spent addressing the customer's needs.

When working with customers, the recovery manager should avoid over-promising. Some recovery managers may try to play the hero; they imagine themselves swooping in during the crisis and saving the project and the organization's reputation with the customer. The danger of this approach is that the recovery manager may make unreasonable promises to the customer about what can be fixed in the situation. Unrealistic promises can come back to haunt the recovery manager, the team, and the organization not only during the current project but also in future business dealings with the customer.

To avoid the risk of overpromising, the recovery manager should:

- Assess and monitor his or her internal need to be viewed as the hero

- Give the customer realistic expectations of what is possible, as this becomes known

- Adopt a positive but realistic tone in communications, stressing all that can and will be done for the customer while accurately describing the limits and extent of recovery possibilities.

Communication Skills

At this point in the project, all stakeholders are aware that things have not been going well and tensions are high. Stakeholders such as project sponsors and customers do not want any surprises. The best approach to dealing with sponsors and customers is to keep them updated with both the good news and the bad news. The project recovery manager must be assertive in reaching out and communicating with key project stakeholders. He or she should provide regular updates and interact frequently with management and with customers.

Project Failure and Project Closure

Even with the best efforts, some project recovery efforts following critical incidents will fail, and the project should be terminated. The recovery effort—and the project—should be terminated when:

- The project has been delayed to the point that the result would be obsolete when completed.

- Final costs outweigh the benefits, or no additional funds are available for recovery.

- The project is so far out of control that it cannot be managed.

- Resources may be better used on other projects.

Although closing down a terminated project is never a pleasant task, it can be handled in an efficient and professional manner. During the closure process, the project recovery manager should have the following goals:

- Provide accurate and timely information.

- Be direct and clear with all stakeholders.

- Display sensitivity when communicating the reasons for the closure to the various stakeholders.

For many stakeholders, the closure will be a personal loss of significant emotional proportion—not to mention the damages to the organization's finances and reputation. The recovery manager's sensitivity when delivering this bad news can help team members maintain a positive personal, team, and organizational image as they move forward to the next project.

Tips for the Project Manager

Critical incidents in the project world require the project manager to address a number of issues and challenges. Project managers should consider the following suggestions when a critical incident or event strikes the project team:

1. Determine whether a critical incident debriefing should be held for team members.
2. During the aftermath of the critical incident, avoid the temptation to make unrealistic promises to team members and stakeholders.
3. Adopt realistic expectations regarding the team members' current ability to perform.
4. Adopt a balanced "yes, but" position with team members, saying in essence: "Yes, we have undergone a crisis, and we are all upset about its implications, but we still must find a way to focus on the tasks of the project the best we can."
5. Gradually set boundaries and limits with the team, acknowledging both the loss and the need to stay focused on the tasks at hand.
6. Monitor individual work performance, and address possible performance issues by talking with struggling team members, reminding them of the goals of the project, and offering internal and external resources that can help them achieve the desired level of performance.
7. As the team begins to stabilize post-crisis, determine whether the critical incident has been sufficiently detrimental to the progress of the project to warrant developing a project recovery strategy, bringing in a project recovery manager, and reassigning the project manager.

Summary

Risk management is an integral part of programs and projects, but many managers overlook risks involving people and instead concentrate on risks involving technical or process-related factors. Critical incidents present major risks when they occur, and though they happen less often than other risks, program and project managers should know how to respond to such events if necessary.

Whenever a program or project manager learns that a critical incident has affected a team member, such as in the case of an illness, the death of a family member, or some other major crisis, he or she should first obtain as much information about the incident as appropriate and then assemble the entire team for a meeting to discuss how it will address the situation. It may be helpful to hold a critical incident stress debriefing and involve the human resource department, which has more expertise in these situations and can facilitate the session and provide counseling services if necessary. It may also be necessary to prepare a recovery plan if the affected team member(s) can no longer complete his or her assigned tasks. Because the critical incident could possibly jeopardize the success of the program or project, it is important to consider and manage the recovery plan very carefully.

If the critical incident affects the program or project manager directly, a senior member of the team or an outside program or project manager may need to assume the manager's duties, work diligently to execute the recovery plan, and involve any stakeholders who can assist in keeping the program or project on track for success.

Discussion Questions

A project manager walked into her office on Monday morning, and her human resources representative immediately told her that one of her team members had died over the weekend following a business trip.

This team member, a telecommunications engineer, had suffered a stroke while traveling. She had been working long hours for months at a time, frequently volunteering to travel to other states to help fellow team members with difficult projects. She had trained many of the junior team members from their first days of employment at the company, and they had looked up to her as a mentor.

As the team members began arriving for work that Monday morning, the project manager wondered what she should do. If you were this project manager:

• How would you share the news with your team?

• What types of reactions and performance issues might you expect from your team members?

Future Issues, Career Management, and Thoughts on Interpersonal Issues

10

Future trends related to interpersonal issues and leadership have implications for portfolio, program, and project managers. Over the past two decades, the emphasis on interpersonal skills as a path to success has grown. As a portfolio, program, or project manager, you need to make conscious efforts to continually improve your performance and to actively manage your career. Paying attention to the basic but profound question of what it means to be a person can enrich your growth as a leader as you and your team members grapple with the many people challenges you will face in your work.

Future Issues and Challenges in Portfolio, Program, and Project Management

The profession of project management continues to grow and change at a rapid pace. In the past decade, we also have seen a greater emphasis on program management and portfolio management, with PMI's issuance of standards for these areas. In 2008, PMI issued new standards for the three portfolio, program, and project areas, along with a standard on organizational project management maturity, to ensure that the four of them would be complementary.

These publications are approved by the American National Standards Institutes as American National Standards.

The profession grows daily. More people are becoming members of PMI, the International Project Management Association (IPMA), and the Australian Institute of Project Management (AIPM). Further, more people are becoming certified by PMI as a CAPM (Certified Associate in Project Management), a PMP, or a PgMP; others are pursuing certifications from IPMA and AIPM. The International Organization for Standardization has certified the PMP and the PgMP programs.

At the same time, organizations are increasingly recognizing that programs and projects are assets to their work and are becoming more project-based. They also are focusing on portfolio management to ensure that they are pursuing the right programs and projects, given capacity limitations and the necessity of ensuring these programs and projects support the organization's strategic goals and objectives. Projects managed through programs provide greater overall benefits and more synergies, interdependencies, and effective resource allocation than if the projects in the program were managed in a standalone fashion.

Organizations are focusing on customer satisfaction, in addition to the triple constraint (on time, within budget, according to specification), and, even more importantly, on the value of portfolio, program, and project management and the enterprise program management office. Many organizations are also integrating business development and knowledge management into their program and project management processes.

As the profession continues its unprecedented growth, challenges are increasing as well. Programs and projects are far more complex than before. With virtual teams becoming the norm and not the exception, organizations have the opportunity to build a 24/7 workforce. Many find the virtual environment an ideal way to ensure that key subject matter experts are available regardless of their locations. The prevalence of virtual work also means we now tend to work with more people from different cultures who have different perspectives.

Downsizing continues, along with mergers and acquisitions. Organizations are performing programs and projects as joint ventures more frequently, often working with former competitors that are now considered valued partners or suppliers. Nothing seems to remain the same! Change is constant, and it should be embraced rather than resisted.

Improving Your Performance as a Portfolio, Program, or Project Manager

While portfolio and program management have become more significant to organizations, the project manager's work remains the cornerstone of the profession. Repeatable, successful projects (and programs) come from good processes and from project managers who continue to learn and improve their personal practices. As noted by Brown, Adams, and Amjad (2007), "successful project management relies almost entirely on the HC (human capital) that is embodied within the project manager as an individual ... project management is concerned with the provision of leadership ... we can expect this to cause project managers to depend on personal knowledge and experience that informs them *how* to lead in a continuously changing project environment" (p. 78).

It is never too late to focus on continuous improvement at any level. Jones (2000) noted that upper management and staff experience has a far greater impact on productivity than do effective methods or processes. At the same time, staff inexperience is much more detrimental to productivity than are ineffective methods or processes. Cockburn (2008) adds to Jones' work by explaining that we have long recognized how success is influenced by the people on a program or project and how they interact with one another and are treated by the leader, but we keep hoping some new process or tool or technique will relieve the need for talent and communication. It is actually the movement of ideas between people that makes projects more efficient.

O'Neill (1999) noted that people in project management spend less than 30 percent of their time on high-priority, value-adding activities. Instead, most of their time is spent coordinating initiatives and working with others—that is, solving people problems. The emphasis on people issues is even greater at the program level: The program manager coordinates the work done at the project level, works to solve escalated issues and risks, and communicates with a wide range of stakeholders. Interpersonal issues abound at the portfolio level, too, because of the continual rebalancing of portfolios and the need to communicate changes as soon as possible to a large number of involved stakeholders and to explain the importance of these changes.

Creating a Personal Improvement Plan

Because portfolio, program, and project managers spend so much time on people issues, it is crucial for every manager (and for team members as well) to craft his or her own personal improvement plan.

The first step in creating such a plan is to establish a baseline of your own level of people skills, knowledge, and competencies (Levin 1999). PMI's *Competency Development Framework*, second edition (2007), can assist in this effort. Also, reviewing the Software Engineering Institute's People Capability Model can be helpful. [Curtis, Hefley, and Miller, 2001].

Assess and document your best and worst performance on projects, with an emphasis on the people skills you used in each case. Note those aspects of your performance that you believed would work well but failed. Also note other situations in which you believed you would not succeed but were in fact successful. These observations will serve as the baseline that will enable you, going forward, to recognize whether your performance is improving or is remaining static.

The next step is to define and establish a personal process you can follow as you perform your work. The purpose of a process is to describe your intentions, which must meet your needs and will help guide your work. Focus on the aspects and areas of your work that you can control and influence as well as productive activities that add value, rather than on circumstances over which you lack control. Keep DeCarlo's words in mind: "The next century will put a premium on back to basics ... challenging us to redirect our energies to focus on those things that are within our power to change. The fact is that we can't change the competitive scene, the course of globalization, or projects that will become increasingly complex" (p. 428, 1997). We live in this new century today.

Establish objective performance criteria for yourself, and compare your own goals with those of your manager, your organization, and your customer. If your organization does not have performance plans, set one up to use for your own improvement. This approach may encourage others to do the same, especially when people notice the improvements you are making.

Strive to answer the following questions when creating your personal improvement plan:

- Where does my work package (if a team member), my project (if a project manager), or my program (if a program manager) fit within the overall strategic plan and portfolio of the organization?

- What is my organization's future strategy?

- Why do some projects or programs in my organization fail?

- Can I improve my own work and the processes I follow to do it by building on the work done by my peers and team members?

- What are the key characteristics of the programs and projects in my organization that succeed?

> While working on a maturity assessment project, a consultant noticed that a vendor's customer had detailed performance plans in place for everyone in the vendor's organization. The consultant interviewed the customer and learned that the customer expected the vendor's staff to have performance plans. The customer wanted the vendor's staff to link their performance plans to its own performance plans at each level. One member of the vendor's team, who was new to the company and had used performance plans in his previous position, created plans for himself and his team. The customer valued the plans and urged the rest of the vendor's staff to follow this project manager's lead. The goal was for everyone on the customer's side and the vendor's side to have common objectives and to pursue them for overall success.

Measure, analyze, and improve your work processes by evaluating the accuracy and effectiveness of your personal plan and processes, making adjustments as needed. Defining, measuring, and tracking work provides insight into your performance, especially your development of people skills (Humphrey 1995). For example, by tracking your work you can determine whether you had to communicate with more stakeholders, work with various team members to improve their performance, or needed more training to improve your own performance. Remember, just as if you were preparing a project plan, you can progressively elaborate your own processes. Keep in mind, also, that one process will not fit all the situations you will encounter in your work. Humphrey, Konrad, Over, and Peterson (2007) write that continuing to follow a process without adapting it as necessary may not benefit your organization; the organization could even miss making its commitments to its customers and users. Your own improvement may have larger implications for your organization.

However, similar to work on a project, you should recognize that even with the best intentions, a detailed plan, and a process, some problems will arise because change is constant. Do not be embarrassed by mistakes you make, but instead recognize that they are lessons learned for future improvement. Analyze your mistakes and accept responsibility for them. Your team will appreciate these efforts, and by accepting responsibility, you will build greater trust and lasting relationships.

Beyond developing a personal improvement plan, you can make additional efforts to further your mastery of people skills:

- Acquire the training you need to pursue a continuous improvement approach; if your organization lacks the resources to fund training courses, see if you can fund them yourself. Participate in some of the numerous free webinars available from PMI and other organizations.

- Search for practice opportunities for testing new skills. Consider your interpersonal skills to be prototypes and work to continually refine them. Ask peers for their support.

- View each program or project and each interaction with a key stakeholder, especially those who may not share your enthusiasm for what you are doing, as a learning opportunity, and share the lessons you have learned with others.

Striving for Excellence

Frame (1999) writes that one of the two or three most significant issues facing organizations today is competence. In the past, getting by was acceptable; today, getting by is a prescription for failure. Individuals must strive to be superlative.

Kevin Cashman urges the pursuit of personal growth, saying, "Too many people separate the act of leadership from the leader. They see leadership as something they do, rather than as an expression of who they are. To be more effective in our people skills with others, we must be more effective with ourselves" (LaBarre 1999) This means making a commitment to your own personal growth. As John Wooden exhorts, "Don't measure yourself by what you have accomplished but by what you should have accomplished with your ability" (Loverro 2002).

Improving Team Members' Performance

As you work on improving yourself and your own people skills, you will also be helping your team members further develop their skills. You will find yourself offering assistance to help them grow in many subtle and indirect ways. To help your team members grow, you must become a guide and create a team culture of success.

Becoming a Guide

The program or project manager must serve as his or her team members' guide. People on your team should understand the big picture of the program or project and should have a clear understanding of how success is defined. As the program or project manager, it is your job to guide your team to this understanding by applying your people skills. To fulfill your role as a guide:

- Meet with team members and foster two-way conversations.
- Talk success and the big picture.

Creating a Team Culture of Success

Success must be central to the team culture (Skulmoski and Levin 2001). One method of building such a culture is to structure activities in a way that makes early successes possible. Early successes will help build a winning attitude and set the direction of the program or project. This effort can help people overcome their fears that this particular program or project simply cannot be successful. With the habit of success established early, team members will be motivated to continue toward success.

Willoughby (2005) suggests breaking each program and project into specific, useful milestones as measures; their completion creates an atmosphere of success.

Foster the habit of success by completing an early milestone quickly so that you can use it to celebrate success with your project team. For example, reconfigure a deliverable so that a portion of it can be completed early in your project.

Career Management for Project Professionals

Your career as a project manager may be just beginning, and you may be enjoying the challenges of developing team leadership skills. Or you may be in the middle of your career, having had some success but not certain what you want the rest of your career to look like. Or, after a long and full career, you may be curious about what professional activities you can engage in during an active retirement.

Regardless of your current career stage, you must take responsibility for the direction of your career; no one else can do that for you. Even if you are currently working under a benevolent mentor, you may come to work one Monday and discover that your mentor has been fired, has been laid off, or has decided to leave the company. Only *you* can really be responsible for your future. Six rules for career management are:

- Rule 1: Actively consider what you want to do.
- Rule 2: Network, network, network!
- Rule 3: The higher you go, the more important chemistry becomes.
- Rule 4: Keep your résumé current and active.
- Rule 5: Put your personal references in order.
- Rule 6: Create your two-minute introduction.

In addition to these six rules, you can also consider an entrepreneurial career.

Rule 1: Actively Consider What You Want to Do

The significance of this career rule becomes evident when you listen closely to people who are considering career changes. Many times, professionals say that they never really set a direction for their career. Things just happened. But if you do not take the time to create a system to consider what you really want to do, you may find yourself in a situation in which:

- You achieve professional success but never attain personal satisfaction and happiness
- Your current path reaches a dead end, with no alternatives in sight
- A major organizational change, such as a merger or downsizing, happens, and you are caught with no survival strategy.

The best way to know what to do with your career is to know who you are. Placing yourself in situations that provide opportunities for formal or informal self-assessment is an excellent way to get to know yourself. Examples of formal self-assessment experiences include career interest and personal style instruments. Consulting psychologists who are skilled in personality assessment as it relates to career planning often use these instruments to help individuals develop their people skills. Traditionally, these psychologists employ tests that evaluate:

- Personality and personal style

- Work and career values

- Interests and skills.

Depending on the size of your company or organization, there may be a consulting psychologist in the organizational development group or the human resources department. Some project professionals value the opportunity to undergo the assessment process with a psychologist who is employed by the company, believing that this person is intimately aware of career issues within that company. Others, however, prefer to consult privately with an outside psychologist, believing this person will bring a more objective view and perspective to the assessment experience.

Informal, more casual self-assessment experiences can be equally valuable. These methods, such as journal writing or going on short, personal retreats are also directed at helping you gain a clear understanding of your personality, your interests, and your values, but they do not involve taking "tests."

Rule 2: Network, Network, Network!

A professional network is a group of people who know you or are familiar with the trends within your profession. Building a vibrant and active professional network before you need it is an essential part of active career management. Many professional jobs come from leads generated through professional networks. When you want to make a career change or transition in the future, a professional network can be an invaluable resource. People who might be part of your professional network include:

- Current and previous coworkers and superiors

- Acquaintances from school, conferences, or professional organizations

- People you know personally or through your community

- People who are known for being thought leaders in the profession.

  There are many ways to develop a professional network. You might:

- Call peers on a periodic basis to find out what is going on in their professional lives.

- Send selected articles to people who have unique interests.

- Set a goal of meeting three new people at the next professional conference you attend.

- Inform people in your network when you receive a promotion or take a new position.

- Consider joining some professional networking websites, such as LinkedIn or Plaxo, and join the sites' portfolio, program, and project management groups.

- Consider joining some of PMI's virtual communities of practice.

- See if your organization has a community of practice set up for project management. If it does not, but has other communities in place, suggest to your knowledge management officer that one be established for project management. If your organization does not have any communities in place, explain to your management that they are a valuable source of ideas for people working on programs and projects and that they promote the sharing of lessons learned.

- Create your own personal "board of directors," a loose association of people you know who can get together periodically (perhaps over a meal) to advise and guide you through the process of career planning and decision-making.

Rule 3: The Higher You Go, the More Important Chemistry Becomes

As you move to higher and higher levels within an organization, the more chemistry between people helps further success. You cannot guarantee good chemistry between you and a key executive, but you can work on creating the people skills that give you the ability to experience positive chemistry. Good chemistry between people takes place when at least one of the two people has sophisticated people skills.

Closely related to good chemistry is the concept of successfully managing upward toward your functional manager, project sponsor, and other executives. The program or project manager who can successfully manage upward is able to:

- Understand the needs of his or her manager

- Achieve goals consistent with these needs

- Find appropriate ways to inform the manager about successes and actions taken to achieve these goals.

For example, if you have a random encounter with an executive or a sponsor, say in the cafeteria or on the elevator, you should be ready to share with that person a two-minute summary—an *elevator speech*—about your current project. Search for other opportunities to give presentations about your project that will keep internal stakeholders informed. Many organizations will have lunch-and-learn sessions for project professionals. If you work in such an organization, plan to attend them. Typically, these sessions are also offered virtually and are recorded so you can view them later. After attending or watching a session or two, ask the organizers if you might present about your work. The organizers will welcome your desire and interest. You may even consider asking some of your team members to present with you to give them an opportunity to speak about their roles on your program or project.

Many people believe they will never encounter the CEO of the organization or a member of the executive team, but typically this is *not* the case. The following story illustrates an excellent—but missed—opportunity for a project manager to deliver his elevator speech.

While working on a consulting project for a Fortune 50 company, a project manager was on site at the firm and riding in the elevator with the customer. When they got off the elevator, the customer said, "Did you know that was our CEO on the elevator?" Of course, he had said nothing to the CEO. The project manager then told the customer about the importance of being ready to deliver an elevator speech. The customer could have mentioned the project manager's visit to the CEO as an opening to talk about what they were doing and why. Later, the customer told the project manager that he again saw the CEO—and this time, he was not afraid to talk with him.

Do not let your fear of speaking up get in the way of speaking with a key executive. Often, these executives really want to know what is happening in the "trenches" and welcome the opportunity to meet staff members one on one. Speaking with them may even encourage them to practice a "management by walking around" approach.

If a particular executive does practice "management by walking around," making an effort to connect with each person, this is all the more reason to have an elevator speech ready. This is a great opportunity to let the executive know about your work and your enthusiasm for it.

Rule 4: Keep Your Résumé Current and Active

Any professional in today's fluid work environment should have an up-to-date, polished résumé. Even when you are not currently in job-search mode, having a current résumé keeps you sharp with regard to recording your accomplishments and prepares you for interviews should the ideal job come along unexpectedly.

Make your résumé results oriented, telling the reader not just what you *did* (such as "served as a project manager for software development") but what you *achieved* (such as "decreased software turnaround time by an average of 13 percent per project; increased ROI by 5 percent; ensured customer satisfaction as noted by repeat business"). A results-oriented résumé:

- Shows that you can set goals and achieve them, realize benefits, and promote value

- Uses action verbs such as "expanded," "improved," "created," "developed," "reduced," "achieved," and "built"

- Uses numbers to quantify and support your listed accomplishments.

Rule 5: Put Your Personal References in Order

An effort related to creating and maintaining an active, vibrant network is identifying people to serve as your professional references. As with your network, your references should be developed and nurtured well in advance of when you will need them. Do not wait until an interviewer asks you for your list of references; that may be too late. Once you have a potential job in mind, you need to qualify your references by talking with them about what they expect to say about you regarding the job you are seeking. Tell them what you think the interviewer would want to know about you. Also, tell them something about the specific job and the company that you are pursuing so that they can tailor their comments accordingly.

When qualifying a reference:

- Choose references who will have credibility with the interviewer and whose backgrounds are relevant to the position for which you are applying.

- Inform your reference of the specific accomplishments, traits, and abilities you think the interviewer should hear about. The fact that you remember these accomplishments does not mean that your reference will also remember them.

- Talk with your reference about areas in which you know you need professional development.

- If you are seeking to leave the organization, inform your references so they are not surprised by referral requests later.

Rule 6: Create Your Two-Minute Introduction

As you begin to inform the outside world about your interest in finding a new position, you should be able to tell your professional story concisely, in about two minutes. A two-minute introduction is the speech you would give to someone who meets you at a conference and asks you to tell them who you are and what you want to do.

Allocate your time wisely when presenting your two-minute introduction. A good rule of thumb is to use about one minute to describe your past and your previous accomplishments and the other minute to describe what you want to do in the future.

The two-minute introduction, tailored to the specific interests and needs of the listener, is designed to quickly give the listener an impression of you as an achiever and as someone who is excited and competent to pursue the next venture. You need not specify a particular job of interest when giving your two-minute introduction, but you do need to provide as many details as you can about the setting, the duties, and the role that you want to assume in your next position.

Consider an Entrepreneurial Career

Trends in the global workplace have led to the creation of a new way of working—an entrepreneurial career. This type of career can be ideally suited to the project professional.

An entrepreneurial career is a career in which the individual is involved in a number of professional activities at one time, conducted under the banner of self-employment. In essence, the professional manages a "portfolio" that holds the various career activities.

Entrepreneurial careers can be exciting for the professional who wants to be involved in a variety of activities and believes that it is not realistic to expect to find a traditional salaried position in which these varied interests will all be satisfied. Examples of activities in one person's entrepreneurial career include:

- One day per week of university teaching
- Independent consulting on portfolio, program, or project management issues
- Coaching project managers on a variety of leadership issues
- Periodic training as a subcontractor for a project management consulting firm
- Writing articles occasionally for professional publications.

Entrepreneurial careers are not for everyone because they have much more variability than salaried positions. In considering an entrepreneurial career, keep in mind that to be suited for such a career, you should:

- Be able to tolerate a lack of predictable structure
- Be comfortable with periods of intense activity (feast) followed by periods of minimal activity (famine)
- Have excellent time-management skills
- Foster customer relationship management at all levels

- Feel comfortable in an entrepreneurial environment in which you must constantly be pursuing business development efforts

- Have outstanding competencies in business development.

Some people find it helpful to move gradually from a salaried position to an entrepreneurial career. This gradual move could start with the salaried person teaching a class in the evenings, followed by a shift to part-time work, then garnering his or her first consulting assignment.

An entrepreneurial career also is one to consider if you are the victim of downsizing in your organization. You might try teaching or consulting as you search for a salaried position, and while doing so, you may find that you are well suited for such work and wish to continue it.

Interpersonal Issues in the Digital Age

When all is said and done, your biggest challenge as a project professional is dealing successfully with people. People determine your successes and your failures. To work effectively with people over time, you need to stay abreast of changes in society. Tapsott (1998) describes the digitally based culture in which today's young people are growing up. The upcoming generation will:

- Exhibit intellectual independence and demand for free expression

- Desire innovation, inclusion, and diversity

- Be motivated by immediate experiences and the acquisition of knowledge.

As a project professional, you should continue to develop interpersonal skills that will enable you to keep up with these changes in priorities and values in an era dominated by technological advancement. The primary people skills that you should continually hone include:

- Being a persuasive communicator, leading through influence as opposed to directives

- Embracing intellectual and cultural diversity without feeling threatened

- Comfortably accepting the fact that younger team members may know more than you about current technology and may even be paid more based on their knowledge and skills.

Refining Your People Skills

To further refine your people skills, Baldoni (2009) suggests looking at your own needs and those of your team. Key questions to consider include:

- What more do I need? Perhaps there are parts of your job you could be doing less and delegating more to others.

- What else should I be doing? It may be necessary to provide your team with more training and additional resources.

- How do I handle feedback? Self-aware leaders do not just accept feedback—they invite it to promote continuous learning.

Baldoni adds that strong leaders acknowledge their shortcomings and strive to make improvements—even though this is hard to do.

Recognize the importance of chemistry on the people side of your work. Better teamwork at any level improves the likelihood of overall success, but effective teamwork takes more than just saying "Let's all work together"; as Willoughby (2005) notes, it is easier said than done. He suggests that teamwork can break down the hidden agendas people may bring to the program or project environment, which allows more problems to be brought forward earlier for resolution. To break down these hidden agendas, the program or project manager should encourage everyone to speak when meetings are held and should ask open-ended questions to uncover possible issues that may be affecting the program or the project.

Finding Meaning in Life

One of the basic challenges we all face is creating a purpose for our lives. The challenge, as we grow and develop, is to define a personal meaning for our individual existence. But what does this need to construct our own personal meaning in life have to do with our work in portfolio, program, and project management? In today's world, people are increasingly defining their life's purpose based at least in part on their professional and career identity. The concept of "who we are" is often intricately related to our job description or our profession.

It is important for portfolio, program, or project managers to remember that:

- Each individual strives for his or her own meaning in life, occasionally in ways that may be unacceptable to you.

- You should look closely to find the individual's contribution; the glass really is half full.

From a purely selfish perspective, remember that the more you can understand about someone's approach to finding meaning in life—and then give them assignments compatible with that approach—the more successful you will be in your own role as a portfolio, program, or project manager.

Coming to Grips with Isolation

Even the most socially active person sometimes feels isolated and alone. Aloneness stems from the truth that no one can ever really know what we are feeling or thinking, regardless of how intent we are in communicating with others. We can try to explain ourselves, but words ultimately cannot bridge this aloneness.

What does this aloneness have to do with portfolio, program, and project management? First, isolation is increasingly more common because of the prevalence of virtual teams. We may not even work in an office setting; more and more people, even those who work for large organizations, work at home. We may not even talk on the phone with anyone during the day; all of our communications may be through email or instant messaging, even if we are on a number of project teams. When someone does call on the phone, it is such a surprise that it is easy for some of us to over-talk and not actively listen to the person who called us, whether he or she is a customer, the program or project manager, a functional manager, or a team member. The human need for social interaction is such that even an introvert may dominate the conversation.

On both co-located and virtual teams, it is vital for each team member to have a sense of identity and commitment to the program or project. Recognizing the vision and mission of the program and project, how one's work supports it, and how it contributes to the overall strategic goals of the organization can help to reduce team leaders' and members' sense of aloneness. In particular, it is important for managers of program and project teams, particularly virtual teams, to conduct regular meetings.

Program or project managers should not underestimate the power that the team has to alleviate individual isolation. Treat the team building process and the team itself with honor, respect, and care. For you and your team members, the team is more than simply a vehicle for accomplishing a task. It is an evolving entity through which individuals can feel part of something greater than themselves and people are offered a chance to work together toward a common purpose, decreasing alienation and isolation.

Managing Beginnings and Endings

Programs and projects and people have one basic quality in common: they have a beginning and an ending. Many of us manage our anxiety about our ultimate demise by becoming very active in our work. This is not necessarily bad. In essence, work becomes a medium through which we can create testimonials to our time on earth, establishing concrete representations of our labors and our achievements that will remain after we are gone.

Work can be an effective means to come to grips with the fact that our life span is limited; this in part explains why people will work outrageous hours or put up with nasty bosses or coworkers. We want to leave this life with some marks of achievement, something that will outlast us.

It is important for you as a program or project manager to realize that each of your team members wants to leave a testimonial through his or her work; this need surfaces on some level over the course of each program or project. Help team members enjoy the experience of leaving a personal legacy or testimonial through their work on each program or project by:

• Helping them have both individual and team successes

• Helping them understand that their work truly makes a difference.

Parting Thoughts

The roles of portfolio, program, and project managers are special and are increasingly recognized as essential. More and more organizations have become project-based and have defined project-management career ladders. The roles of the portfolio, program, or project manager go beyond ensuring that the portfolio is optimized or the program or project is successfully completed to the customer's satisfaction. You influence the lives of people who are looking to you for guidance, and you affect the vibrancy, level of excellence, and future capabilities of your company or organization.

Try using the tools and approaches presented in this book. Above all, remember that solving interpersonal issues requires you to use your interpersonal skills as an artist would. Practice, experiment, integrate, and trust your intuition. Portfolio, program, and project management can be highly rewarding on both the professional and personal levels.

References and Recommended Resources

Adams, J.R., S.E. Barndt, and M.D. Martin. 1979. *Managing by project management.* Dayton, Ohio: Universal Technology Corporation.

Adams, J.R., and B.W. Campbell. 1982. *Roles and responsibilities of the project manager.* Upper Darby, PA: Project Management Institute.

Aitken, A., and L. Crawford. 2007. Coping with stress: Dispositional coping strategies of project managers. *International Journal of Project Management* 25 (7): 666–673.

Allen, C. 2009. Plan of attack. *PM Network* 23 (12): 19.

Argyris, C. 1957. *Personality and organizations: The conflict between system and the individual.* New York: HarperCollins.

Armstrong, S., and S. Beecham. 2008. Studying the interplay between the roles played by stakeholders, requirements and risks in projects. *Project Perspectives: The Annual Publication of the International Project Management Association XXIX,* 46–51. http://www.pry.fi/html/02_documents/Project_Perspectives_2007-08_final.pdf (accessed March 28, 2010).

Baccarini, D. 1999. The logical framework method for defining project success. *Project Management Journal* 30 (4): 25–32.

Baker, R.J.S. 1962. *The management of capital projects.* London: Bell. Quoted in Wearne, S. 2008. Stakeholders in excellence in teaching and learning of project management. *International Journal of Project Management* 36 (37): 326–328.

Baldoni, J. 2009. How to crack the self-awareness paradigm. *Harvard Business Review* blogs. http://blogs.hbr.org/baldoni/2009/12/cracking_the_self_awareness_pa.html (accessed March 28, 2010).

Blake, R.R., and J.S. Mouton. 1964. *The managerial grid: The key to leadership excellence.* Houston: Gulf Publishing.

Bourgault, M., N. Drouin, and E. Hamel. 2008. Decision-making within distributed project teams: An exploration of formalization and autonomy as determinants of success. *Project Management Journal (Supplement) Special PMI Research Conference Edition* 39: S97–111.

Bredin, K. 2008. People capability of project-based organisations: A conceptual framework. *International Journal of Project Management* 26 (5): 566–576.

Brown, A.W., J.D. Adams, and A.A. Amjad. 2007. The relationship between human capital and time performance in project management: A path analysis. *International Journal of Project Management* 25(1): 77–89.

Bruce, P., and S. Pederson. 1982. *The software development project.* New York: John Wiley & Sons.

Buber, M. 1970. *I and thou.* New York: Charles Scribner's Sons.

Bugental, J.F.T. 1990. *Intimate Journeys: Stories from life-changing therapy.* San Francisco: Josey-Bass.

Byrd, T.A., and D.E. Turner. 2001. An exploratory analysis of the value of the skills of IT personnel: Their relationship to IS infrastructure and competitive advantage. *Decision Sciences.* 31(1): 21–54.

Cheney, P.H., and N.R. Lyons. 1980. Information systems skills requirements: A survey. *MIS Quarterly* 4 (1): 35–43.

Chiocchio, F. 2007. Project team performance: a study of electronic task and coordination communication. *Project Management Journal* 38 (1): 97–109.

Cicmil, S., T. Cooke-Davies, L. Crawford, and K. Richardson. 2009. *Exploring the complexity of projects: Implications of complexity theory for project management practice.* Newtown Square, PA: Project Management Institute.

Cleland, D.I., and L.R. Ireland. 2007. *Project management strategic design and implementation.* 5th ed. New York: McGraw-Hill.

Cockburn, A. 2008. Good old advice. *Crosstalk* 21(8): 7–10.

Csikszentmihalyi, M. 1990. *Flow: The psychology of optimal experience.* New York: HarperCollins.

Curtis, B., W.E. Hefley, and S.A. Miller. 2001. *People Capability Maturity Model® (P-CMM®).* Version 2.0, CMU//SEI-2001-MM-01. Pittsburgh, PA: Carnegie Mellon University, Software Engineering Institute.

de Abreu, A., and D. Conrath. 1993. *The role of the stakeholders' expectations in predicting information systems implementation outcomes.* Paper presented at the 1993 Proceedings on Computer Personnel Research, St. Louis, Missouri. ACM Portal database.

DeCarlo, F.D. 1997. *It's gonna be a jungle out there managing projects in unfriendly cultures: How to survive and thrive in the next century.* Proceedings of the 28th Annual Project Management Institute Seminars and Symposium, Chicago.

Delisle, C.L., J. Thomas, K. Jugdev, and P. Buckle. 2001. *Virtual project teaming to bridge the distance: A case study.* Proceedings of the 32nd Annual Project Management Institute 2001 Seminars and Symposium, Nashville.

Department of Defense. 2005. *The national defense strategy of the United States of America.* http://www.globalsecurity.org/military/library/policy/dod/nds-usa_mar2005.htm (accessed June 10, 2007).

Drouin, N., M. Bourgault, and S.B. Sauders. 2009. Investigation of contextual factors in shaping HR approaches and determining the success of international joint venture projects: Evidence from the Canadian telecom industry. *International Journal of Project Management* 27: 344–354.

Etzioni, A. 1961. *A comparative analysis of complex organizations on power, involvement and their correlates.* New York: Free Press.

Filey, A.C. 1975. *Interpersonal conflict resolution.* Glenview, IL: Scott Foresman and Company.

Fisher, B.A. 1970. Decision emergence: Phases in group decision-making. *Speech Monographs* 37: 55–66.

Fisher, B.A. 1974. *Small group decision-making: Communication and the group process.* New York: McGraw-Hill.

Flannes, S.W. 1998. *Choosing the team that really works: How an understanding of personal style helps your team succeed.* Proceedings of the 29th Annual Project Management Institute Seminars and Symposium, Long Beach, CA.

Flannes, S.W., and D. Buell. *Coaching skills for the senior human resource professional.* Unpublished paper and seminar presented to the Northern California Human Resources Association. August 12, 1999. San Francisco.

Flannes, S.W., and G. Levin. 2001. *People skills for project managers.* Vienna, VA: Management Concepts.

Flannes, S.W., and G. Levin. 2005. *Essential people skills for project managers.* Vienna, VA: Management Concepts.

Frame, J.D. 1999. *Project management competence: Building key skills for individuals, teams, and organizations.* San Francisco: Jossey-Bass.

Frame, J.D. 2002. *The new project management: Tools for an age of rapid change, complexity, and other business realities.* 2nd ed. San Francisco: Jossey-Bass.

Freeman, R.E. 1984. *Strategic management: A stakeholder approach.* Boston: Pittman/Allinger.

French, W.L., and C.H. Bell, Jr. 1973. *Organization development: Behavioral science interventions for organization improvement.* Englewood Cliffs, NJ: Prentice-Hall.

Friedman, M. 1996. *Type A behavior: Its diagnosis and treatment.* New York: Plenum Press.

Frooman, J. 1999. Stakeholder influence strategies. *Academy of Management Review* 24 (2): 191–205.

Godin, S. 1995. *Wisdom, Inc.: 26 business virtues that turn ordinary people into extraordinary leaders.* New York: HarperBusiness.

Greengard, S. 2008. Lessons in leadership. *PM Network* 22 (8): 59–63.

Hallgren, M., and T.L. Wilson. 2008. The nature and management of crises in construction projects: Projects-as-practice observations. *International Journal of Project Management* 26 (8): 830–838.

Handy, C. 1995. Trust and the virtual organization. *Harvard Business Review* (May–June): 40–50.

Harvey, J. 1974. The Abilene paradox: The management of agreement. *Organizational Dynamics* 3 (1): 63–80.

Heglund, J., D.R. Ilgen, and J.R. Hollenbeck. 1998. Decision accuracy in computer-mediated versus face-to-face decision-making teams. *Organizational Behavior and Human Decision Processes* 76 (1): 30–47.

Herman, J.L. 1992. *Trauma and recovery: The aftermath of violence, from domestic violence to political terror.* New York: Basic Books.

Herzberg, F. 1968. One more time: How do you motivate employees? *Harvard Business Review* 46 (1): 55–62.

Hollingsworth, S. 1987. Communications management. *Project management body of knowledge (PMBOK® Guide) of the Project Management Institute.* Upper Darby, PA: Project Management Institute.

Humphrey, W.S. 1995. *A discipline for software engineering.* Reading, MA: Addison-Wesley.

Humphrey, W.S., M.D. Konrad, J.W. Over, and W.C. Peterson. 2007. Future directions in process improvement. *Crosstalk* 20 (2): 17–22.

Jepsen, A.L., and P. Eskerod. 2009. Stakeholder analysis in projects: Challenges in using current guidelines in the real world. *International Journal of Project Management* 27 (4): 335–343.

Jones, C. 2000. *Software assessments benchmarks and best practices.* Reading, MA: Addison-Wesley.

Jones, T. 2009. Double duty: Lean teams are learning to juggle like never before. *PM Network* 23 (9): 53–59.

Juhre, F. 2001. *Global companies, global resource allocation, global challenges—how to manage global projects.* Proceedings of the 32nd Annual Project Management Institute 2001 Seminars and Symposium, Nashville.

Karlsen, J. 2002. Project stakeholder management. *Engineering Management Journal* 14 (4):19–25.

Katzenbach, J.R., and D.K. Smith. 1993. *The wisdom of teams.* New York: HarperBusiness.

Kerzner, H. 2009. *Project management: A systems approach to planning, scheduling, and controlling.* Hoboken, NJ: John Wiley & Sons.

Kerzner, H., and F. Salidis. 2009. *Value-driven project management.* Hoboken, NJ: John Wiley & Sons.

Kirby, L.K., N.J. Barger, and R.R. Pearman. 1998. Uses of type in organizations. In *MBTI manual*, ed. M.H. McCaulley, N.L. Quenk, and A.L. Hammer, 325–365. Palo Alto, CA: Consulting Psychologists Press.

Kirchof, N.S., and J.R. Adams. 1982. *Conflict management for project managers.* Upper Darby, PA: Project Management Institute.

Kolby, J. 2000. *Vocabulary 4000: The 4000 words essential for an educated vocabulary.* Los Angeles: Nova Press.

LaBarre, P. 1999. How to be a real leader. *Fast Company* 24 (April 30). http://www.fastcompany.com/magazine/24/cashman.html (accessed April 24, 2010).

Levin, G. 1999. *Aspiring to peak performance: A personal improvement model for project management professionals.* Proceedings of the 30th Annual Project Management Institute Seminars and Symposium, Philadelphia.

Levin, G. 2008. *Guidelines to create a culture to promote successful use of virtual teams.* Proceedings of the 2008 Project Management Institute World Congress North America, Denver.

Levin, G. 2009. *Team building strategies for the project team.* Proceedings of the 2009 Project Management Institute World Congress North America, Orlando, Florida.

Levin, G., and A. Green. 2009. *Implementing program management templates and forms aligned with the "Standard for Program Management—Second Edition (2008)."* Boca Raton, FL: CRC Press.

Levin, G., and P.F. Rad. 2007. *Moving forward with project management: A knowledge management methodology.* Originally published as part of the 2007 Global Congress Proceedings, Atlanta. Newtown Square, PA: Project Management Institute.

Lewin, K. 1947. Frontiers in group dynamics: Concept, method, and reality in social science; social equilibria and social change. *Human Relations* I (1): 5–40.

Loverro, T. 2002. *The quotable coach: Leadership and motivation from history's greatest coaches.* Franklin Lakes, NJ: The Career Press.

Mallak, L.A., and H.S. Kurstedt, Jr. 1997. Planning for crisis in project management. *Project Management Journal* 28 (2): 14–24.

Maslow, A. 1954. *Motivation and personality.* New York: Harper and Brothers.

Mayer, M. 1998. *The virtual edge.* Newtown Square, PA: Project Management Institute.

McClelland, D. 1961. *The achieving society.* New York: Free Press.

McElroy, B., and C. Mills. 2003. Managing stakeholders. In *People in project management,* ed. R.J. Turner, 99–118. Aldershot, UK: Gower.

McGregor, D. 1960. *The human side of enterprise.* New York: McGraw-Hill.

Mehrabian, A. 1968. Communication without words. *Psychology Today* (September): 53–55.

Meredith, J.R., and S.J. Mantel, Jr. 2009. *Project management: A managerial approach.* 6th ed. Hoboken, NJ: John Wiley & Sons.

Meyerson, D., K.E. Weick, and R.M. Kramer. 1996. Swift trust and temporary groups. In *Trust in organizations, frontiers of theory and research,* ed. R.M. Kramer and T.R. Tyler, 166–195. Thousand Oaks, CA: Sage Publications.

Midler, Christophe. 1995. Projectification of the firm: The Renault case. *Scandinavian Management Journal* 16 (4): 363–375.

Milosevic, D.Z. 2003. *The project management toolbox tools and techniques for the practicing project manager.* Hoboken, NJ: John Wiley & Sons.

Milosevic, D.Z., R.J. Martinelli, and J.M. Waddell. 2007. *Program management for improved business results.* Hoboken, NJ: John Wiley & Sons.

Mishra, A. 1996. Organizational responses to crisis: The centrality of trust. In *Trust in organizations, frontiers of theory and research*, ed. R.M. Kramer and T.R. Tyler, 261–287. Thousand Oaks, CA: Sage Publications.

Mitchell, R.K., R.A. Bradley, and D.J. Wood. 1997. Toward a theory of stakeholder identification and salience: Defining the principle of who and what really counts. *Academy of Management Review* 25:27–287.

Noer, D. 1995. *Healing the wounds: Overcoming the trauma of layoffs & revitalizing downsized organizations.* San Francisco: Jossey-Bass.

Nutt, H., N. Kessler, and G. Levin. 2003. *The business development capability maturity model.* 2nd ed. Farmington, UT: Shipley Associates.

Ogden, C.K. 1930. *Basic English: A general introduction with rules and grammar.* London: Paul Treber & Co., Ltd.

O'Neil, J. 1999. Short-staffed? Maximize scarce resources with knowledge resource planning. *PM Networks.* 13:37.

Parker, G.M. 1994. *Cross-functional teams: Working with allies, enemies, and other strangers.* San Francisco: Jossey-Bass.

Patton, N., and A. Shechet. 2007. Wisdom for building the project manager/project sponsor relationship: Partnership for project success. *CrossTalk* 20 (11): 4–9.

Peters, T. 2004. Nix the spreadsheet. *PM Network* 18 (1): 13.

Peters, T. 2008. The top 27: Twenty-seven practical ideas that will transform every organization. PowerPoint presentation. http://www.tompeters.com/slides/uploaded/Top_27_120408.ppt (accessed May 11, 2009).

Project Management Institute (PMI). 1987. *Project management body of knowledge (PMBOK® Guide) of the Project Management Institute.* Upper Darby, PA: Project Management Institute.

Project Management Institute (PMI). 2004. *A guide to the project management body of knowledge (PMBOK® Guide).* 3rd ed. Newtown Square, PA: Project Management Institute.

Project Management Institute (PMI). 2006. Decision-making in project management. *PM KnowledgeWire* (1).

Project Management Institute (PMI). 2007. *Project manager competency development framework.* 2nd ed. Newtown Square, PA: Project Management Institute.

Project Management Institute (PMI). 2008a. *A guide to the project management body of knowledge (PMBOK® Guide).* 4th ed. Newtown Square, PA: Project Management Institute.

Project Management Institute (PMI). 2008b. *The standard for portfolio management.* 2nd ed. Newtown Square, PA: Project Management Institute.

Project Management Institute (PMI). 2008c. *The standard for program management.* 2nd ed. Newtown Square, PA: Project Management Institute.

Project Management Institute. 2009a. The in crowd. *PM Network* 23 (6): 18–19.

Project Management Institute. 2009b. *Leadership through project management.* Newtown Square, PA: Project Management Institute.

Rad, P.F., and G. Levin. 2003. *Achieving project management success using virtual teams*. Boca Raton, FL: J. Ross Publishing.

Rad, P.F., and G. Levin. 2006a. *Metrics for project management formalized approaches*. Vienna, VA: Management Concepts.

Rad, P.F., and G. Levin. 2006b. *Project portfolio management tools & techniques*. New York: IIL Publishing.

Rapport, A. 1960. *Fights, games, and debates*. Ann Arbor: University of Michigan.

Reich, B. 2007. Managing knowledge and learning in IT projects: A conceptual framework and guidelines for practice. *Project Management Journal* 38 (2): 5–17.

Reid, J. 2000. *Crisis management: Planning and media relations for the design and construction industry*. New York: John Wiley & Sons.

Robbins, S.P. 2003. *The truth about managing people … and nothing but the truth*. Upper Saddle River, NJ: Prentice Hall.

Schein, E. 1990. *Career anchors: Discovering your real values*. San Francisco: Jossey-Bass/Pfeiffer.

Schmid, B., and J. Adams. 2007. *Motivation in project management: The project manager's perspective*. http://www.pmi.org/pdf/pp_schmid.pdf (accessed March 28, 2010).

Shellenbarger, S. 2003. Juggling too many tasks could make you stupid. CareerJournal.com: The Wall Street Journal Executive Career Site. http://208.144.115.170/columnists/workfamily/20030228-workfamily.html (accessed March 28, 2010).

Shenhar, A.J., O. Levy, D. Dvir, and A.C. Maltz. 2001. Project success: A multidimensional strategic concept. *Long Range Planning* 34:699–725.

Shenhar, A.J., D. Milosevic, D. Dvir, and H. Thamhain. 2007. *Linking project management to business strategy*. Newtown Square, PA: Project Management Institute.

Skulmoski, G., and G. Levin. 2001. Creating the environment for successful projects: 5 key ingredients for project managers and project participants. *ESI Horizons* 2 (9).

Smith, L.W. 2000. Project clarity through stakeholder analysis. *CrossTalk* 13 (12). http://www.stsc.hill.af.mil/CrossTalk/2000/12/smith.html (accessed April 24, 2010).

Strom, W.L. 2009. The human realities of corporate downsizing. *Graziadio Business Report*. http://gbr.pepperdine.edu/981/downsizing.html (accessed March 28, 2010).

Stuckenbruck, L.C., and D. Marshall. 1985. *Team building for project managers*. Upper Darby, PA: Project Management Institute.

Tapsott, D. 1998. *Growing up digital: The rise of the net generation*. New York: McGraw-Hill.

Thamhain, H.J. 2009. The future of team leadership in complex project environments. In *Project management circa 2025*, ed. D.I. Cleland and B. Bidanda, 365–381. Newtown Square, PA: Project Management Institute.

Thamhain, H.J., and D.L. Wilemon. 1975. Conflict management in project life cycles. *Sloan Management Review* (Summer): 31–49.

Thomas, K.W., and R.H. Kilmann. 1974. *Thomas-Kilmann conflict mode instrument.* Palo Alto, CA: Consulting Psychologists Press.

Thompson, K., and T. Border. 2007. The gauge that pays: Project navigation and team building. *CrossTalk* 20 (11): 14–18.

Tuckman, B.W. 1965. Developmental sequence in small groups. *Psychological Bulletin* 63:384–399.

Tuckman, B.W., and M.A. Jensen. 1977. Stages of small-group development revisited. *Group Organizational Studies* 2:419–427.

Turner, R., M. Huemann, and A. Keegan. 2008 Human resource management in the project-oriented organization: Employee well-being and ethical treatment. *International Journal of Project Management* 26 (5): 577–585.

Verma, V.K. 1997. *Managing the project team.* Newtown Square, PA: Project Management Institute.

Weinberg, G.M. 1992. *Quality software management:* Volume 1—*systems thinking.* New York: Dorset House.

Wellman, J. 2007. Leadership behaviors in matrix environments. *Project Management Journal* 38 (2): 62–74.

Willoughby, K.A. 2005. Improvement in project expediting: There must be a better way. *International Journal of Project Management* 23 (5): 231–236.

Index

Managing Complex Projects: A New Model
Kathleen B. Hass, PMP

For organizations to thrive, indeed to survive, in today's global economy, we must find ways to dramatically improve the performance of large-scale projects. *Managing Complex Projects: A New Model* offers an innovative way of looking at projects and treating them as complex adaptive systems. Applying the principles of complexity thinking will enable project managers and leadership teams to manage large-scale initiatives successfully. *****Winner of the 2009 Project Management Institute David I. Cleland Project Management Literature Award.*****

ISBN 978-1-56726-233-9, Product Code B339, 298 pages

How to Save a Failing Project:
Chaos to Control
Ralph R. Young, Steven M. Brady, and Dennis C. Nagle, Jr.

Poor project results are all too common and result in dissatisfied customers, users, and project staff. With countless people, goals, objectives, expectations, budgets, schedules, deliverables, and deadlines to consider, it can be difficult to keep projects in focus and on track. *How to Save a Failing Project: Chaos to Control* arms project managers with the tools and techniques needed to address these project challenges. The authors provide guidance to develop a project plan, establish a schedule for execution, identify project tracking mechanisms, and implement turn-around methods to avoid failure and regain control.

ISBN 978-1-56726-239-1, Product Code B391, 234 pages

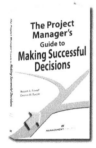

The Project Manager's Guide to Making Successful Decisions
COL Robert A. Powell, PhD, and Dennis M. Buede, PhD

Decision-making is critical in project management. Lack of decision-making knowledge, avoidable mistakes, and improper definitions can negatively impact your company's ability to generate profit. *The Project Manager's Guide to Making Successful Decisions* is a practical handbook that focuses on the significance of project decision-making skills that will allow you to reach workable and effective results. This valuable resource highlights various techniques that facilitate the decision-making process, provides an overview of decision analysis as it relates to project management, and much more!

ISBN 978-1-56726-234-6, Product Code B346, 311 pages

Metrics for Project Management: Formalized Approaches
Ginger Levin, DPA, PMP, and Parviz F. Rad, PhD, PMP

Metrics for Project Management: Formalized Approaches offers a comprehensive set of project management metrics in an easy-to-read format. Through a unique presentation of metrics categorized as things, people, and enterprises, you'll learn how metrics can guide you toward informed decisions, help the enterprise recognize the sum of its collective capabilities, link efforts of individual team members with the overall success of a project, and indirectly promote teamwork and improve team morale.

ISBN 978-1-56726-166-0, Product Code B663, 365 pages

Essential People Skills for Project Managers
Ginger Levin, DPA, PMP, and Steven Flannes, PhD

Essential People Skills for Project Managers brings the key concepts of interpersonal skills into sharp focus, offering specific, practical skills that you can grasp quickly, apply immediately, and use to resolve difficult people issues. Derived from the widely popular original book, *People Skills for Project Managers*, this new version provides condensed content and a practical focus.

ISBN 978-1-56726-168-4, Product Code B68X, 181 pages